SYMPHONY AND SONG

Symphony

Could I revive within me
Her symphony and song,
To such a deep delight 'twould win me
That, with music loud and long,
I would build that dome in air,
That sunny dome, those caves of ice . . .

from "Kubla Khan"
by Samuel Taylor Coleridge

and Song

The Saint Louis Symphony Orchestra

THE FIRST HUNDRED YEARS: 1880–1980

by Katherine Gladney Wells

THE COUNTRYMAN PRESS

© Copyright 1980 by the Saint Louis Symphony Orchestra
Library of Congress Cataloging in Publication Data
Wells, Katherine Gladney, 1918–
    Symphony and song.
    Discography: p.
    Includes index.
    1. St. Louis Symphony Orchestra. I. Title.
ML200.8.S152S949   785'.06'277866   80–14322
ISBN 0–914378–62–7
Printed in the United States of America

ACKNOWLEDGMENTS

I AM GRATEFUL to the *St. Louis Post-Dispatch* and the *St. Louis Globe-Democrat* for much interesting information from their pages, and for providing copies of certain news photographs;

to Virgil Thomson for permission to quote his review of the 1950 Carnegie Hall concert of the Saint Louis Symphony Orchestra;

to the librarians of the Missouri Historical Society's Library, who steered me toward much valuable information;

to the staff at Powell Symphony Hall for all kinds of miscellaneous assistance;

and to the following individuals who gave me their time in conversations pertinent to the preparation of this book:

James N. Cain	David J. Hyslop	Carl Schiebler
John S. Edwards	Oscar Johnson	George Silfies
Harry Farbman	Henry Loew	Leonard Slatkin
Alfred Fleishman	Morton D. May	Herbert Van den Burg
Leigh Gerdine	Edward Murphy	Ben H. Wells
Elmer Gesner	Peter Pastreich	Robert Wykes
Stanley Goodman		

Obviously, hundreds more could be mentioned: the Orchestra personnel—one by one—the chairmen of the Board committees, the managers, the various heroes and heroines in emergencies, professional and volunteer alike. Because of the impossibility of giving each individual credit where credit is deserved, only a handful of names has been brought into the saga. It is simply a matter of limited space. Undoubtedly there are scores of clear-memoried individuals who could add anecdotes and statistics. To those who felt they might have been interviewed, apologies from the author. The spirit was willing, but the number of pages just too few.

CONTENTS

FOREWORD

THE BAKER, in *The Hunting of the Snark*, was asked to tell his tale but was told not to digress.

> "My father and mother were honest though poor—"
> "Skip all that!" cried the Bellman in haste.
> "If it once becomes dark, there's no chance of a Snark—
>   We have hardly a minute to waste!"
>
> "I skip forty years," said the Baker, in tears,
> "And proceed without further remark
>   To the day when you took me aboard of your ship
>   To help you in hunting the Snark."
>
> from Fit the Third of
The Hunting of the Snark,
by Lewis Carroll

In preparing these pages, I have felt for the Baker—so much to tell and so much *not* to tell. No particular forty years has had to be skipped, but much has had to be left out through the entire hundred years.

This story of the Saint Louis Symphony Orchestra was not written as a scholarly dissertation, but as an informal, affectionate biography of a great symphony orchestra in its own setting, St. Louis, Missouri. Material for this volume has come from a variety of sources: the Symphony Archives (that is to say, the concert programs bound as a volume for each year beginning in 1904), personal interviews, newspaper clippings, books on St. Louis history (to be found in the library of the Missouri Historical Society), and miscellaneous published works by diverse authors. As the completion of this book drew near, the realization of how much had to be omitted or skipped over was disturbing. Many a colorful personality within the personnel rosters of the Saint Louis Symphony Orchestra through the years would provide material for a full-length biographical tome. Many an outstanding subscription concert, many a "special" concert could be described in detail. The celebrities who have come to St. Louis to conduct the Orchestra, and the rehearsal antics involved, would make good reading. The Summer Pops, the Baroque Series, the Little Symphony Concerts, the chamber music concerts, the open air concerts in the summer, the intermittent Sunday afternoon Pops—any of these could be dealt with separately with great interest. And, of course, accounts of the recording sessions—beginning in the days of Rudolph Ganz—might make the most lively narration of all.

In sifting and sorting through the multitude of facts and material, one course seemed to emerge. That is the course which has been pursued: the course of attempting to record the progress, the growth, the "life and times" (you might say) of the Saint Louis Symphony Orchestra through its conductors and its principal thrust—the subscription concerts. Without them there would be no "extra" series, no summer concerts, no recording sessions, no orchestra identity—no center from which these could emanate. It is through the two primary avenues, the conductors and the subscription concerts, that the continuity and life's blood of an orchestra must surely be traced and found.

The Orchestra's strength also lies in the concertmasters, the managers and stage managers, as well as in the volunteer presidents of the Board, presidents of the Women's Division, chairmen of the Junior Division, and program annotators, all of whose names are recorded in the Appendix. For those who do not ordinarily get backstage, a verbal tour of Powell Hall has been included. Photographs of all the members of the Centennial Orchestra (up to press time), by section, may be found on pages 166 through 179.

K.G.W.

DA CAPO

Before 1880

IT WAS the Germans who made the most music. To these new Americans, who had left the world of Bach, Mozart, and the more modern Beethoven, music-making was an essential aspect of life. When Wilhelm Robyn, one of St. Louis' earliest music enthusiasts, arrived here in 1837, there were only 15,000 people settled in this river town. Even so, Robyn, who played the cello, double bass, clarinet, flute, horn, trombone, and trumpet, managed to get a music job. He joined the pit orchestra of Ludlow and Smith's theater troupe,[1] a professional company which presented an annual summer season in St. Louis. Robyn played bass fiddle for Ludlow and Smith and was paid $12 a week. Not long afterwards, the talented German was engaged by St. Louis University to teach in its new music classes.[2] In short order Robyn began to present the Masses of Haydn and Mozart. Whatever Robyn produced was handled with taste and high standards, and displaying an interest in music became rather fashionable.

Two years after Robyn settled in St. Louis, Charles Balmer, a pianist, emigrated from Germany. Balmer was followed shortly thereafter by Henry Weber. Together these three Germans—Robyn, Balmer, and Weber—did much to kindle early St. Louis' appreciation of music. Balmer set up a music publishing business, in which Weber later joined him. Robyn, in addition to his teaching and his programs at St. Louis University, organized a brass band for which he wrote and arranged scores. The results of his determination to elevate musical standards were wide in range. Very soon after his arrival in St. Louis, he had attended an Odd Fellows funeral at which the trio of musicians played an E-flat clarinet, a violin, and a bass drum. To compound what Robyn regarded as a musical disgrace, the trio played "Adeste Fideles" as the funeral march.[3] Two years later, after Robyn had organized the "St. Louis Brass Band," he was asked to participate in an Odd Fellows burial service. He not only agreed, but composed two funeral marches and, conducting a double quartet of male voices accompanied by three trombones, helped put the dead to rest with two chorales sung at the graveside.[4]

In 1845, Robyn became the music director of the new St. Louis Polyhymnia

Society, the most ambitious musical undertaking the city had known to that date. Dr. Johann Georg Wesselhoeft, one of the leading German journalists in the country during this period, was a prime mover in the formation of this organization. Among the young members of the group were George Engelmann, Dr. Adolph Wizlisenius, Dr. S. Gratz Moses, and Emile Karst.[5] (The last, very much in the minority, was the French Consul.) The first concert of the Polyhymnia, on October 8, 1845, included Mozart's Overture to *Don Juan*, Rossini's Overture to *La Gazza Ladra*, and vocal selections from the opera *Acteon* by Auber.

In addition to presenting its own concerts, the Polyhymnia accompanied visiting singing celebrities. One of these was Jenny Lind, who came in 1851, arriving on the steamboat *Lexington*. The Swedish star, who was managed by P. T. Barnum, gave five concerts in Wyman's Hall (on Market Street between Fourth and Fifth Streets) to sell-out crowds at $5 a ticket.

Presenting more instrumental than vocal music, the Polyhymnia lasted only about ten years. Its demise is best explained by a sentence from Robyn's autobiography: "We continued to give our monthly concerts, but as we could give only instrumental concerts—for no amateur lady singers could be induced at that time to appear before the public—the people lost interest in it, and in 1855 we discontinued."[6]

A second concerted attempt to establish a permanent musical organization took place in 1859 when the St. Louis Philharmonic Society was founded. The following year, the organization engaged the services of Eduard Sobolewski, a fifty-two-year-old German who had been in Milwaukee for two years. Sobolewski, "an eccentric but profound musician,"[7] assembled about one hundred singers from various choirs and more than fifty orchestra pieces. Sobolewski's salary is recorded as one thousand dollars per season. Sobolewski resigned as music director after six seasons. There were efforts made to keep the Philharmonic going, first by August Waldauer (a violinist and conductor), and later by Egmont Freulich (composer and conductor), but the organization was forced to disband in 1870 because of "a decline in subscriptions and ever increasing expense, caused by the engagement for each concert of foreign artists, who received more remuneration than the Society or its treasury could afford."[8] (After a twenty-three-year gap, the forerunner of the present-day Philharmonic Society of St. Louis came into being, in 1893. This organization, changing its name in 1909–1910 to "The St. Louis Orchestra Club," continued annually until 1923 when it took the name "The Philharmonic Society of St. Louis.")[9]

Another music group, one that did not involve singers, began and ended during the 1870's. The Haydn Orchestra, an amateur ensemble organized by a violinist and conductor, Robert Sauter, presented, in the fall of 1871, the first of what was to be annual seasons. These lasted only seven or eight years, and shortly after the dissolution of the Haydn Orchestra, another group of instrumentalists—one that figured very specifically in the beginnings of the Saint Louis Symphony Orchestra—banded together to form the St. Louis Musical

Union. This group managed to raise a rather impressive fund of $8000 with which to get started. Although one source gives the date of origin of the St. Louis Musical Union as 1879,[10] while another places it at 1881,[11] both concur that the founders were August Waldauer and Dabney Carr, an amateur flutist, and that the concerts were played at Mercantile Library Hall every month from November to May. The records also show that dress rehearsals, held the day before each performance, were well attended.

In spite of the difficulties in keeping alive a large musical group, particularly one involving instrumental music, there was no shortage of smaller singing groups. In 1872, St. Louis played host to the National Triennial Sängerbundfest (Singing Society Convention). The Convention's sessions were held in a large frame convention hall constructed on a vacant lot bounded by Washington, St. Charles, 11th, and 12th Streets. At that time, local singing groups included the Druid Männerchor, Chouteau Valley Männerchor, Hungary Sängerbund, Swiss Männerchor, Jägar Sängerbund, Sängerbund of the Sons of Herman, and the Liederkranz Singing Society. St. Louis had a population of 313,301 in 1870; one-sixth of these St. Louisans were of German origin.

If this preamble to the beginning of the Saint Louis Symphony Orchestra seems confused, two facts should be clear. One is that the city's appetite for music grew considerably in the years between Wilhelm Robyn's arrival in 1837 and the birthdate of the Orchestra in 1880. The other is that the Saint Louis Symphony Orchestra, like the great Mississippi River surging past its city, is what it is because of innumerable small feeder streams, flowing into it and contributing to its ultimate size and importance.

Joseph Otten

JOSEPH OTTEN

The Symphony Years 1880–1894

NOW WE COME to the beginning of what we know as the Saint Louis Symphony Orchestra. The year was 1880. The East coast had developed a sophisticated (for the times) social and economic culture that was over 250 years old. American Independence was 104 years old. Here, near the center of the continent, the town of St. Louis—really a city by 1880—was 116 years old, with a population of 350,518.

Eads Bridge had been in use for six years. Forest Park, as an entity, was five years old. Public cleaning and sprinkling of the streets had been initiated. There were 600 working telephones in the city.[1]

In the international world of music, Franz Liszt was going strong; Giuseppe Verdi and Richard Wagner were well established, although the latter was not universally admired; Tchaikovsky had yet to write his Fifth Symphony; and Stravinsky and Shostakovich were still to be born.

The American inventors, one in particular, had come up with various devices that would play significant roles in the fostering of concert music everywhere. Thomas Alva Edison had, in the decade preceding 1880, invented the Cylindrical Record Phonograph, the stock ticker, the cash register, and the incandescent lamp. Without St. Louis realizing it, the stage was set for the inception of the Saint Louis Symphony Orchestra.

Not only was the stage set, the time was right. For the westward-bound travellers, St. Louis had burgeoned as a pass-through city. For large numbers of European families seeking a new life in America away from the crowded port cities of the East coast, it was a come-and-settle place. It was a community known for its handsome residences and its congenial citizens. It was also already a blend of nationalities. In addition to the large German population, there were the Irish, who had made their way to St. Louis in the early part of the century, the Italians, who had begun to settle in large numbers during the last half of the century, and the French, who had founded the town and who still flourished. In addition, smaller contingents from Russia and various Central European countries gave St. Louis a particularly appealing flavor, a colorful personality that would enhance it indefinitely.

By 1880, the New York Philharmonic (the only American symphony orchestra founded earlier than the Saint Louis Symphony Orchestra) was thirty-eight years old, and already experiencing various ups and downs. The energetic and peripatetic Theodore Thomas had been engaged as the Philharmonic's conductor. A relevant digression at this point is to give a few brief facts about Theodore Thomas since, in a way, his presence figures in the early days of the Saint Louis Symphony Orchestra. Thomas came to this country from Germany when he was ten years old, thus his adult musical career can be classed as American. A violinist with an unwavering determination to present good serious concert music, he eventually established his own orchestra and developed as a proficient conductor. The Thomas Orchestra, as it came to be known, was founded in 1864 and was the first orchestra in this country to guarantee a full year's employment to the musicians. At the time the New York Philharmonic took him on as conductor, he was still presenting his own series with his own orchestra. In 1878, he agreed to head up a new musical college in Cincinnati and subsequently agreed to commute regularly between Cincinnati and New York—a complicated maneuver in 1879. In any event, with Thomas as conductor, the New York Philharmonic was solidly on its feet (artistically, at least) and playing to audiences of considerable sophistication.

Here in St. Louis, a place which many Easterners regarded (and perhaps still do) as an outpost, the public's interest in music was, though less cultivated, nonetheless persistent. By 1880, Joseph Otten, a twenty-eight-year-old German organist, had been in St. Louis for one year. Educated at the Liège Royal Conservatory of Music in his native Holland, and having later studied with Albert Becker in Berlin, Otten was expert in the field of choir direction and accompaniment. In St. Louis, he became director of a small choral society which dissolved after only six weeks of existence even though Otten offered to continue his services without a salary. Determined to establish an organization which he could guide and shape into a fine quality musical group, Otten gathered a group of interested citizens, and on September 1, 1880, the St. Louis Choral Society was founded. Although no skyrockets were fired and no particular notice of the date was taken by the press, this event was the coming-into-existence of the Saint Louis Symphony Orchestra. It was the beginning of a century (to this present date) of concert seasons without breaks in continuity.

The directors of the new organization were L. L. Tebbets, President; R. Chauvenet, Vice-President; Thaddeus Smith, Secretary; and A. A. Schnuck, Librarian.[2]

The local singers' activities in 1880 commanded the public's interest to such an extent that they were recounted in the press. In routine listings of church services, the names of the various soloists were included. On May 2, 1880, *The Republican* published various little tidbits about what some of the singers were planning for the summer. The St. Louis Quartet Club, for instance, was to go on an excursion to Hermann, Missouri, where "they expect to be received with brass bands, a deputation of citizens, and the fire department." Readers of the paper were also informed that "next Tuesday the Epstein brothers and the

West End Quartet will give a concert at Webster Groves on the Missouri Pacific railroad."[3] (It is hoped that they were either in the depot or *beside* the track!) At that time, the Catholic churches, as a rule, did not have paid singers. The Protestant churches were the ones with the paid soloists, most of whom had trained in the Catholic choirs.[4] From a large heterogeneous group of vocalists, Otten formed a choir of some fifty men and women, which rehearsed at Trinity Church, at 11th and Washington. The first concert—Handel's *Dettingen Te Deum*—was presented in Mercantile Library Hall on March 24, 1881. The concert, with E. M. Bowman at the organ, was repeated on April 26.

In the second season, Otten added orchestral accompaniment to his four programs. A review of a December concert (which presented the Beethoven "Egmont" Overture, the March and Chorus from *Tannhäuser*, and the entire Beethoven Mass in C) pronounced the ensemble of eighty voices "nearly equally balanced, with the single exception that the alti were somewhat weak in numbers and in power." The review went on to say, "the orchestra of 19 strings and 12 wind and reed instruments, was complete in its constitution except only that the fagotti, which St. Louis does not afford, were necessarily replaced by 'celli. Mr. Otten, who appeared for the first time as an orchestral conductor, had his band thoroughly in hand, and accompanied and supported his choir without drowning it; an excellence which should be especially remarked in St. Louis, where orchestral accompaniments have, far too often, been distinguished more for noise than for more excellent qualities. . . . The list of associate members now numbers over 200, thus providing a fund for the season of over $2000—a sum quite sufficient to assure the success of the four concerts promised."[5]

During the same winter, the St. Louis Musical Union was presenting its concerts, generally on Thursday evenings, with dress rehearsals opened to audiences on the preceding Wednesday mornings. These concerts, like the Choral Society programs, took place in Mercantile Library Hall. The Musical Union charged $20 for a season subscription which included three tickets for each concert and three for each rehearsal.

In 1882, Otten's group performed one of the more ambitious programs of his tenure, Mendelssohn's oratorio *Elijah*. According to a review of the performance, Otten brought it off quite successfully. "Mr. Otten is a true musician, who inclines somewhat to the modern school but who, nevertheless, is an admirer of Palestrina and Bach. He has the qualities which go to make a good director—painstaking, zealous, and tireless; what he lacks in personal magnetism is made up by energy, enthusiasm, and thorough knowledge of his work."[6] In this performance, Carl Froelich had had to fill in for Edward Dierkes, in the lead, when Dierkes became ill. Froelich had had little or no rehearsal, and managed to perform the part by sight-reading it. The review concluded, "We doubt if any other man could be found, west of New York, who could have done this."

During the 1882–1883 season, the Choral Society presented Schumann's cantata, *Paradise and the Peri*. Although Otten had taken the chorus through fifteen rehearsals before the performance, the instrumental accompaniment had apparently not had as thorough a going-over. As one critic saw it, "The orchestration of this work is so beautiful that more time ought to be devoted to rehearsing the orchestra than there is. The uncertainty of attack, the obscurity of some of the figures, and the close attention paid to the music, with scarcely any time to glance at the director, is the inevitable outcome of insufficient rehearsals."[7]

Obviously, Otten's forte was the choral aspect of the music, and, in this area, he was excellent. Working with an augmented chorus of 300, Otten rehearsed the singers for a performance of Gounod's *Redemption* under the baton of the ubiquitous Theodore Thomas (May 1883). This large production took place not in Mercantile Library Hall but in Armory Hall in order to accommodate the much larger than usual audience. Otten was given high marks for this concert by a review which read, "Next to Mr. Thomas, Mr. Joseph Otten deserves the most praise for the extremely efficient work of the Choral Society on this occasion. Never, I think, has such fine chorus singing been heard in St. Louis."[8]

Otten had his troubles. Before a performance of the *Messiah* (in December 1883) he issued a statement that "no person will be allowed to sing in the concert who has not attended enough rehearsals to know the work thoroughly."[9] Later that year, the Society gave a repeat performance of Schumann's *Paradise and the Peri* (it had been presented during the previous season) with disastrous results. "The chorus and the orchestra sang and played as if they had never heard of the work before, and were giving it a reading rehearsal." One of the sopranos "in the very first number began a third above her note, and Mr. Otten was compelled to start her solo for her." The tenor failed miserably. "He seemed never to know when to come in or what the pitch of his note should be." The flutes and oboes were out of tune. "Mr. Porteus did not sing four notes correctly, making a complete failure. One of his solos had so many errors they had to do it over. . . . Altogether the performance was the worst that the Choral Society ever gave."[10]

In 1884, Robert S. Brookings, a philanthropist who had built up considerable means through the growth of his company (Samuel Cupples Wooden Ware Company), became the fourth president of the Society's board and "placed the finances on a more solid footing."[11] The three men who had preceded him were L. L. Tebbets, Nat Hazard, and William S. Stuyvesant. Although Tebbets and Stuyvesant were business executives, Hazard was a clerk, and a tenor who directed the choir of Central Presbyterian Church.

Significant metamorphoses took place during Brookings' presidency. For one, the principal orchestral organization in St. Louis, the Musical Union, disbanded. Various factors brought about its end. It had been extremely difficult to keep attendance up, perhaps because those citizens interested in concerts were still more oriented toward choral music. And, Waldauer, the guiding spirit behind the orchestra, was in failing health. In any event, the Musical Union sold its rights, title, instruments, and library to the Choral

Society, in 1890.[12] After absorbing the Musical Union, the Choral Society unofficially changed its name to the St. Louis Choral-Symphony Society. To return to the analogy of the Saint Louis Symphony Orchestra and the Mississippi River, the actual fountainhead of the Symphony Orchestra was the Choral Society, and the largest early tributary was the Musical Union.

The Musical Union orchestra had acquired a certain familiarity with standard orchestral works—sometimes performing entire symphonies, sometimes single movements. In the ten years of its existence, the Union had performed four Beethoven Symphonies (the Third, the Fifth, the Sixth, and the Seventh), Mozart's *Jupiter* and G Minor Symphonies, and Mendelssohn's *Scotch* and *Italian* Symphonies, to mention only a few. The St. Louis Choral-Symphony Society now more or less alternated its programs between the orchestral and the vocal.

The St. Louis Choral-Symphony Society was formally incorporated in 1893, Brookings remaining president. The original incorporators were Otto Bollman, Brookings, D. H. Clark, A. D. Cunningham, R. D. Kohn, George D. Markham, Hugh McKittrick, Jr., Otten, Richard Perry, Henry S. Potter, W. D. Simmons, and W. E. Zella.

Although the number of subscription concerts had been as high as nine (during Otten's eleventh and twelfth seasons) the annual deficit had become such that, by the fourteenth season, the number was reduced to seven. The Board of the newly incorporated group felt it only prudent to schedule no more than four choral and two orchestral concerts for the next season. Otten, unwilling to face this cut-back, resigned at the end of the 1893–1894 season.

Alfred Ernst

ALFRED ERNST

The Symphony Years 1894–1907

WHATEVER THE OBSTACLES and complications were, the St. Louis Choral-Symphony Society was not going to be allowed to collapse. The organization had fourteen years of continuous history behind it by now, and although it was a critical milestone to have its original conductor depart, the Board, under the leadership of Robert S. Brookings, secured another conductor.

The new leader was Alfred Ernst, a twenty-six-year-old German pianist who had arrived in New York in 1893. Again, the title "conductor" was really a courtesy inasmuch as the individual, like Otten, was not an experienced wielder of the baton. Although Ernst, after some musical studies in Leipzig, had—at age nineteen—been appointed conductor of the Court Opera at Gotha, this did not necessarily prepare him for the kind of job he undertook in St. Louis. The orchestra for a small court opera, undoubtedly performing for limited audiences, was a far cry from what the St. Louis musical organization had become. Here, at the time Ernst came, the orchestra contained ten first violins, eight second violins, five violas, four cellos, four double basses, two flutes, two oboes, two clarinets, three bassoons, four horns, three trombones, two trumpets, harp, timpani, and drums.[1] Ernst was a talented musician who grew with the job. The concerts numbered six a year during Ernst's first three years, increasing to twelve concerts the fourth season. The years from 1899 to 1903 were "seasons" of ten programs each year.

During the late nineties, the Orchestra had the usual financial troubles, but, as each year passed, the organization had more stature in the community. In 1898, the following eloquent plea appeared in *The Mirror*: "It is a lamentable fact that, in spite of unremitting work on the part of the Board of Management, the Choral-Symphony Society has not this season had the support of the public which has been extended to it in former years. The subscription of $10,000 necessary to avoid financial disaster has not, as yet, been secured. . . . A permanent orchestra more than any one thing indexes the real culture and refinement of a community. It may be argued that there are not enough people interested in music in St. Louis to support a permanent orchestra, but an institution whose scope is as broad as that of the Choral Society deserves the support not only of the music loving portion of the population but of every public spirited citizen."[2] *The Mirror* also carried a blow-by-blow argument, among readers, as to whether or not the Choral-Symphony Society's progress was hampered by the presence of too many amateur musical clubs. There were readers who felt that the smaller groups were stealing the limelight by hiring soloists and presenting concerts that were aimed to be competitive. There were others who insisted that more groups kept more people interested in music. In any event, the controversy stirred up attendance for the Choral-Symphony Society's programs.

Ernst, like Otten before him, had to take the brickbats with the plaudits. Following a concert in January 1898, which had consisted of Tchaikovsky's *Pathetique* Symphony, Servais' *Fantasia* for cello and orchestra, Handel's Largo from *Xerxes*, Goddard's *Berceuse* for cello and orchestra, and Wagner's *Huldigungsmarsch*, Ernst and the orchestra got what must certainly be called a mixed review. (Bear in mind that the Tchaikovsky B Minor Symphony had been composed only five years before this time.) The critic wrote: "Rough places were to be found . . . but taking into consideration one thing with another, never before has a local orchestra given so excellent a performance of any work. . . . Daring in its originality, at times lurid in its sensationalism, the Tchaikovsky B Minor Symphony still stands as one of the greatest orchestral works of modern times." The reviewer went on to say that Bruno Steindel played the Servais *Fantasia* in a "masterly fashion," although the reviewer considered the music "at best, trivial." Things got worse as the concert went on, and the critic continued, "The Largo of Handel, well known and well beloved, received brutal treatment at the hands of the orchestra. The arrangement for orchestra by Mr. Fischer is acceptable but its performance was execrable. Mr. Gecks played badly on the violin, but Miss Ghio's performance on the harp was positively wicked. Many excuses are offered for the fiasco, but none are legitimate. If Miss Ghio's broken string could not be replaced in time, as is alleged, either Mr. Fischer or Mr. Ernst should have played the harp part on the piano. Mr. Gecks was undoubtedly somewhat influenced by the vagaries of the harpist, but his strident tone was inexcusable. . . . The accompaniment to the *Berceuse* was not satisfactory—that unfortunate harp again! From the numerous smiles and nods he distributed among the audience, I infer that Mr. Steindel's friends were well represented. This, no doubt, is very gratifying to the artist, but would it not be better to defer his greetings to them until after the concert?"[3]

Ernst periodically tried his hand at composing, not always with a great deal of success. After another concert, when the soloist had been Georg Buddeus, who played a piano concerto by Schytte and a short piece by Ernst called "Gondoliera," the reviewer was far from excited by the Ernst composition. Of it he said, "as a composition it is conventional and rather commonplace, and did not reveal any new qualities in the pianist's work."[4]

1904 was a significant year in the history of the city of St. Louis. It was also a signal year in the annals of the Saint Louis Symphony Orchestra. The Louisiana

Frederick Fischer at the celesta. In addition to his skill at the keyboard, Fischer was bassoonist and Assistant Conductor under Ernst, Zach, and Ganz.

Purchase Exposition, commonly and rather carelessly referred to as the St. Louis World's Fair, was an event of enormous ramifications in this city. After three years of consideration and discussion of the project, Congress passed a bill which enabled St. Louis to play host to the hundredth-year anniversary celebration of the Louisiana Purchase. The city, fourth in population ranking in the United States in the 1900 census, flew into action for the International Exposition. In time for the Fair, there were ninety-four hotels in operation— some new, some old (the Jefferson Hotel dates from this period). Over 1200 acres in Forest Park (and adjoining it) had been set aside for the grounds. All the American states and Territories exhibited, as did many foreign countries.

Alfred Ernst and the Orchestra became deeply involved in the musical activities of the Fair. In the eighty-two-member official Exposition Orchestra, fifty-two of the musicians were the fifty-two members of the St. Louis Choral-Symphony Society. This Exposition Orchestra played popular concerts daily

ORCHESTRA.

ALFRED ERNST, Conductor.
CHARLES GALLOWAY, Organist.

FREDERICK FISCHER, Ass't Conductor and Manager
J. S. McCONATHY, Librarian.

First Violins.
Christ Jacob
(Concert Meister).
Mrs. L. K. Burg.
E. Vollrath.
Chas. Kaub.
P. L. Donath
V. Lichtenstein
A. Pesold.
O. Kuetine.

Second Violins.
O. Thumser.
P. Haskell.
J. Blumenberg.
A. Davidson.
C. F. Steinkuehler.
G. Bergsterman.
H. Brandt.
W. Oberkircher.

Violas.
C. Tholl.
L. Kielsmeier.
H. Falkenheiner.
F. Goll.
H. Lanznar.

Violoncellos.
P. G. Anton.
Chas. Mayer.
C. Froehlich.
N. Gobelet.

Double Basses.
R. Buhl.
H. Broekaert.
C. Thul.
F. Freiermuth.

Harp.
Mme. Emily Grey.

Flutes.
J. Kiburz.
L. Mack Close.

Oboes.
J. Wouters.
J. S. McConathy.

Clarinets.
A. Meyer.
A. Steppan.

Bassoons.
Frederick Fischer.
Noel Poepping.

Horns.
F. Hoefer.
W. Helmholz.
Paul Thaens.
L. Paudert.

Trumpets.
G. Heim.
N. Pearson.

Cornets.
A. Banbridge.
B. Tarrantino.

Trombones.
O. Hallback.
D. Bittner.
F. Henniger.

Tuba.
O. Ostendorf.

Tympani.
R. Venuto.

Drums.
Geo. Eckhardt.

Ernst's Orchestra in 1905. One woman in the first violins, and one woman at the harp. Note the advertised price of the Steinway upright; also the availability of transportation of the period.

(except for Fridays) at the Tyrolean Alps restaurant. On Friday, the ensemble played a more serious concert in the Festival Hall. Ernst was engaged to conduct the Friday symphony concerts. Three guest conductors assisted in these twenty-five concerts. They were Emil Mollenhauer, Walter Damrosch, and Frank Van der Stucken.[5]

The popular concerts were conducted by Richard Heuberger of Vienna and Karl Komzak of Baden-Baden. These programs were made up of sure-fire favorites such as Strauss waltzes and familiar operatic melodies, and it was considered entirely acceptable for the customers to accompany the music by beating with their spoons on their beer steins.[6]

This endeavor of the Orchestra (at the Fair) had all sorts of competition in that there was much going on in the way of small groups playing nationalistic music in the various exhibition buildings. In addition, there was the occasional presence of a visiting dignitary such as John Philip Sousa. John McCormack made his American debut in The Irish Village. Although these concerts which were performed in the Tyrolean Alps may have been woefully lacking in sophistication, they did serve to keep the money coming in and to build an eventually wider audience.

In 1896, after twelve years in office, Robert S. Brookings had finally bowed out as head of the Society's Board. He was followed by John T. Davis (for two years), William McMillan (for two years), Corwin H. Spencer, and John Schroers, serving one year each. In 1903, Mrs. John T. Davis, Jr. took over. The women of St. Louis had played a serious part in the over-all aspects of the Fair, with their own committees and as adjuncts to their husbands' various committees. (The St. Louis Woman's Club had been founded in 1903, partly in the realization that facilities would be needed to entertain the visiting V.I.P.'s who were to be in the city.) Mrs. Davis remained Board President for four years, from 1903 to 1907.

These years following the Fair were an interesting chapter in the story of the Saint Louis Symphony Orchestra. The Odeon, which had been built in the mid-Nineties at the corner of Grand and Finney, was the hall used for the concerts, and, by this time, the printed programs were very formal and proper, replete with program notes on the music as well as advertisements and announcements.

As to the actual music being presented, an example is the program of January 23, 1905—the second concert of the season. The selections were Tchaikovsky's Symphony No. 4 for the opening number and Elgar's *Pomp and Circumstance* for the closing number. In between there were no less than Joseph Hoffman playing Rubinstein's Piano Concerto in D minor with the Orchestra, solo piano pieces by Chopin, Liszt, and Moszkowski—played by Hoffman, and Herbert's "Love Scene" from *Serenade Suite*, played by the strings only.

The third subscription concert had Fritz Kreisler playing Beethoven's D Major Concerto, op. 61, with the Orchestra, and Kreisler playing four miscellaneous pieces by Sulser, Porpora, Dvorak, and Paganini, accompanied by Alfred Ernst himself on the piano. This program opened with the Prelude to *Die*

From program of 1904–1905 season. The special notice was full of rules and regulations, including the statement that patrons were not to leave the auditorium during the performance of any number. The horses had to circle around if the carriage owner wasn't waiting at the carriage landing.

Meistersinger and included the chorus singing "Unfold ye Portals" from *The Redemption* by Gounod. It was varied, to say the least.

The musical activities in St. Louis in this period are nicely mirrored in the advertisements which appeared regularly in the programs. In addition to the Kroeger School of Music, housed in the Odeon, there were various conservatories listing their services. Strassberger's Conservatories of Music, on 2200 St. Louis Avenue, with a branch at Grand and Cleveland, had Alfred Ernst and his wife on the faculty. Conrath's Conservatory of Music, at 3400 Lindell, announced: "Instruction imparted from the very beginning to the highest point of artistic development in Piano, Violin, Vocal, Harmony and Composition, Organ, Cello, Cornet, Flute, Zither, Mandolin, Guitar, etc." It further promised "Diplomas, Gold and Diamond Medals." The Weltner Conservatory of Music, on Finney near Grand, offered instruction in "All branches of Music, Dramatic Art, Modern Languages, Etc." All varieties of pianos were advertised including the Bahnsen piano, made in St. Louis. A Steinway "Verte Grand" piano (an upright) could be bought for $500, a Steinway "miniature grand" for $750. The Odeon itself had an "entertainment Hall" which was available for rent for "Balls, Musicales, Germans, Lectures, and Entertainments of Every Description." There were individual "notices" offering music instruction from all sorts of vocalists and instrumentalists, including one from Mrs. Lulu KunkelBurg, a violinist with the Symphony Orchestra and the only woman in the organization except for the harpist, Mme. Emily Gray.

Ernst was reported to have demonstrated a hair-trigger temper at rehearsals, and his gift for epithet and castigation was apparently a modest forerunner of that of Arturo Toscanini. Toscanini, in his celebrated diatribes years later, spoke to his personnel in Italian. Ernst obviously used German, which scarcely eased the blows when you consider that the names in his orchestra were Vollrath, Lichtenstein, Blumenberg, Steinkuehler, Brandt, Oberkircher, Falkenhainer, Froelich, Broekaert, Freiermuth, Helmholz, to name a few.

In these early days, the names of the boxholders were printed routinely in the program. In 1904, for instance, the holders of boxes A to Z were:

Mr. E. G. Cowdrey	Mrs. Kate M. Howard	Mr. D. R. Francis
Mr. Festus J. Wade	Mrs. Andrew Sproule	Mrs. G. C. Castleman
Mr. H. M. Blossom	Mr. A. B. Hart	Mrs. A. L. Chauvenet
Mrs. Alfred Bradford	Mrs. E. H. Semple	Mrs. John Fowler
Mrs. J. C. Moon	Mr. Robt. S. Brookings	Mrs. John T. Davis
Mr. Adolphus Busch	Mr. Murray Carleton	Mrs. Thos. H. McKittrick
Mrs. Wm. McMillan	Mr. Daniel Catlin	Mr. Henry C. Scott
Mrs. John D. Davis	Mrs. Claude Kilpatrick	Mr. W. F. Boyle
Mr. Henry S. Potten	Mr. W. K. Bixby	Miss M. R. Tutt
Mr. Robt. McK. Jones	Mr. Thomas West	Mr. E. C. Simmons
Mrs. J. F. How	Judge Adams	Mr. D. M. Houser
Mrs. McKittrick	Mrs. Wm. Huse	Mr. Samuel Cupples
Mr. Geo. D. Markham	Mr. D. C. Nugent	

In a setting where the Southern Railway advertised that it had the shortest line, by forty-three miles, from St. Louis to Louisville, when a six-foot-tall hall clock with an eight-day movement could be bought at Mermod, Jaccard and King for $10.50, when banks advertised 2 per cent on current deposits and 3 per cent interest on savings deposits, the audience members were instructed and admonished in every program with the following words:

SPECIAL NOTICE

The concert will begin promptly at 8:15 and will close at 10 o'clock.

Patrons are requested not to leave the auditorium during the performance of any number.

It is expected that all persons will leave their hats, cloaks, coats, umbrellas and wraps in the wardrobe room, where they will be securely guarded without charge.

Response to encores will be at the discretion of the conductor.

An Intermission of 15 minutes will occur between the first and second parts of the program.

After the performance carriage numbers will be called on both sides of the foyer as the carriage enters the north driveway, giving ample time for patrons to reach the carriage landing by the time their vehicle is ready to receive them. Should the owners of the carriages not be ready at the time their number is called, we must insist on their carriage driving out again and driving back in turn.

NOTE: If any subscriber, not receiving one of these Programme Books in advance of the Concert, will notify the Secretary, a book will be sent regularly.

Meanwhile, the Orchestra (which was still going under the name "St. Louis Choral and Symphony Society") worked up to a subsidiary series of eleven Sunday Afternoon Popular Concerts, from January through March of 1906. These programs presented local singers, instrumental soloists from the Orchestra, single movements from some of the great symphonies, and a variety of musical subject matter that would capture the more casual public's interest. Frederick Fischer, bassoonist in the Orchestra, was not only the Orchestra Manager but the Assistant Conductor who shared the Sunday podium with Ernst.

In spite of the fact that Ernst had built up his organization to an orchestra of fifty-five and a chorus of 200 by 1900–1901, in spite of the facts that the Fair of 1904 had spurred on the effort and the concerts (both subscription and "popular") had gradually gathered momentum—in spite of all this which Ernst might well have regarded as achievements through his personal efforts, the transplanted German leader, like many another European conductor, never quite got used to his American environment. At a time when long-distance travel was not undertaken lightly or often, Ernst found St. Louis, Missouri, to be a long, long way from home. In 1907, he returned to his native Germany where he continued his music career, primarily in the production of opera. He died in 1916 in Berlin, from injuries sustained during World War I.[7]

PROGRAMME SECOND CONCERT.

January 23, 1905.

PART I.

1. Symphony No. 4 in F Minor, Op. 36 — Andante Sostenuto; moderato con anima. / Andantino in modo di canzona / Scherzo: Pizzicato obstinato. / Finale: Allegro con fuoco. — *Tschaikowsky*
ORCHESTRA.

INTERMISSION.

PART II.

2. Concerto for Piano in D Minor . . . . *Rubinstein*
JOSEF HOFMANN AND ORCHESTRA.

3. "Love Scene" from "Serenade" Suite, ... *Herbert*
STRING ORCHESTRA.

4. FOR PIANO — *a* Funerailles . . . . *Liszt* / *b* Berceuse . . . . *Chopin* / *c* Caprice Espagonle . . . . *Moszkowsky*
JOSEF HOFMANN.

5. March—"Pomp and Circumstance" . . . . *Elgar*
ORCHESTRA.

Program from Ernst's eleventh season. Note description of singing method taught by Robert Pattterson Strine.

MAX ZACH

The Symphony Years 1907–1921

FOLLOWING the departure of Alfred Ernst, the conductor engaged to carry on was Max Zach, first chair viola player with the Boston Symphony Orchestra. The Board of the Society, with Hanford Crawford as president, had high hopes for the future quality of the Saint Louis Symphony Orchestra, as the official name had become in 1907.

Not only had Max Zach been the principal violist in Boston, he had also (for ten years) been a member of the Adamowski Quartet. He had been brought to Boston in 1886 (at the age of twenty-one) by Wilhelm Gericke, the second permanent conductor of the Boston Symphony Orchestra (which had come into being in 1881). Gericke was a disciplinarian and a dyed-in-the-wool classicist who taught both his orchestra and his audiences to expect and appreciate high quality in performance. Zach brought with him to St. Louis not a little of his mentor's aura.

Another element Zach brought with him, one which was totally new to the twenty-seven-year-old orchestra, was his expertise as a conductor. He had conducted the Boston Popular Concert series for ten years. He knew how he wanted a piece to sound and, moreover, he knew how to get that sound out of the musicians. The rehearsals became more businesslike than they had ever been before, and the musicians were put on a regular seasonal paycheck. Although Zach "inherited" much of his orchestra from Alfred Ernst, he infused new blood into it with additional players. One of the most notable of these was Hugo Olk, a violinist and composer who had performed as a soloist in Europe in his youth and had been concertmaster of the Kiev Symphony Orchestra in Russia. Later he had been a member of the Louisiana Purchase Exposition Festival Orchestra here in St. Louis and had subsequently held various elevated positions: he had been concertmaster of Henry Savage's "Parsifal" Opera Orchestra, and had spent two seasons each (as concertmaster and soloist), first with the Philadelphia Orchestra, and then with the Cincinnati Symphony Orchestra. With Zach as conductor and Hugo Olk as concertmaster, the Saint Louis Symphony Orchestra was to start shedding its perhaps somewhat provincial image.

Max Zach

In his first season, 1907–1908, in St. Louis, Max Zach did not find himself in a desert devoid of musical sustenance. It was a time when the great soloists and opera companies looked upon touring as a routine way-of-career. The St. Louis Odeon had its share of bookings, over and above what the Symphony Orchestra was doing there. The great Paderewski played a recital at the Odeon in January of Zach's first year here. The Milan Grand Opera Company appeared at the

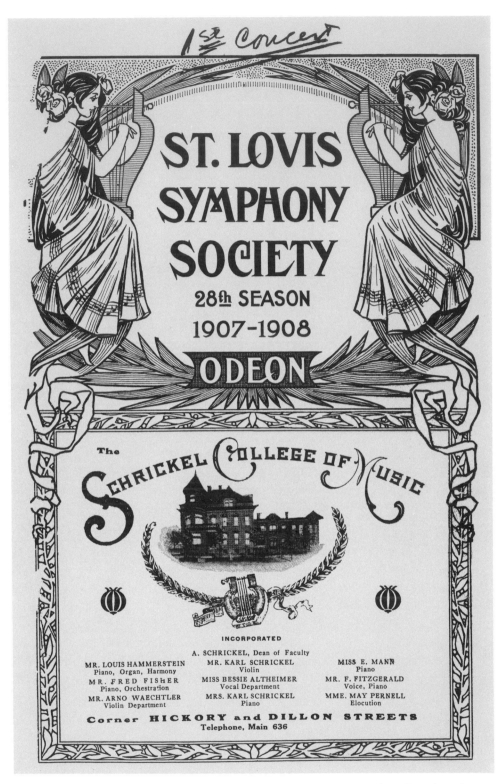

Early program cover. Handwritten "1st concert" at top was apparently written by whoever saved this particular program, which became part of the archives.

ORCHESTRA

MAX ZACH, Conductor
FREDERICK FISCHER, Assistant Conductor and Manager
HUGO OLK, Concert Master

FIRST VIOLINS
1 Hugo Olk
2 Arno Waechtler
3 Victor Lichtenstein
4 Charles Kaub
5 Emil Vollrath
6 Arnold Pesold
7 Alfred Davidson
8 Benjamin F. Clay
9 Ernst Lange
10 Julius F. Silberberg
11 Alfred T. Braun
12 Maurice Speyer

VIOLONCELLOS
P. G. Anton
Charles Mayer
Edward A. Storman
Edward Clay
Frederick G. Albers
Joseph Kern

OBOES
Jacques Wouters
James S. McConathy

BASS-CLARINET
Gustave Guentzel

HORNS
Franz Hoefer
Carl Schinner
Karl Peter
George Zaenglin

TROMBONES
Oscar Hallback
David Bittner
Oswald Forkert

SECOND VIOLINS
Carl Steinkuehler
Guido Bergsterman
Karl Schrickel
Harry Brandt
Louis F. Stocker
Otto H. Dierker
H. Scott Harrington
Valentin Schopp
Harry Gieselmann
Samuel Kippel

DOUBLE BASSES
Robert Buhl
Henry Broeckaert
Fritz Freiermuth
Charles Mayer
Carl Thul
Valentino Trovato

ENGLISH HORN
Jacques Wouters

BASSOONS
Frederick Fischer
Noel Poepping

TRUMPETS
George Glessner
Nils Pearson
John Schopp

TUBA
Clarence Beatty

LIBRARIAN
James S. McConathy

VIOLAS
Carl A. Tholl
Louis Kielsmeyer
Henry Falkenhainer
Oswald Thumser
John Boehmen
William A. Kaltenthaler

HARP
Miss Wilhelmina Lowe

FLUTES
Leopold Broeckaert
John Kiburz
Mack L. Close

PICCOLO
John Kiburz

CLARINETS
Antonio Sarli
Gustav Guentzel
Valentino Trovato

DOUBLE BASSOON
Noel Poepping

CORNETS
Noah Tarrantino
John Schopp

TYMPANI.
Charles H. Vet

BATTERY
Moritz Waechtler
Adolph Burg

Zach's Orchestra during his first season here. Victor Lichtenstein, in the first violins, was also music critic, writing reviews of the concerts in *Reedy's Mirror*.

Odeon in December 1907, presenting the classic repertoire consisting of *Lucia*, *Aïda*, *Faust*, *Rigoletto*, *Bohème*, *Carmen*, and *Pagliacci*. The Thomas orchestra, conducted by Frederick Stock, played a series of six concerts at the Odeon. And, no doubt for a different kind of audience, John Philip Sousa and his band played a series of three concerts, also at the Odeon.

Zach started out with eight symphony concerts and eighteen popular concerts. The proportion of Pops concerts to regular, or subscription, concerts was to change as Zach built up the music level of his audiences. The usual schedule in his later years was to become fifteen or twenty pairs of subscription concerts —depending on the year's finances—the Pops series remaining at twenty or slightly less. Frederick Fischer, the bassoonist and still the Assistant Conductor, conducted many of the Pops concerts.

Several years after the Zach reign began, Arthur J. Gaines, a young accountant, audited the books for the Saint Louis Symphony Orchestra. He was immediately hired to be the manager, and he remained in that office for ten years. (Arthur Gaines was a significant figure in the story of the St. Louis Symphony Orchestra, having been its manager in two different sessions—from 1912 to 1922, and again from 1931 to 1938. In a way, we shared him with the Minnesota Orchestra—then called the Minneapolis Symphony—as he also served that organization as manager through two long, significant periods in its history.)

With Zach as Conductor and Gaines as Manager, the Saint Louis Symphony Orchestra made enormous strides. Max Steindel, a twenty-one-year-old cellist, came in as Principal in 1912. A member of a family highly regarded in professional music circles, Steindel had an uncle and a brother in the Theodore Thomas Orchestra. Except for a short hiatus during World War I, Steindel was to remain with the Saint Louis Orchestra for over forty years.

The guest-artist list in this decade read like a musical "Who's Who." Wilhelm Bachaus, Jacques Thibaud, Fritz Kreisler, Olga Samaroff, Ossip Gabrilovitsch, Josef Lhevinne, Albert Spalding, Sergei Rachmaninoff, Ernestine Schumann-Heink—such names appeared on the programs repeatedly. In 1913, Zach (and Gaines) started taking the Orchestra out on tours—on a modest basis at first, but increasing the number of towns visited each year. In 1913, one tour into Illinois took the Orchestra to Springfield, Peoria, Jacksonville, Galesburg, and Bloomington, plus a spur trip into Burlington, Iowa. Obviously, that having been the age of the railroad, they went where the trains went.

That the money to keep the Orchestra going was hard to come by was not an unusual condition, to say the least. The income from ticket sales did not, of course, suffice and the operation was supported by contributions in a "Guarantors' List," published regularly in each concert program. In 1914, the exchequer received a boost when it was announced that the Business Men's League had assisted the Symphony Society in raising a Guarantee Fund of $45,000 per year, for the next four years, "for the support and improvement" of the Symphony Orchestra. In 1915–1916 the deficit, out of an $82,509 total expense, was $32,348. (Salaries were listed at $55,646, soloists fees at $6,708.)

Program in Zach's first season. Advertisement on back cover is lost to posterity.

Eleventh Symphony Program

FRIDAY AFTERNOON, FEBRUARY 13th, AT 3:00
SATURDAY EVENING, FEBRUARY 14th, AT 8:15

Soloist—SERGE RACHMANINOFF—Pianist

The present generation has not produced a more interesting musical figure than Serge Rachmaninoff. As Pianist, Composer, and Conductor, he is pre-eminent. His Symphonies, Concertos, Piano pieces, and Songs, occupy prominent places on the best musical programs throughout the world. As Conductor of the Imperial Opera at Moscow he established a reputation that was later enhanced by his wonderful leadership of the famous Philharmonic Orchestra of the same city. He came to America a year ago and played a few concerts in the larger cities and it is safe to say that no Pianist, since the palmy days of Paderewski, has created such a great sensation.

The patrons of these concerts will enjoy the unusual treat of hearing this great artist interpret one of his own, and perhaps his greatest work for the piano, at next week's concerts.

The Complete Program

Brahms.."Tragic" Overture, Op. 81

Schumann..Symphony No. 2, C Major, Op. 61
  I—Sostenuto assai: Allegro ma non troppo
  II—Scherzo: Allegro vivace
  III—Adagio espressivo
  IV—Allegro molto vivace

Rachmaninoff..Concerto for Piano, No. 2, in C Minor, Op. 18
  I—Moderato; allegro
  II—Adagio sostenuto
  III—Allegro scherzando; presto

Single Admission Tickets for these concerts: Parquet, $2.00; Box seats, $2.50; Balcony, $1.50 and $1.00. No War Tax. Sale opens Monday, February 9th, at Baldwin Piano Co., 1111 Olive Street. Telephones: Olive 4370, Central 6765. Mail orders accompanied by check or money order payable to St. Louis Symphony Society, filled in order of receipt. Enclose stamped addressed envelope if you wish tickets mailed.

Program from Zach's thirteenth season. It was Rachmaninoff's second American tour. Note informal reference to Paderewski's popularity.

St. Louis Symphony Orchestra

SEASON 1919-1920

MAX ZACH, Conductor

VIOLINS

MICHEL GUSIKOFF,
          Concert Master
ARNO WAECHTLER
ELLIS LEVY
CHARLES A. KAUB
ALFRED DAVIDSON
EMIL VOLLRATH
JOHN FREIERMUTH
ISADORE COHEN
ALBIN STEINDEL
BENJAMIN CLAY
JULES LEPSKE
CLARENCE MAURER
FRANK KELLENBERGER
HARRY GOLD
LOUIS DRUZINSKY
CARL M. BERGMANN
ARMIN AUFFARTH
OSCAR MARK, JR.
OTTO KUETTNER
BENJAMIN RADER
EDWIN NIES
JOE WINTER
M. D. AQUINO
EARL GOTTSCHALK
FRANCIS VAN RAALTE
DAVID BITTNER, JR.
ANDREW J. GILL
OTTO REINERT
JOSEPH CATARNICHI

VIOLAS

HUGO OLK
CARL A. THOLL
LOUIS KIELSMEIER
OSWALD THUMSER
H. J. FALKENHAINER
CHRISTEN KNUDSEN
PAUL ROSSOW
VICTOR HUGO
NILS PEARSON

VIOLONCELLOS

H. MAX STEINDEL
ABRAHAM TORGOVE
CHARLES MAYER
FRANK H. MENGES
EDWARD CLAY
EDWARD A. STORMAN
LEO TORGOVE
ARNESS SELKIRK

BASSES

ROBERT BUHL
OLE L. OATMAN
ANDREA CASERTANI
LOUIS TORGOVE
WILLIAM STEIN
JOSEPH ZOTTARELLE
JOHN OSMAK
SALVATORE CAMPIONE

HARP

IDA DELLEDONNE

FLUTES AND PICCOLOS

JOHN F. KIBURZ
OSCAR W. NEFF
L. MACK CLOSE

OBOES

ADOLPH BERTRAM
PAUL STANDKE

ENGLISH HORN

JACQUES WOUTERS

CLARINETS

TONY P. SARLI
ALEXANDER HALBMAN

BASS CLARINET

ERWIN HARDER

BASSOONS

FREDERICK FISCHER
DOMENICO DELLEDONNE
NOEL POEPPING

CONTRA BASSOON

NOEL POEPPING

HORNS

PELLEGRINO LECCE
JOHN UGRIN
WALDEMAR HELMHOLZ
ALBERT A. GILCHER
OSCAR A. BABBE

TRUMPETS AND CORNETS

DAVID GLICKSTEIN
JOE CARIONE
NILS PEARSON
OTTO KUETTNER

TROMBONES

OSCAR H. HALLBACK
PAUL VEGNA
EUGENE KIEFER

TUBA

RALPH E. WALKER

TYMPANI

OTTO KRISTUFEK

PERCUSSION

ELMER GESNER
WILLIAM GILCHER
EMIL VOLLRATH

Orchestra Manager—FREDERICK FISCHER   Librarian—EUGENE KIEFER

Zach's Orchestra in his second-to-last season. Hugo Olk, former concertmaster, is now principal viola. Max Steindel and Elmer Gesner are already in the roster.

At the bottom of the page bearing the budget figures some plain statements were printed. These read: "Every Symphony Orchestra has a deficit. Our Orchestra is one of the best, but in spite of that fact the deficit is the smallest of any of the large orchestras. There has been subscribed to the Guarantee Fund for this year $23,794. Any subscription is appreciated. Subscriptions run from $5.00 to $1,000. We have eleven of the latter. We need twenty." What could be more direct!

By 1917–1918 (we were then officially involved in World War I) the concert-goers' programs gave a running account of the state of the deficit throughout the season. Early in the season, the Guarantee Fund deficit was estimated to be $40,000. Later in the year, the estimate of shortfall was $50,000. A little later it dropped to $46,000. By mid-March, a bit more than $40,000 had been raised.

As to what was happening on the stage, the concerts had pretty well leveled off to fifteen pairs of subscriptions and twenty Pops. There had been some talk of changing the subscription concerts from Friday afternoons and Saturday nights to Friday afternoons and Thursday nights, but the season ticket holders had been polled and had rejected the change. Michael Gusikoff had replaced Hugo Olk as Concertmaster, Zach (and Arthur Gaines) were inviting the concert-goers to mail in preferences for "request programs."

The mid-winter tour of the 1919–1920 season took the Orchestra not only to various smaller towns but into Orchestra Hall in Chicago.

It seems fair, from almost any point of view, to credit Max Zach with having been the principal architect in the construction and development of the Saint Louis Symphony Orchestra as a major name in the world of American symphony orchestras. Various accounts picture him as a man who could never quite throw his whole personality into the so-called Romantic Repertoire, and as one who never gracefully adjusted to the interpretive liberties which the great soloists took with the scores. It is inaccurate, however, to fault him for inflexibility and for holding too closely to the classic tradition, when one scans a listing of some of the repertoire which he offered, for the Orchestra, during this period, presented first local performances of music by Tchaikovsky, Glazounov, Berlioz, Rachmaninoff, Debussy, Bruckner, Sibelius, and R. Strauss, to mention a few. Zach not only programmed such relatively "new" European music as this, along with the classic repertoire, but he also saw to it that the American composers were recognized, and he presented works by Ernest Bloch, John Alden Carpenter, George W. Chadwick, Charles T. Griffes, St. Louis' own Ernest Kroeger, and a conglomeration of others, many of whom have faded out of the picture since that time.[1]

It is interesting to note that Zach, for all his stern classic background, actually wound up limiting Beethoven music to about eight per cent of total repertoire, and Brahms to about six per cent.[2] During this era, this was considered rather progressive.

A sidelight here has to do with Max Zach, his first association (Boston Symphony Orchestra), and the current events of the period. Zach's tenure in St. Louis obviously included World War I. While the Bostonians were building up

ALTHOUGH the *Symphony Orchestra* will show an operating loss on the season's concerts of approximately $43,000.00, this must not be looked on as a LOSS or WASTE of money or energy.

In its largest sense it is an actual PROFIT to the City of St. Louis. It shows the world that this community is made up of people whose civic pride is so intense that they do not hesitate to put up the necessary funds to maintain a musical organization whose aims are purely altruistic.

ESTIMATED EXPENDITURE for Season 1919-20:

Salaries of Conductor, Orchestra and Soloists	$ 90,725.00
Hall Rent, Advertising, Management Salaries, Office Expense, Music, Printing, Stationery and Postage, Interest and Miscellaneous Expense	27,236.37
Total Estimated Expenditure	$117,961.37

ESTIMATED INCOME for Season 1919-20:

Subscriptions (Season Tickets)	$ 52,000.00
Symphony and Popular Concert Door Sales	20,000.00
Extra Concerts and Tours	3,000.00
Total Estimated Income	$ 75,000.00

ESTIMATED DEFICIT for Season 1919-20 .... $ 42,961.37

Every Symphony Orchestra in America operates at a deficit. This is necessary because the cost of maintaining an orchestra is very heavy, but the price of tickets must be placed at such a reasonable figure that all may attend the concerts. The Orchestra aims to furnish music at a low cost to the man with a small purse as well as to those of greater means. *If every seat in the Odeon is sold for every concert there will still be a deficit of $25,000.00.*

The deficit must be met by voluntary and liberal donations from people who believe the Orchestra is filling a recognized need in the civic life of St. Louis.

FORM OF GUARANTEE FUND SUBSCRIPTION

St. Louis, Mo.,..............19...

The undersigned, desiring that the Symphony Orchestra be maintained and continued, subscribes for the benefit and use of the ST. LOUIS SYMPHONY SOCIETY the sum of...Dollars ($.................), and agrees to pay the said sum on demand of the said Society.

NAME   ADDRESS

....

Return to ST. LOUIS SYMPHONY SOCIETY, 210 University Club Bldg., Grand and Washington Aves.

From program during Zach's thirteenth season. Note opening paragraph.

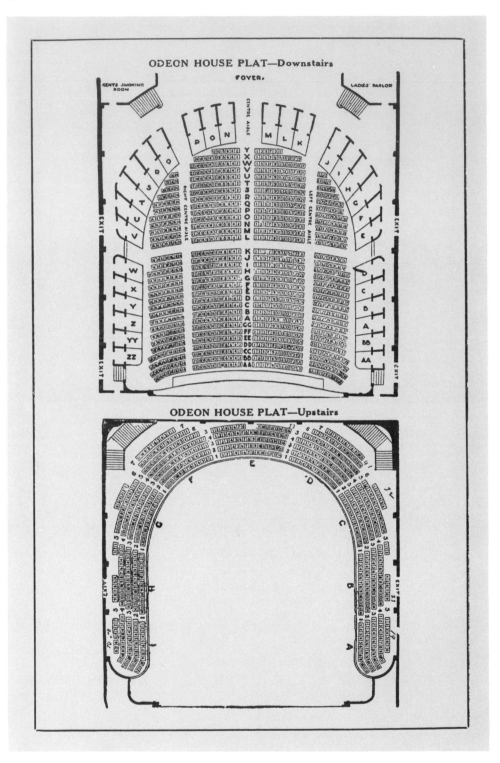

This plat of the Odeon was printed in most of the early programs, through the 1920's.

a nationalistic resentment of their conductor, Dr. Karl Muck—a German and a distinguished Wagner interpreter—St. Louisans were not inclined to fight the war at the level of artistic interest. Zach was never regarded as a representative of "the enemy"—German music was not under fire. Dr. Muck, on the other hand, was a victim of anti-German sentiment: he was even accused of playing "The Star-Spangled Banner" with a lack of proper respect. And as a conductor he was eventually drummed out of the world of music in America and returned to Germany.[3] In St. Louis, perhaps because of the large, stable German population—citizens who had neighbors and friends all over the community—the war was not fought by turning the concert stage into a battlefield. True, the street name "Berlin" was changed to "Pershing," but the German-born conductor of the Saint Louis Symphony Orchestra did not become an object of suspicion.

Zach's elevation of the quality in orchestral performances was recognized by the audiences and reported by the critics. A review of a concert during Zach's seventh season is more or less typical. After a January concert featuring Carl Friedberg as soloist, playing Schumann's Piano Concerto in A Minor, the reviewer wrote, "The accompaniment by the orchestra was masterly; and Mr. Zach's reading was filled with authoritative tonal, rhythmical and interpretive power. The orchestra, so far this season, has displayed an improvement and development over previous years that is little short of astonishing, and now ranks with the foremost organizations of the kind in any part of this country."[4]

It seems a fairly reliable guess that Max Zach's national reputation would have grown enormously had his life not been cut short at age fifty-six, an age when many conductors are hitting their stride with the most vigor. Zach, in the winter of the 1920–1921 season, had to have a tooth extracted and died on February 3, 1921, from infection in the gum.[5] There were no "miracle drugs." It was fourteen years too early for sulfas.

The remainder of the 1920–1921 season was conducted by the Assistant Conductor Frederick Fischer and three guest conductors—Theodore Spierin, Dirk Foch, and Rudolph Ganz.

The dignified, formal, and rather formidable man, who lived alone at the Jefferson Hotel and commuted to the Odeon by street car, left his name permanently in St. Louis. Look at any current program: almost all of the old "standards" of the serious concert stage will be listed as having been first performed by the Saint Louis Symphony Orchestra with Max Zach conducting.

Rudolph Ganz

RUDOLPH GANZ

The Symphony Years 1921–1927

AFTER ZACH'S DEATH, the guest conductor who made the greatest impact on St. Louis was Rudolph Ganz. He was engaged to open the 1921–1922 season as the fourth Permanent Conductor. Ganz, born in Zurich in 1877, had been a double-threat child prodigy, performing both as a cellist and as a pianist. He gravitated toward the piano and made his debut as a mature soloist in 1899 with the Berlin Philharmonic Orchestra. (He played, on this occasion, both the Beethoven E Flat Concerto and the Chopin E Minor Concerto.) He had subsequently made extensive tours in Europe and in America, and was a well-known personality in professional music circles. From 1910 to 1915 he was head of the piano department at Chicago Musical College, after which he continued his widespread touring, including Canada in his itinerary. As a soloist, he took great pride in playing the works of new and relatively unestablished composers. He introduced new works by Debussy, D'Indy, Ravel, Busoni, and Bartok, to mention only a few. He was already a "name," a "star," when he was engaged to lead the Saint Louis Symphony Orchestra.

The appointment of Ganz as Permanent Conductor did not represent first choice, since the powers-that-were had tried unsuccessfully to acquire Fritz Kreisler for the post.[1] Obviously, the principal concern was to come up with a soloist, a "celebrity" who would draw in the crowds by sheer virtue of a famous name. Ganz had a sparkling personality, a sense of showmanship, and plenty of social know-how. He was a fine concert pianist. He was also a composer. He was not, however, a top-flight conductor when he was hired.

St. Louis in 1921 was a musically active city and growing more and more musically sophisticated. The Symphony Orchestra was contending with friendly competition. Among the local professional entrepreneurs was Elizabeth Cueny (a member of the National Concert Managers' Association) who brought to St. Louis such luminaries as the tenor John McCormack, Josef and Rosina Lhevinne (in a joint piano recital), Sergei Rachmaninoff, and Fritz Kreisler. Arthur Gaines (Manager of the Symphony Orchestra)—wearing his second hat as an independent manager—presented, among others, Joseph Hoffman and the baritone Emilio de Gogorzia.

A sign of the times was the astonishing number of musicians advertising as soloists and teachers in the regular symphony programs. The instrumentalists were, for the most part, members of the Symphony orchestra. The singers were primarily those who had earned some kind of reputation as performers and were settling down to teaching, or "coaching." Many of the instrumentalists were managed privately by Arthur Gaines and offered their services not only for instruction but for performance in private-home concerts. The singers—most with their studios in the Musical Art Building—included such names as Madame Vetta-Karst, Mrs. Karl Kimmel, Mrs. Stella Kellog Haines, John W. Bohn, and Eugenia Getner. For some of the musicians, offering their teaching skills was their fulltime activity. For the Orchestra musicians, it was a means of augmenting an income that was far from being an adequate full year's salary.

Another sidelight, a rather frivolous one, on the musical activities of the early Twenties was the vogue (revived somewhat in the Seventies) of the "player piano." Supposedly, familiarity with the sounds emanating from a piano roll would improve one's own keyboard technique. Kieselhorst Piano Company was selling the A. B. Chase Reproducing Piano. Aeolian was selling the Duo-Art Reproducing Pianola, and the Baldwin Piano Company was offering a player piano named Manualo.

Ganz inherited a pattern of concerts which he retained—fifteen pairs of subscription concerts and twenty Pops. He wore his mantle of conductor lightly, at first, freely admitting to the Orchestra that he knew very little about what to do with a baton. Obviously his skill increased as he grew more accustomed to the podium. His principal claim to fame, as conductor in St. Louis, came by way of a rather unexpected avenue. It turned out that he had an instinctive rapport with juvenile audiences. He cajoled them, encouraged them, and showed enormous patience with their restless behavior during concerts. In his first year here, Ganz conducted five Free Children's Concerts (played on Saturday mornings and sponsored by the *St. Louis Post-Dispatch*) and four children's concerts in Kansas City when the Orchestra was on tour.

By 1921, when Ganz took over, World War I was far enough in the past that it was no longer necessary to prove patriotism by performance of American music. Max Zach, the German-born, had ended his tenure with the Orchestra with approximately twelve per cent of its repertoire being American music. Ganz, with the pressure off, reduced the percentage to five per cent, a much more expected and normal ratio.[2]

Of the soloists who appeared in subscription concerts during Ganz' first year, Ganz himself (playing the Tchaikovsky B-flat Minor Concerto in the Fourteenth Concert) was by far the best known. The others were either bright lights of the period who never achieved a lasting fame, or were soloists from the Orchestra itself. There were no guest conductors, although Ganz occasionally had a reprieve when Frederick Fischer (the valuable legacy from the time of Alfred Ernst and the time of Max Zach) conducted.

Arriving in Jackson, Mississippi, on tour in 1922. Left to right, Frederick Fischer (Assistant Conductor and bassoonist), Arthur Gaines (Manager), Mme. Margaret Namara (soprano soloist), Mrs. N. N. Banks (mother of Mme. Namara), and Rudolph Ganz. Pullman porter behind them is Morris Brooks, who was known as "the guardian Angel" and who made the entire tour with them. Note wooden train car. (*St. Louis Post-Dispatch* photograph, April 22, 1922)

The tours, which under Zach had usually involved six or eight concerts each, began to expand in numbers of concerts and in distances travelled. Ganz took the Orchestra on a month-long Spring Tour in 1922 during which they played twenty-seven concerts. The group went south first, into Texas, Louisiana, Mississippi, and Tennessee. After a six-day, catching-the-breath interval at home in St. Louis, they took off again, heading this time north into Iowa. Strenuous tours of this magnitude gradually became the expected thing in Ganz' era.

Among the personalities that played significant if often background roles during these times and for many years thereafter, were the Gesner brothers, Clarence and Elmer. Elmer had joined the Orchestra in 1916, under Zach, as a

1926–1927 Orchestra, Rudolph Ganz, Music Director. Ganz seated in center, to the left of two seated women.

percussionist, when one of the percussion players had died suddenly. He became a regular member of the Orchestra the next season. Clarence, a clarinetist, entered the ranks of the Orchestra several years later in 1922. Clarence became the Stage Manager, Elmer the Librarian.

Between the two of them, they handled most of the incredible logistics of getting a big orchestra out on tour. There were the trunks to be accounted for and safely delivered. These trunks not only held each player's instrument but often a good many personal effects. The trunks had to be conveyed to the railroad station, put safely aboard the baggage car, and carefully unloaded and transported to wherever the Orchestra was to play. In addition to this there was, of course, the music. The sheets had to be sorted, packed, conveyed, unpacked, and placed on the individual stands on whatever stage the next concert was to be performed. The Gesners did all of this. Moreover, musicians being mere human beings with common human failings, items got forgotten—essential items. The Gesners could always handle the emergency, be it a forgotten pair of black shoes, a white shirt, a necktie, or an emergency headache remedy. Over a period of years, the brothers developed a kind of tongue-in-cheek penalty list which they posted backstage, listing who had needed what and who had forgotten what. Behind the scenes it was called the "Dumb Cluck List." Nobody really minded. The orchestra members were handled with such tender loving care by the Gesners that they were very willing to take a little chiding. (At the end of the 1953–1954 season Clarence Gesner left the Orchestra and went to the West Coast. Elmer Gesner remained as Librarian until 1968. Clarence was with the Orchestra thirty-one years, Elmer fifty-one years.)

Although touring was (and still is) an obvious upheaval in the musicians' lives, it was recognized in these early days as an essential element in the life of a

major symphony orchestra. Much of the same music was played from city to city and town to town, so rehearsals weren't as burdensome as they were for the "at home" performances. The acoustics in the hall, gymnasium, auditorium, or wherever they were playing, were occasionally horrendous, but nothing could be done except to be sure the musicians were forewarned. Usually, some of them would go to the place a few minutes early to clap their hands and test the sound for themselves. Sometimes the musicians slept on the train, which was parked and waiting for them, about to take off for the next town. Other times, accommodations—not on the train—were less than luxurious. Occasionally the space provided for sleeping would be one large, barracks-like room. In spite of the absence of comforts, Ganz enjoyed the tours and, consistent with his fondness for young listeners, he is said to have shaken hands with all 10,000 students who attended a concert in Des Moines.[3]

One of the soloists introduced by Ganz at the popular concerts in his first year here, was a young St. Louisan, a soprano named Helen Traubel Carpenter. In short order, she began to be featured on the tours. As Helen Traubel (she dropped the name Carpenter after a divorce) she rose, through the Twenties, to considerable eminence. Ganz—invited to be Guest Conductor of a Stadium Concert of the New York Philharmonic—presented her as soloist there. She captivated an audience of 10,000. The young performer, later to distinguish herself as a great Wagnerian opera singer, was sponsored by an interested St. Louisan, Mrs. J. A. Haskell, who resolutely kept the fact of her patronage under wraps.

Financial problems were ever-present, as customary. The monetary need, according to the Society Board, in the 1921–1922 season, for instance, was $90,000 of which $6800 had been pledged by 1028 subscribers. The projected need was for $100,000 in each of the next two years. If this amount seems modest (in comparison to figures quoted in Symphony reports in the Seventies) one can take note of a full-page advertisement placed in the Symphony Program by one of the banks which stated, in early spring, "Deposit $20 per month, and by July or August, you will have enough for a vacation."

During Ganz' last season the subscription concert series was still holding on at fifteen pairs, and nineteen popular concerts. The Student Concerts numbered ten under the auspices of the Saint Louis Symphony Society and five sponsored by the Board of Education.

When Ganz left, at the end of the 1926–1927 season, he returned to the Chicago Musical College as vice-president. (Ten years later he was to conduct the Young People's Concerts of the New York Philharmonic Society.)

Ganz had lent color and visibility to the Saint Louis Symphony Orchestra, but he was lacking in the conducting mystique and skill which shape a good orchestra into a truly great one. Even the public—the supposedly untutored, unprofessional public—can spot something that falls short of excellence. At the time of Ganz' departure, there was a noticeable sag in audience enthusiasm and support. Some of the disaffection with Ganz was reported more than forty years after the fact in an article in the *Post Dispatch* by Frank Peters. The story read, in part: "It was Ganz who introduced the Saint Louis Symphony audience to Stravinsky, Ravel, Schoenberg, Mahler, Honegger, Respighi, Vaughan-Williams, and Richard Strauss. Ganz took jovial responsibility for the shocks he gave the audience, and invited the subscribers to hiss if they didn't like this or that contemporary piece. . . . Ernst Krohn, the peppery old musician and historian of St. Louis music affairs, . . . says he and various critics of Ganz circulated petitions for the conductor's removal, and collected an impressive number of signatures, including those of orchestra musicians. The Symphony Society got wind of the petition, Krohn says, and being already concerned at audience apathy, invited Ganz to a board meeting, at which he immediately offered his resignation."[4]

First

Symphony Program

_____

FRIDAY AFTERNOON, NOVEMBER 11, AT 3:00
SATURDAY EVENING, NOVEMBER 12, AT 8:15

_____

Dramatic Overture, "Patrie," Op. 19...Bizet
(First time)

Symphony in E Minor, No. 5, Op. 64...................................Tschaikowsky
    I.   Andante; Allegro con anima.
   II. Andante cantabile, con alcuna licenza.
  III. Valse: Allegro moderato.
  IV. Finale: Andante maestoso; Allegro vivace.

INTERMISSION

Prelude to "Lohengrin"...Wagner

"Waldweben," from "Siegfried," Act II, Scene 2............................Wagner

Prelude to "Die Meistersinger von Nuernberg"..............................Wagner

NO SYMPHONY CONCERTS NEXT FRIDAY AND SATURDAY
as the orchestra appears in the first Kansas City concerts next week.

    Next concerts on Friday and Saturday. November 25 and 26. Popular concerts every Sunday as usual.

    No encores by the orchestra. The artist may grant one encore if the audience expresses a desire for it.

    Hats must not be worn or put on during concerts. Ushers have instructions to enforce this rule.

    Holders of Season tickets, when unable to attend, are urged to see that the tickets are used. It is not difficult to find a friend who will be glad to have the opportunity of hearing a concert.

Ganz's first season. Ushers were to enforce the rule that hats must not be worn during concerts, and permission is granted the soloist to play one encore.

SEVENTH REGULAR PROGRAM

THURSDAY EVENING, JANUARY 3, AT 8:15
FRIDAY AFTERNOON, JANUARY 4, at 3:00

Soloist—OSSIP GABRILÓWITSCH—Pianist

1. Overture to "Der Freischütz"..Weber

2. Symphony No. 8, in F Major, Op. 93............................Beethoven
   I.   Allegro vivace e con brio.
   II. Allegretto scherzando.
   III. Tempo di menuetto.
   IV. Allegro vivace.

3. Prelude and Isolde's "Love Death," from "Tristan und Isolde,"
   Wagner

(Intermission Thursday Night)
(No Intermission Friday Afternoon)

4. Concerto No. 2, in B-flat Major, for Pianoforte and Orchestra,
   Op. 83..Brahms
   I.   Allegro non troppo.
   II. Scherzo: Allegro appassionato.
   III. Andante.
   IV. Finale: Allegretto grazioso.

MASON AND HAMLIN PIANO USED

FUTURE REGULAR SYMPHONY DATES AND SOLOISTS (Thursday Evenings at 8:15 and Friday afternoons at 3:00, respectively)—January 10-11, Gusikoff, Violinist; January 17-18, Ganz, Pianist; January 31-February 1, Orchestral program (no soloist); February 7-8, Friedman, Pianist; February 21-22, Leginska, Pianiste; February 28-29, Morini, Violinist; March 6-7, Hempel, Soprano; March 13-14, Schwartz, Baritone.

The artist may grant one encore if the audience desires it. All concerts begin promptly as announced—Thursdays, 8:15; Fridays, 3:00 and Sundays, 3:15. Hats must be removed during the concerts.

Do Not Waste Your Symphony Tickets—Subscribers who are unable to attend are urged to co-operate with the Ladies Friday Musical Club in giving deserving students an opportunity of hearing good music. Tickets should be sent at least two hours in advance of concert or the locations of tickets can be telephoned to MRS. DAVID KRIEGSHABER, 4939 WASHINGTON AVE., Forest 2594-W.

SEASON TICKETS

for the remaining eight (8) Thursday Evening or Friday Afternoon Symphony Concerts
still may be obtained

PRICES $6.40, $7.50, $9.60, $13.35

Make reservations at
THE AEOLIAN COMPANY or SYMPHONY ORCHESTRA OFFICE
1004 Olive St.   Olive 9103——302 Odeon Building——Lindell 2907

Ganz's fourth season. Gabrilowitsch's wife, Olga Samaroff, also an established soloist of the period, was a native St. Louisan.

THE ST. LOUIS SYMPHONY ORCHESTRA
Personnel for 1925-1926

First Violins
Michel Gusikoff
Concertmaster
Ellis Levy
Assistant Concertmaster
Joseph Faerber
John Freiermuth
Charles Kaub
Harry Gold
David Hochman
Kirk Frederick
Isadore Grossman
Louis Druzinsky
Benj. Grosbayne
Joseph Johnson
F. C. Lathrop
Emil Vollrath

Second Violins
Edwin Nies
Principal
J. F. Claiborne
Earl Gottschalk
M. Halbman
Jack Fielderman
John Halk
C. A. Preusse
Paul Schreiber
Simon Poles
Sam Morris
Robert Burger
Maurice Sacks
Joseph Loebker

Violas
Jacques Tushinsky
Principal
Carl Tholl
Oswald Thumser
H. Falkenhainer
Christen Knudsen
Victor Hugo
Paul Rossow
John Hartl

Violoncellos
Max Steindel
Principal
Pasquale De Conto
Abraham Torgove
Domenick Sotille
Leo Torgove
Carl Rossow
W. R. Ammann

RUDOLPH GANZ, Conductor

FREDERICK FISCHER
Assistant Conductor

Basses
Joseph Krausse
Principal
Karl Phil Auer
Robert Buhl
Andrea Casertani
Albert Ravagnani
Earl Hyna
Salvatore Campione
Meyer Pitchersky

Harps
Graziella Pampari
Principal
W. L. Spyer

Flutes
John Kiburz
Principal
Peter Altmeyer
L. M. Close

Piccolo
L. M. Close
Principal

Oboes
Ermete Simonazzi
Principal
Joseph Spada
Vincent Rifici

English Horn
Vincent Rifici

Clarinets
Louis DeSantis
Principal
Clarence Gesner
Charles Camacho

Bass Clarinet
Charles Camacho

Bassoons
Max Fuhrman
Principal
Herman Beilfuss
Noel Poepping

Contra Bassoon
Noel Poepping

Horns
Pellegrino Lecce
Principal
Emilio Stango
Joseph Rescigno
William Miller

Trumpets
Joseph Gustat
Principal
Joseph Carione

Trombones
Oscar Hallback
Principal
Joseph Valetic
Charles Meier

Tuba
Vincenzo Vanni

Tympani
Ben Vitto

Percussion
Elmer Gesner
W. G. Albers

Librarian
Elmer Gesner

Orchestra Manager
Frederick Fischer

Ganz's Orchestra in his fifth season.

From 1925–1926 season program. Ganz developed extremely successful young people's concerts. Note the "Guessing the Instruments Contest."

From program of 1926–1927 season.

The symphony orchestra is really an orchestra on the new Orthophonic Victrola

THROUGH the Orthophonic Victrola, you can bring the great symphony orchestras to your home, *precisely* as you would hear them at their public performance.

Realistic! You can almost *see* the rise and fall of the violin-bows . . . the pulsing beat of the padded hammers on the kettle-drums!

Visit your nearest Victor dealer and have him play some of the new Orthophonic recordings of the world's greatest symphonies as played by foremost orchestras. Build a symphonic library of records in your own home for your entertainment—and your friends'.

The most famous symphony orchestras are recorded by Victor, and their recordings include all the favorite movements from all your favorite symphonies. The following selections are also of particular interest:

Country Dance No. 1 (from *Nell Gwyn*) (German)

Pastoral Dance No. 2 — The Merry-makers' Dance No. 3 (from *Nell Gwyn*) (German)
GANZ—ST. LOUIS SYMPHONY ORCHESTRA

Song of India (Rimsky-Korsakow)
Minuet (Bolzoni)
GANZ—ST. LOUIS SYMPHONY ORCHESTRA

Barber of Seville—Overture—Parts 1 and 2 (Rossini)
GANZ—ST. LOUIS SYMPHONY ORCHESTRA

VICTOR TALKING MACHINE COMPANY, CAMDEN, NEW JERSEY, U. S. A.

From 1927 program. Some Ganz recordings with the orchestra were available.

Our Conductor
RUDOLPH GANZ

Excerpts from the Daily Press Upon
Mr. Ganz's Work as Conductor

"I found in Mr. Ganz a leader keen in his understanding of the music he sought to interpret, alert, sensitive, and aristocratic. He is direct and simple, and displays no frills."
—Pierre Key, in a syndicated article.

"Mr. Ganz's technic with the baton is as neat as it would be were he using a piano, his phrasing, his accenting, have the finish of the soloist."
—New York Times.

"He leads with great verve and zest and the result is an unusual clarity and sharpness of outline in everything he conducts."
—New York Evening Post.

"Mr. Ganz's reading was admirable, with a beautifully elastic tempo subtly varied, with the result of contributing greatly to the expressiveness of an eloquent performance."
—New York Herald-Tribune.

"He is signally an interpretative artist."
—Christian Science Monitor.

"Ovations, rare even from enthusiastic Hollywood Bowl audiences, acknowledged the art of Rudolph Ganz."
—Los Angeles Evening Examiner.

"Mr. Ganz enjoyed unrivaled popularity while in Hollywood and his programs comprised one of the outstanding achievements of the season."
—Hollywood Citizen.

"He is the virtuoso-composer at all times and characteristic of no one but Ganz."
—Los Angeles Evening Herald.

"Mr. Ganz was triumphant, and the orchestra was at its lucid, sensitive, communicative best."
—St. Louis Times.

"Mr. Ganz won a signal triumph yesterday afternoon with the first symphony of Johannes Brahms."
—St. Louis Post.

"At the conclusion of the concert the audience fairly shouted approval, and in the ensuing tumult great bouquets of flowers were showered on the conductor, by which demonstration even this artist experienced in public manifestations, was somewhat taken back."
—St. Louis Globe-Democrat.

Mr. Ganz will conduct the Popular Concert the coming Sunday, Nov. 7th, at 3:15.

MAKE EVERY EFFORT TO ATTEND—TELL A FRIEND

(For Program see Inside Back Cover)

Ganz's sixth and last season.

AFTER GANZ,
THE GUEST CONDUCTORS

The Symphony Years 1927–1931

FOR FOUR YEARS after the departure of Ganz, the orchestra performed under various guest conductors. There were seven conductors who did the major portion of concerts from 1927 to 1931. Four of them were German, one British, one Italian, and one Spanish. Their ages varied from the early thirties to the late sixties. These men were William Van Hoogstraten, Carl Schuricht (a conductor perhaps better known in Germany than in America), Emil Oberhoffer (who had been the first conductor of the Minneapolis Symphony Orchestra in 1903), Eugene Goossens (the English maestro who became the head of the Cincinnati Orchestra in 1931), Bernardino Molinari (the great expert in Italian opera, and he of the fiery temper), Enrique Arbos (one of the few established conductors from the Iberian Peninsula), and George Szell, who made his American conducting debut at age thirty-two with the Saint Louis Symphony Orchestra, and who later (1946) became the renowned conductor of the Cleveland Orchestra. These were the men who really kept us afloat while we were without a principal conductor. There were others whose appearances were less frequent than those mentioned above. One in particular was to become the mainstay of the Saint Louis Symphony Orchestra for many years to come.

The Board, in its endeavors to choose a new permanent conductor, sought advice from experts in all directions. Walter Damrosch (Permanent Conductor of the New York Symphony which merged in 1928 with the New York Philharmonic) and Serge Koussevitsky, then Permanent Conductor of the Boston Symphony Orchestra, recommended Vladimir Golschmann, a thirty-seven-year-old Frenchman of Russian parentage.[1] Golschmann had established his reputation in Paris as a kind of elite "whiz kid," having single-handedly devised, promoted, and conducted a successful series of programs called "Concerts Golschmann." He was a strong proponent of the music of his generation, but he could also handle the standard repertoire with great skill, even though his repertorial preference leaned toward French Impressionistic music. He had

had great visibility as guest conductor of a good number of American orchestras, and when he guest-conducted here, the Board liked what it heard and saw.

Golschmann was certainly to become the second major architect in the development of the Saint Louis Symphony Orchestra, his mark being the most telling and advantageous since that of Max Zach. His appointment in 1931 ushered in a whole new era, one characterized by acknowledgment of the classic repertoire, introduction of many new works, and, more than anything else, continuity. Unlike the present times when conductors can hold down two podiums at once, when travel time, even trans-oceanic, is reduced to a mere few hours, when even a permanent conductor doesn't conduct more than a fraction of concerts in his so-called "home town," things were different in the 1930's. It was an age when a permanent conductor or music director more or less stayed put, and the reputation of his orchestra grew because of his steadying hand and regular presence. To be sure, conductors travelled all over to perform as guest conductors. But the great orchestras had, in their resident conductors, fixed images. The Chicago Symphony was still going strong with Frederick Stock, who, as the young assistant conductor, had succeeded to the job of Permanent Conductor after the death of Theodore Thomas in 1905. Koussevitzky had been in Boston since 1924; he was to stay until 1959. Sokoloff had been in Cleveland since 1918. Ossip Gabrilovitch had been in Detroit since 1917, Stokowski had been in Philadelphia since 1912.

It was essential for a top-quality orchestra to be identified with a top-quality conductor. The Saint Louis Symphony needed such an identity and got it when the Society appointed Vladimir Golschmann as Principal Conductor in 1931. Golschmann stayed for twenty-seven years. His tenure with the Orchestra covered, roughly, the third quarter of the Symphony's one hundred year history.

THE SUNDAY CONCERTS

೧৶

Sixteen Sunday afternoon concerts, at popular prices, will be given in the Odeon during the course of the season, six of them beginning November 6, coming on consecutive Sundays before the Christmas Holidays, and ten of them beginning January 8, coming on consecutive Sundays until March 11. These concerts will mark in quality a decided advance on most of those which have been given in past years. In the belief that "Popular Concerts" given by a Symphony Orchestra should not be "Popular" in the vulgar sense of inferior music, it is the idea of the Management that there is a wide public in St. Louis which will gladly hear good music and yet cannot afford the regular Symphony concerts. It is also the belief of the Management that a very considerable percentage of the patrons of these concerts in the past will welcome a heightening of the artistic quality of the programs.

To this end, these concerts will be made, in a sense, "Little Symphony Concerts," not so serious, not so heavy, as the regular Symphony Concerts on Fridays and Saturdays, but yet having their programs contain certain works which, heretofore, have been limited to the Symphony Concerts, and also delving into the rich and varied literature of delightful music which has not been deemed quite serious enough for a regular program.

For example, the series will begin next Sunday (November 6) with a Tschaikovsky program, the principal items on which will be the thrilling Fourth Symphony and the ever charming Nutcracker Suite. On the following Sunday, a delightful list of works, announced elsewhere in this program, has been prepared and so it will go through the season. Mr. Oberhoffer's last Sunday program, which he will play on November 27, will be composed entirely of Wagnerian music.

Mr. Oberhoffer will conduct four of these concerts; Mr. Schuricht, three; Mr. Molinari, one; Mme. Ethel Leginska, one; Mr. Fischer, six and Mr. Steindel, one.

Great care and pains have been taken in the engagement of soloists. All who are to appear are artists of unquestionable standing. Although the list is not yet complete, those who have been engaged are; *Pianists*: Princess Jacques de Broglie, Katherine Gorin, Mieczyslaw Münz and Ethel Leginska (who will play the piano as well as conduct); *Violinists*: Thelma Given and Frances Berkova; *Violoncellist*: Madeline Monnier; *Singers*: Bernard Ferguson, Isabelle Molter, Grace Leslie, Harriet Van Emden and Jerome Swinford.

These Sunday Concerts will be a most admirable auxiliary to the Symphony Concerts and they are offered to the public by the St. Louis Symphony Society at nominal prices. The entire floor will be fifty and seventy-five cents, all seats reserved. The balcony will be twenty-five cents, unreserved.

From 1927–1928 season. The last half of the first paragraph spells out the philosophy.

FIFTH PAIR OF SYMPHONY CONCERTS

FRIDAY AFTERNOON, DECEMBER 14, 3:00

SATURDAY EVENING, DECEMBER 15, 8:30

EMIL OBERHOFFER, *Guest Conductor*

Soloist—VLADIMIR HOROWITZ—*Pianist*

PROGRAM

Beethoven ....Overture to "Egmont"

Brahms..Symphony No. 3 in F Major

INTERMISSION

Tschaikovsky............Concerto for Piano and Orchestra, in B-flat minor. No. 1

TICKETS—$1.00, $1.50, $2.00, $2.50

On Sale at 1004 Olive Street; Telephone JEfferson 8610

VLADIMIR HOROWITZ

A year ago the real sensation of the season, not only in St. Louis but wherever else in the country he appeared was the stupendous pianism of the young Russian, Vladimir Horowitz. In him seems to have been born the pianistic giants of a past generation. Hence the importance of his return as soloist with our Orchestra when he will play that most thrilling of works for piano and orchestra, Tschaikovsky's Concerto in B-flat minor.

GIVE THE IDEAL CHRISTMAS GIFT
A SEASON TICKET TO THE SYMPHONY CONCERTS
*For Particulars Call JE*FFERSON 8610

From interim period of guest conductors, between Ganz and Golschmann. Program took place in December 1928. Horowitz, who had made his American debut the previous spring, was twenty-four years old.

THE
ST. LOUIS SYMPHONY ORCHESTRA

Personnel for 1929-1930

First Violins

Alexander Thiede,
  Concertmaster
Ellis Levy
Joseph Faerber
John Freiermuth
Ludwig Gunder
Isadore Grossman
Edward Shalett
Jacob Levine
Max Buzatesco
Ladislav Nagy
Arthur Baron
Sol Kranzberg
David Rizzo
Charles Kaub
Francis Jones

Second Violins

Louis Druzinsky
  Principal
Paul Schreiber
Carl Nagel
Simon Poles
Rudolph J. Magin
Anton Votava
Louis Etzkow
Carl Preusse
Meyer Lipsitz
James Adair
Carl F. Hugo
Robert Burger

Violas

Philip Neeter
  Principal
Carl A. Tholl
George Goldstein
Victor Hugo
Henry Falkenhainer
Stellario Giacobbe
Oswald Thumser
John Hartl

Violoncellos

Max Steindel
  Principal
Pasquale De Conto
Emile Simon
Carl Rossow
Gustaf Keller
Igor Geffen
Antonio LaMarchina
Joseph Tonar

Basses

Carl Auer
  Principal
Waldemar F. Helmholz
Robert Buhl
Andrea Casertani
Earl Hyna
Karl Schoenfeld
George Altschuh

Harp

Graziella Pampari

Flutes

John Kiburz
  Principal
Oscar W. Neff
L. M. Close

Piccolo

L. M. Close

Oboes

Ermete Simonazzi
Joseph Antonucci
Alfred H. Hicks

English Horn

Alfred H. Hicks

Clarinets

Rocco M. Zottarelle
  Prineipal
C. L. Gesner
Charles Camacho

Bass Clarinet

Charles Camacho

Bassoons

Louis Pietrini
  Principal
John E. Ferrell
Noel Poepping

Contra Bassoon

Noel Poepping

Horns

Edward A. Murphy
  Principal
Emilio Stango
Robert L. Gustat
Wm. C. Gebhardt
George L. Scott

Trumpets

Joseph Gustat
  Principal
Joe Carione
Carl F. Hugo
John Hartl

Trombones

Oscar Hallback
  Principal
Joe Valetic
Charles Meier

Tuba

Adam Spiller

Tympani

William Ehrlich

Percussion

Elmer Gesner
William Albers
Louis H. F. Schick

Librarian

Elmer Gesner

Orchestra Manager

Frederick Fischer

73

No conductor listed. This was one of the interim years between Ganz and Golschmann, with all guest conductors.

NO SYMPHONY CONCERTS NEXT WEEK

FOURTH PAIR OF SYMPHONY CONCERTS

FRIDAY AFTERNOON, NOVEMBER 29, 3:00
SATURDAY EVENING, NOVEMBER 30, 8:30

E. FERNANDEZ ARBOS
GUEST CONDUCTOR

Soloist—NATHAN MILSTEIN—*Violinst*
(*His first appearance in Saint Louis*)

∽

Program

1. *Cherubini* .... Overture to "Anacreon"

2. *Bloch* .... Concerto Grosso for String Orchestra
   (*First Performances in St. Louis*)

3. *Albeniz-Arbos* .... { (a)   L'Albaicin
                                                            { (b)   Fête-Dieu à Seville
   (*First Performances in St. Louis*)

Intermission

4. *Glazounov* .... Concerto for Violin and Orchestra
   MR. MILSTEIN

5. *Rimsky-Korsakoff* .... Spanish Caprice

TICKETS—$1.00, $1.50, $2.00, $2.50

On Sale at 1004 Olive Street; Telephone, JEfferson 8610

THE sensation of the early musical season in the East has been the playing of Nathan Milstein, the young Russian violinist who has come to America for the first time. A close friend and fellow student of the astounding Horowitz who returns to St. Louis later in the season, he bids fair to rival the popularity of that pianistic genius . His appearance with our orchestra is awaited with keenest interest.

NATHAN MILSTEIN

Program during interim period of guest conductors, between Ganz and Golschmann. This was Milstein's first American tour. Note the price of the tickets.

ELEVENTH PAIR OF SYMPHONY CONCERTS

FRIDAY AFTERNOON, JANUARY 31, *at* 3:00

SATURDAY EVENING, FEBRUARY 1, *at* 8:30

GEORG SZELL

General Music Director of Prague, Czechoslovakia

Guest Conductor and Soloist

ⁿᵖ

PROGRAM

1. *Cherubini*............................Overture to "Ali Baba, or the Forty Thieves"

2. *Mozart*......................Concerto in A major for Pianoforte and Orchestra
    - I.   Allegro.
    - II. Andante.
    - III. Presto.

MR. SZELL

Intermission

3. *Ravel*..Le Tombeau de Couperin
    - I.   Prelude.
    - II. Forlane.
    - III. Menuet.
    - IV. Rigadaun.

(*First Time in St. Louis*)

4. *Kodaly*...Suite from the Opera: "Háry Janos"
    Prelude. The Tale Begins—Viennese Musical Clock—Song—The Battle and Defeat
    of Napoleon—Intermezzo—Entrance of the Emperor and His Court
    (*First Time in St. Louis*)

STEINWAY PIANOS USED

The concerts will begin promptly on the hour announced—**FRIDAYS AT 3:00,
SATURDAYS AT 8:30, SUNDAYS AT 3:15.** None will be seated during the performance of the work. Patrons having to leave before the end of a concert will
kindly do so between numbers. Hats **must** be removed during the concert.

Only **one** encore will be granted a soloist

DO NOT WASTE YOUR SYMPHONY TICKETS

Subscribers who are unable to attend are urged to cooperate with the Ladies'
Friday Musical Club in giving deserving students an opportunity to hear good music.
Tickets should be sent as early as possible but at least two hours in advance of concert, to MRS. DAVID KRIEGSHABER, 4939 WASHINGTON BLVD., FOREST
2594-W, or the location phoned to her.

Program from interim period between Ganz and Golschmann. This concert was Szell's American
conducting debut.

SIXTEENTH PAIR OF SYMPHONY CONCERTS

FRIDAY AFTERNOON, MARCH 14, *at* 3:00

SATURDAY EVENING, MARCH 15, *at* 8:30

EUGENE GOOSSENS
Guest Conductor

Soloist: MISCHA ELMAN: *Violinist*

ໜ

P R O G R A M

1. *Weber*..Overture to the Opera "Der Freischütz

2. *Mozart*..Eine Kleine Nacht Musik (for strings)
    I.   Allegro
    II. Romanza: Andante.
    III. Menuetto: Allegretto
    IV. Rondo: Allegro

3. *Debussy*.......................................La Mer: Trois Esquisses Symphoniques
                                           ("The Sea" Three Symphonic Sketches)
    I.   De l'aube à midi sur la mer ("From Dawn to Noon upon the Sea")
    II. Jeux de vagues ("Sport of the Waves")
    III. Dialogue du vent et de la mer ("Dialogue of Wind and the Sea")

Intermission

4. *Tschaikovsky*...........................Concerto for Violin in D major, Op. 35
    I.   Allegro moderato
    II. Canzonetta: Andante
    III. Finale: Allegro vivacissimo.

MR. ELMAN

MR. ELMAN *uses the* STEINWAY PIANO

The concerts will begin promptly on the hour announced—**FRIDAYS AT 3:00, SATURDAYS AT 8:30, SUNDAYS AT 3:15.** None will be seated during the performance of the work. Patrons having to leave before the end of a concert will kindly do so between numbers. Hats **must** be removed during the concert.

Only **one** encore will be granted a soloist

DO NOT WASTE YOUR SYMPHONY TICKETS

Subscribers who are unable to attend are urged to cooperate with the Ladies' Friday Musical Club in giving deserving students an opportunity to hear good music. Tickets should be sent as early as possible but at least two hours in advance of concert, to MRS. DAVID KRIEGSHABER, 4939 WASHINGTON BLVD., FOREST 2594-W, or the location phoned to her.

Goossens was one of the regular guest conductors during the interim years between Ganz and Golschmann.

Vladimir Golschmann

VLADIMIR GOLSCHMANN

The Symphony Years 1931–1958

THE SAINT LOUIS SYMPHONY ORCHESTRA, its thrust and growth having been splintered by too many conductors, was hungry for an upswing. The four years of guest conductors following the Ganz departure had coincided with the stock market debacle of 1929 and the beginning of the subsequent depression, leaving the exchequer in worse shape than usual. There *had* to be a new look—a new look and a new sound, a new era that would stimulate the community both in attendance and in general support. The Board of the Society had great expectations of its new choice as Music Director, hopes in his public image, and faith in his musicianship. The Board's expectation, hopes, and faith were not to be disappointed.

As for the public image, no board member nor patron could have asked for anything more. Vladimir Golschmann and his wife, Odette, virtually took St. Louis by storm. Their arrival in the fall was a public event. Excitingly French from the tips of their shoes to the tops of their well-coiffed heads, the two were photographed and interviewed repeatedly in the newspapers. They made friends easily with board members, patrons, and members of the orchestra. They were entertained by everyone. Early in the season, Golschmann was speaker at a meeting of the French Society of St. Louis, where he announced plans to broadcast a series of ten special concerts over KMOX radio.

That both Golschmanns were extremely attractive was a factor which was not essential but which certainly did no harm. Golschmann had a slight limp (it was *never* mentioned), the result of a cycling accident in his youth although legend and rumor had it that it was a war injury. This very minor impediment in no way detracted from his sartorial elegance. Mme. Golschmann was the personification of what American women tend to admire wistfully in their French counterparts. She was fastidiously well-groomed and always dressed in exactly the proper costume, whatever the occasion. She was gracious, charming, and witty, and appeared to be more than willing to join into the customs and mores of her husband's new milieu. It may seem somewhat irrelevant to mention the impact of a conductor's wife on the community, since that aspect is not usually considered in the deliberations concerning engagement of the conductor. Sometimes there is no wife, and certainly—if there is one—it is not demanded of her that she be her husband's working partner in the matter of public relations. However, when things work out as they did when the Golschmanns came to St. Louis, it is indeed a bonus.

When they first arrived, the Golschmanns settled in at the Coronado Hotel on Lindell Boulevard. In those days the Coronado was an elegant choice, having played host to Queen Marie of Rumania when her international travels brought her to St. Louis.

All of this is, of course, subsidiary to the important aspect of Vladimir Golschmann's presence in St. Louis. What was most significant was what started to happen to the music.

Fourteen new musicians joined the Orchestra. Of these, three were principals. There were Scipione Guidi, Concertmaster; Herbert Van den Burg, Principal Viola, and Rene Corn, Principal Oboe. Guidi had been recruited by Arthur Gaines, who had returned to begin his second period of managing the Saint Louis Symphony Orchestra. At the time he came here, Guidi had been Concertmaster of the New York Philharmonic for ten years. The Principal Violist of the Saint Louis Orchestra, Philip Neeter, had been killed in a car accident in St. Louis in September, leaving the First Viola Chair open. Golschmann had met Herbert Van den Burg in the east and invited him to come to St. Louis. Van den Burg, Dutch, had come to America to study at the Curtis Institute with Louis Bailly.

The season's programs were laid out—eighteen pairs of subscription concerts, four popular concerts, and miscellaneous high school and students' concerts, in addition to the ten radio concerts on KMOX and a brief tour consisting of three concerts, in Indianapolis, Urbana, and Quincy.

The scheduled soloists for the subscription series were four singers—Janet Vreeland, John Charles Thomas, Paul Althous, and Friedrich Schorr; four violinists—Scipione Guidi, Albert Spalding, Adolf Busch, and Samuel Dushkin; three pianists—Myra Hess, Ossip Gabrilovitsch, and Vladimir Horowitz; and Max Steindel, cellist.

The program of Golschmann's first concert as the permanent conductor was as follows: Overture to *Der Freischütz* by Weber, Brahms' Symphony No. 2, *Tod und Verklärung* by Richard Strauss (which was played In Memoriam for Frederick Fischer, the venerable bassoonist and assistant conductor—under both Max Zach and Rudolph Ganz—who had died that year) and Rimsky-Korsakoff's *The Russian Easter*. Although Golschmann had, for obvious reasons, a strong penchant for French music and particularly for French impressionistic music, he shied away from it in the opening concert and showed the audiences and the musicians that he could handle other music with sensitivity, skill, and élan.

As a conductor, Golschmann was extremely sensitive to the total impact of the music. He was constantly aware of his audience—some say he even feared the audiences. The effect of the music on his listeners was of paramount

SAINT LOUIS SYMPHONY ORCHESTRA

Season 1936 - 1937

VLADIMIR GOLSCHMANN, Conductor
SCIPIONE GUIDI, Assistant Conductor

FIRST VIOLINS

Scipione Guidi,
  Concertmaster.
Joseph Faerber
Francis E. Jones
Felix Slatkin
Isadore Grossman
David Salomon
Harry Lookofsky
Ladislav Nagy
Sol Turner
Edward Shalett
Meyer Schumitzky
Jacob Levine
Sol Kranzberg
Arthur Baron
L. Ernest Walker, Jr.

SECOND VIOLINS

Louis Druzinsky,
  Principal.
Paul Schreiber
Carl Nagel
Simon Polca
Irvin Rosen
David J. Rizzo
Meyer Lipsitz
Louis Erzkow
Rudolph J. Magin
Charles A. Kaub
Jerome Rosen
Carl A. Preusse
Joseph F. Oswald, Jr.
Robert Burger

VIOLAS

Herbert Van den Burg,
  Principal.
Carl A. Tholl
Garry White
Alvin Dinkin
Victor Hugo
Stellario Giacobbe
Walter S. Roehrborn
Henry J. Falkenhainer
John Hartl

LIBRARIAN

Elmer Gesner

PERSONNEL MGR.

Max Steindel

VIOLONCELLOS

Max Steindel,
  Principal.
Pasquale De Conto
Martin Teicholz
Carl Rossow
Igor Geffen
Gustaf Keller
Antonio La Marchina
Carl Steppi
Abe Kessler
Joseph Tonar

BASSES

Oscar G. Zimmerman,
  Principal.
Waldemar F. Helmholz
Salvatore Campione
John Klima
Karl P. Auer
Robert Buhl
Clinton Manning
Earl Hyna

HARP

Graziella Pampari

FLUTES

Laurent Torno
Harry H. Moskovitz
John F. Kiburz

PICCOLO

John F. Kiburz

OBOES

Pierre Mathieu
Joseph Antonucci
Alfred H. Hicks

ENGLISH HORN

Alfred H. Hicks

CLARINETS

Rocco M. Zottarelle
C. L. Gesner
Charles E. Camacho

BASS CLARINET

Charles E. Camacho

BASSOONS

Henry Cunnington
Nat Reines
John E. Ferrell

CONTRA BASSOON

John E. Ferrell

HORNS

Edward Murphy
Joseph Vegna
John B. Dolan
Robert L. Gustat
John Mountz

TRUMPETS

Samuel G. Krauss
Joseph Gustat
Joseph Carione
Frank Miller
John Hartl

TROMBONES

Merritt W. Dittert
Oscar H. Hallback
Charles F. Meier

TUBA

John Bambridge

TYMPANI

William Ehrlich

PERCUSSION

Elmer Gesner
William Albers

PIANO AND CELESTA

Corinne Frederick
Joseph F. Oswald, Jr.

Golschmann's Orchestra in his sixth season. Felix Slatkin in first violins.

importance to him. This is not to say that he shaped music to suit the rank and file; far from it. He wanted to communicate at peak level with the responsive listeners, the knowledgeable concert-goers, and he wanted others in the audience to be quickened to a point where they moved up a notch or two as listeners. The effect was compelling. Thomas Sherman, music critic for the *St. Louis Post-Dispatch*, wrote of one concert, that in the excerpts from *The Fire Bird* (Stravinsky) "the orchestra played with a coruscating brilliance that could only have been the result of a complete assurance on the part of the conductor. . . . The same cutting incisiveness, clarity of parts, balance of dynamics and expressiveness of orchestral tone was manifested in Ravel's *La Valse*. This is certainly Mr. Golschmann's *pièce de résistance*. Nobody alive can do it better."[1] In another review, referring to the orchestra's playing of the Mozart G Minor Symphony, Sherman wrote, "Above all, Mr. Golschmann's taste was irreproachable. It is harder to steer a Mozart Symphony between the Scylla of an effeminate refinement and the Charybdis of a complacent virility than to play all of the Strauss Tone Poems at one sitting."[2]

As to his stick technique, he used an extremely long baton (which Sir Thomas Beecham, here as a visiting conductor once, referred to as a "fishing pole")[3] and did not have particularly definitive movements with his hands. One of the first chair players, in referring to Golschmann as the most sensitive conductor he had ever played under, said that "he had a miserable beat but it *worked!*"[4] His whole attitude, facial expressions, hand movements—all elements combined to translate precisely what he wanted to the orchestra. He was, in the vernacular, a quick study on the scores. He sometimes got his assistant conductor to take the Orchestra through a new piece while he sat out in front and listened, after which he had a clear and exact picture of how he wanted the over-all to sound.

The Great Depression was casting its pall over everything including the Saint Louis Symphony Orchestra. The Orchestra members agreed to accept reductions of 10 per cent in salaries. Manager Arthur Gaines and the office staff, small as it was, were in on this retrenchment, which was expected to save $20,000 in the expense budget. The Women's Association, which had been founded in 1925, jumped valiantly into the sea of problems and worked industriously to increase the number of subscribers and donors to the Guarantee Fund, as it was then called. Golschmann's first year saw an actual upswing in numbers of donors to the Guarantee Fund: from 1300, the number increased to 1800, and there were an additional 1250 ticket subscribers. This helped, and the organization kept going.

L. Warrington Baldwin, then head of the Missouri Pacific Railroad, had been president of the Society since 1928. He remained president until the Orchestra was launched on its new chapter and Golschmann had completed his first season. Mr. Baldwin's successor was J. D. Wooster Lambert, one of the sponsors of Charles Lindbergh's solo flight to Paris in 1927. He came into office during a year of musical heights and financial doldrums. Many years later, Mr. Lambert recalled going to Musicians' Hall on weekends with a satchel of money, paying the players off in cash—in an almost hand-to-mouth ritual. Unfortunately, after one year in the office, when Mr. Lambert was just getting the "feel" of the job, his business commitments brought about his moving to New York. The Board decided to ask a young neophyte, Oscar Johnson, Jr., to take over as president.

Oscar Johnson, whose father had been a founder of one of St. Louis' large shoe companies, was visiting in California when the long-distance call came asking him to be president of the Saint Louis Symphony Society. His immediate reaction was to say "no" inasmuch as he was only twenty-eight years old (much younger than most) and, moreover, felt totally unqualified to take on the responsibilities involved. His mother, a long-time patron of the Symphony Orchestra, insisted that he accept, and so he did.[5] He remained board president for twenty-one years, resigning only two years before Golschmann left.

That a close friendship developed between the new conductor and the new board president was no surprise. Oscar Johnson, who was unmarried, fond of fast automobiles, and professed no deep-seated musical knowledge, began to pay a great deal of attention to the affairs of the Saint Louis Symphony Orchestra. In these lean years, he (with his mother) did a vast amount of entertaining of the visiting dignitaries as well as the Orchestra, at after-concert receptions. He began to accompany the Orchestra regularly on the tours, which was certainly a new practice.

Oscar Johnson also began to make up the deficit at the end of each fiscal year. At the risk of laboring the point, it should be mentioned again that this was a terrible era for symphony orchestras financially. Potential patrons (those who hadn't already formed the habit of helping) were frightened by the signs of depression around them and were cautious. Orchestra support from national or state organizations was off in the dim future. Mr. Johnson became an "angel" when one was desperately needed.

The first decade of Golschmann's regime was a kind of see-saw, with musical highs and financial lows. There were salutary occasions on the stage—appearances of Rachmaninoff (he came five times in the Thirties), Heifetz, Horowitz, Piatigorsky, Kreisler, Menuhin, and Prokofiev. (Prokofiev, here in January 1937, played and conducted his own Piano Concerto No. 3). There was the 1933 concert when the Russian Ballet, accompanied by the Symphony Orchestra, performed in the Odeon Theater. Arthur Gaines, Manager until 1938, and a confirmed balletomane, engineered that event, extremely innovative for the times, and so successful that the Russian Ballet returned annually to St. Louis for years thereafter.[6]

A Saint Louis Symphony Chorus led by William Heyne was formed in 1934 and began to participate in the programs. The number of concert-goers grew from 75,000 in 1930 to 225,000 by 1936. The tours continued to expand to the point that the orchestra played as many as thirty-two engagements out of town, performing not only in the smaller towns, where no symphony orchestra existed, but in places such as Chicago, Memphis, Dallas, and Houston, all of which had orchestras of their own.

Meanwhile, the financial situation of the Orchestra was annually aired in the papers in a kind of "Perils of Pauline" sequence. In the spring of 1933, it was announced that the Orchestra would be disbanded the following year unless 3000 people subscribed. It was further stated that no Guarantee Fund would be initiated unless the subscribers were forthcoming. The local newspapers co-operated by carrying editorials championing the cause at the lowest moments in the crisis. The Women's Committee involved itself diligently in the problem, helping with ticket sales as well as recruiting new donors to the Guarantee Fund.

The musicians were tempted to leave, tempted through many avenues. Other orchestras were increasing their seasons' numbers of weeks, and some were paying more. The members of the orchestra moonlighted at whatever they could find, with part-time jobs in the winter and whatever employment they could get in the summer, musical or otherwise. The Little Symphony started up in 1934. This was a small-scale orchestra, made up primarily of Symphony Orchestra musicians. Its concerts were originally performed in the amphi-theater of John Burroughs School. (The concerts were later moved to the quadrangle on the campus of Washington University.) Many played in the Little Symphony orchestra, although it did not provide a full summer's work. Many played in the orchestra of the Municipal Opera in Forest Park. Some went elsewhere to play summer music. The fact was that an Orchestra musician had to like what he was doing quite a lot in order not to quit and do something else entirely different. It was a time when a $5 a week raise was a big one. One big temptation, waving a lure under the eyes of the players in any symphony orchestra—not just St. Louis—was Hollywood. This was the heyday of the movies and California studios were capable of paying salaries that made ordinary orchestra pay checks look even more pallid. In the early Thirties, for instance, an average-to-good salary from the Saint Louis Symphony Orchestra was somewhere in the range of $2300 for the season. The studios in California were offering an annual salary of $8000. Some players succumbed. Many stayed.

In 1934 the city of St. Louis completed construction of a municipal audi-torium on Market Street—Kiel Auditorium, named after Mayor Henry F. Kiel. The Symphony Society leased the Opera House in this building and from 1934 on, the "at home" concerts were played here. The Odeon had had a seating capacity of something under 2000. The building had fine acoustics and—with renovations—might have continued to serve the Orchestra longer than it did, had it not been plagued by several fires. The Opera House in Kiel Auditorium seated 3500, a factor which was obviously a plus on nights starring a celebrated soloist, and a large minus at concerts when the attendance was down. Parking in the 1930's was not a problem, since public transportation was still available in various forms and the automobile had not proliferated to its present num-bers. Thus the available garages and parking lots were more than adequate. One of the biggest drawbacks to the Kiel Auditorium was that the Opera House backed up to a mammoth convention hall, capable of seating 10,000 persons and also frequently adapted for sports events. This Convention Hall was separated from the Opera House by a supposedly sound-proof partition between the two stages. That this partition was not totally sound-proof became painfully evident whenever a symphony concert coincided with, say, a basketball game. The orchestra members had considerable difficulty hearing one another through the muffled din just behind them. Occasionally, the sounds of the athletic contest rose above the sounds of the whole orchestra, even to the ears of the audience.

St. Louis, and America, were scarcely beginning to pick themselves up off the carpet as the Depression lifted when the entire world became embroiled in World War II. Shortly after the war in Europe started (September 1, 1939), the Golschmanns were aboard the last westward crossing of the *Ile de France*. Piatigorsky and Milstein were also aboard the vessel, and needless to say, all the men were very much aware of the possibility of German naval action aimed at the ship. Golschmann is reported to have commented to his two music confrères that at least there would be world-wide publicity if the ship went down with the three of them on it. The other two failed to see the humor.

The first Pension Fund Benefit Concert had been played in 1935 and became an annual event. In March 1940, the Benefit Concert was one the likes of which has not been seen before or since. The Orchestra members were dressed in outlandish costumes, some heavily disguised and some attacking the wrong instruments. Golschmann played the kettledrums and Oscar Johnson conducted, after having been introduced as a guest conductor. Golschmann and Johnson had originally intended to use the Overture to *The Marriage of Figaro* for the *pièce de résistance*, but decided that this music was too good to be subjected to the horseplay.[7] Instead, they presented "Hail to the Conquering Hero." Needless to say, an encore was *de rigueur*, so the "Beer Barrel Polka" was forthcoming. It was a night to remember!

With America's involvement in the War, the Symphony Orchestra had to tighten its collective belt even more. The season was cut from twenty-three to twenty-one weeks, a seemingly small cut, but one felt by the musicians. Competitive pay in the major symphony orchestras had already become an important issue, and with the shortened season, there followed a considerable turnover in the Saint Louis Orchestra, the more established players leaving for better salaries and less experienced ones being hired to fill the gap. The Women's Committee (it was later named the Women's Association) was having fund-raising difficulties because of the wartime restrictions. Many of the women carried out their solicitations personally, by automobile, and what with gasoline and tire rationing, their activities were curtailed. Moreover, women had naturally involved themselves in numerous activities supportive of the American war effort, and just plain didn't have as much time for their symphony volunteer work.

In the middle of the 1941–1942 season, Golschmann fired his once close friend, Scipione Guidi, the Concertmaster. He fired him onstage, during a rehearsal—a dramatic scene which could not conceivably take place today.

Recording session, 1942. John Crawford, recording engineer. (*St. Louis Post-Dispatch* photograph by Art Witman, April 12, 1942)

According to those present at the time, Guidi's playing at the moment was more than adequate, although Golschmann had challenged the way he had played a certain passage. Apparently the contretemps was the culmination of a long-smoldering set of circumstances: Guidi was exceedingly knowledgeable about the scores, was a sensitive interpreter of phrasing and how various parts of the music should be handled; Golschmann, in the early days, had often asked his opinion and asked it often enough that Guidi was not above volunteering his opinion. It was a dangerous situation to have been allowed to develop, and on the particular day of the firing, Golschmann undoubtedly boiled over in a build-up of resentment.

The violinist engaged as Concertmaster, beginning with the next season, was Harry Farbman. He was a musician from New York City, where he had been playing under Alfred Wallenstein, then the music director of WOR Radio. Farbman had formed his own ensemble, the Farbman Sinfonietta,[8] which had made its debut in Town Hall and was recognized for its high quality. Farbman stayed for nineteen years, during which time he did a prodigious amount of conducting—subscription concerts, when Golschmann was out of town, the Pops concerts, and many of the Student Concerts. He was also head of an orchestra which played on KSD TV, the first television station in St. Louis.

Sunday Free Concert in Kiel Auditorium. (*St. Louis Post-Dispatch* photograph, November 22, 1942)

(Laclede Gas was the local sponsor willing to gamble on this new communications medium.)

In 1943, Mrs. Clifford Gaylord, chairman of the Society's directors and, in effect, in charge while Oscar Johnson (still president) was on leave of absence in the United States Navy, persuaded Mayor William Dee Becker to let the orchestra have the use of Kiel Auditorium free of charge, in exchange for four free concerts. This eased the budget for a short time, but in May 1943, it was announced that the Orchestra would go under, that contracts could not be renewed unless the remaining $40,000 (needed for the next season) could be raised for the Maintenance Fund. St. Louis wasn't the only troubled orchestra. The Philadelphia Orchestra was showing a deficit of almost $70,000 because of declining attendance.

The music, fortunately, continued without a break while the directors struggled with the money problems. The start of the 1943–1944 season saw twelve newcomers join the Orchestra. The important element of this statistic is that five of them were women. Heretofore, the presence of women on the stage had been limited to the harp (for many years played by the dramatic Graziella Pampari) and an occasional string player. Now with the shortage of civilian males, the women were needed and therefore recognized. The new principal

Nathan Milstein with Golschmann. (*St. Louis Post-Dispatch* photograph, November 12, 1944)

oboist was a woman, Lois Wann. (She had been first chair oboe player with the Pittsburgh Symphony Orchestra.) The other four women were two violinists, one harpist, and one string bass player. Incidentally, there were three new first chair players at the start of this particular season. In addition to the oboist, Lois Wann, there were Louis Pallendino (principal trombonist) and Emil Herbert (principal string bass).

Golschmann had little patience with or interest in Pops concerts and there were few of them—perhaps three or four a year during the Thirties and Forties. Student concerts fluctuated in number, but if anything grew more numerous during this period. The tours kept going no matter what. They did not always offer a surcease from the backstage problems at home. On one tour in the south, the Orchestra was startled to see Mrs. Clifford Gaylord appear on the stage during a rehearsal to make a desperate appeal to the musicians. She asked them to accept a shortened season, and, further, to accept a reduced weekly paycheck. She vowed that the Orchestra would not go under, not if the women (herself included) "had to scrub floors."[9] The orchestra acquiesced.

Golschmann was an inveterate poker player and, on tour, there was always a game going on in the front car with Golschmann, Oscar Johnson (except for the stretch when he was away in the Navy), and whoever else happened to be in the area. Johnson was in an ironic position when he happened to be the winner

Beer and Pretzels Pension Fund Concert, Kiel Auditorium. (*St. Louis Post-Dispatch* photograph, March 4, 1944)

Farbman Sinfonietta about to take off on a tour in the late 1940's. Harry Farbman and Edith Schiller Farbman to right of center, dark satchel on pavement in front. Members of Saint Louis Symphony Orchestra identifiable in photograph include John B. Dolan, Rex Clark, Joseph Vegna, Frances Jones (assistant concertmaster), Murray Schwartz, Isador Grossman, Robert Wisneskey, Robert Weatherly, and Sol Kranzberg. (Photograph courtesy of Harry and Edith Farbman)

since, as perennial but unpublicized "angel," he seemed to see the money travelling in both directions. The stakes were somewhat limited in these tour games, which was not the case with the poker group of St. Louis businessmen with whom Golschmann played when back at home.

The behind-the-scenes management changed several times during Golschmann's years. When Arthur Gaines resigned in 1938 to return to the Minneapolis Symphony, the business affairs of the Orchestra were managed for one year by Donald S. Foster, who was followed by John Edwards (who later, in 1967, became the legendary manager of the Chicago Symphony). Edwards was Acting Manager during 1939–1940, and Manager from 1940 to 1942. He had also worked for the *St. Louis Globe-Democrat* and his journalistic know-how combined with his musical knowledge (acquired from a love affair with the concerts of the Boston Symphony Orchestra when he was a graduate student at Harvard) were such a fortunate blend that he wound up writing the concert program notes as well as handling the business affairs of the orchestra.

Edwards later recalled this period as a kind of age of innocence for him—a kind of "Garden of Eden" period.[10] It was not his first job but it was his first involvement in the world of professional musicians, a complex world that was to become his milieu. Edwards got nothing but experience in return for writing the program notes. His predecessors had been paid. His notes were highly regarded by all readers, including Golschmann. During an arduous rehearsal of some difficult measures in a Sibelius symphony, Golschmann finally told the Orchestra, "Stop worrying so much about this place. All you have to worry about is the conductor and the program notes."[11]

When Edwards was wooed away by the National Symphony Orchestra, the man who took over the management was the public relations man who had shared an office with him, William Zalken. Zalken remained in charge of booking and business affairs and all the expected and unexpected management crises for twenty-four years. During this long period, it was felt by many who were familiar with the situation that Zalken held the Saint Louis Symphony together with his bare hands, Scotch tape, and glue.

As has been indicated earlier in this account, the music played on the tours was not particularly challenging to the musicians. It was old stuff to them since they frequently repeated much of the programs from city to city. This is not to say that they didn't play it well. It was just that repetition made it easy. One selection played at Fort Leonard Wood on a tour during the 1942–1943 season was a world prèmiere, however. Golschmann had been told that a Corporal Rudolph Uhlig, the Post organist on the base, had written a piece called "My Country." Whether the composer had scored the brief music for an ensemble or whether Golschmann took it over and orchestrated it is not known. Whatever the case, Golschmann and the Orchestra performed the composition in the concert there.

Things were more challenging in the subscription concerts. Isaac Stern made his first appearance with the Orchestra in January of 1944, Harry Farbman conducting. (Golschmann was away at the time, having been invited to conduct the Boston Symphony Orchestra in seven concerts in January of that year.) Symphony No. 1 by the Russian composer Tikhon Khrennikov was given its first St. Louis performance. In 1944–1945, the Orchestra accompanied such high-powered soloists as Piatigorsky, Rubinstein, Szigeti, Casadesus, Spalding, and Helen Traubel, then a celebrated Wagnerian diva. That same year, Sir Thomas Beecham came to conduct the Annual Pension Fund Concert, and presented a variety of selections including the Delius Piano Concerto with Lady Beecham at the piano. For various reasons, 1944–1945 was a year with no tours. There were the usual twenty pairs of subscription concerts, four Pops concerts, eleven Student and High School Concerts, two special concerts conducted by André Kostelanetz, two concerts on radio, the Pension Fund Concert, and one concert at Missouri University, but no tour.

1950 Bus Tour about to take off. (*St. Louis Post-Dispatch* photograph, February 27, 1950)

In 1950 the Orchestra went to the East coast for the first time. The highlight of the tour was the concert played in Carnegie Hall on March 8. Golschmann had prepared an extremely varied program consisting of Couperin's Overture and Allegro (orchestrated by Milhaud), Mozart's Symphony No. 40 in G Minor, *Magic Manhattan* by Manuel Rosenthal, *Verklärte Nacht* (for strings) by Schönberg, and DeFalla's *Dances from "The Three-Cornered Hat."* The composer Virgil Thomson was the music critic of the *New York Herald Tribune* at the time. His review of the concert was not only informative concerning the music, but highly complimentary concerning the performance of the Orchestra. His account of this concert explained that the Rosenthal piece, written two years earlier, was "a companion piece to Gershwin's 'American in Paris.' It represents a Frenchman's visit to New York." His critique of the concert as a whole proved that Golschmann knew what he was talking about when he said that he would never take the Orchestra to New York until he was sure the Orchestra was ready. The opening paragraph of Thomson's review read: "The Saint Louis Symphony Orchestra, second oldest organization of its kind in the country, now in its seventieth year, gave its first New

York concert last night in Carnegie Hall. A brilliant concert it was, too, both as to program and to playing. Vladimir Golschmann, now in his twentieth year as conductor of the St. Louis body, directed with verve and all musical elegance. His orchestra is not quite the equal of our Eastern Big Three nor, perhaps, even of Cleveland now nor of Chicago in its best days; but it is an accomplished and well-trained group, sensitive as to nuance and rich of tone; and Mr. Golschmann is a conductor with life in him as well as musicianship. His concert was for this reviewer one of the most delightful of the season."[12]

The Carnegie Hall triumph was a pinnacle not necessarily being reached in every subscription concert, for in the early 1950's it became apparent to those who paid close attention to such matters that the Saint Louis Symphony Orchestra was no longer in its ascendancy. Attendance and support had frequently been off in the past, but the problems could usually be attributed to such external circumstances of the times as war, depression, and recession. Vladimir Golschmann had, by 1954, been here twenty-three years and the problems, at that point, seemed different and more ominously significant. His was, at that time, a longer tenure than that of any other American symphony conductor, except for Koussevitzky's in Boston. It takes an extraordinary human being to keep the fires alive that long. David Wooldridge, the British conductor and composer, in referring to Koussevitzky's tenure says, that "it was remarkable (as that of his colleague Leopold Stokowski was legendary)— not by reason of the turbulence of his personality or his self-assured caprice (though such factors did of course provide incidental stimulus), but for that sense of pride which has already been referred to and which Koussevitzky generated and maintained among his players and the community at large. This ability to restore the belief of his musicians in the jaded classic and sustain it through the rehearsals and performances of initially antipathetic contemporary works, is the essential and seemingly uneventful aspect of truly great conducting."[13] To say that Golschmann didn't have the staying power to keep the sense of excitement and growth going is not to discredit him or to take away from the enormous good which he *did* bring about. It was just too long a stay. There is an old rumor, perhaps apocryphal, that when Golschmann was appointed, he was given an unwritten agreement that he would remain twenty-five years. Obviously this was too long, for the truth remains that Golschmann, for all his undisputed talents, for all that the Orchestra rose to new and wonderful heights under his hand in the Thirties and Forties—for all this, Golschmann in the last few years was inadvertently resting on his oars. It was said that he felt that the Board didn't do enough, that the decline of the Orchestra was virtually out of his hands. Whatever the combined reasons, some felt that he grew careless and somewhat apathetic in routine details. He had to be reminded constantly to get the programs set up and planned and ready for the printer, for instance. Those close to the situation felt that Zalken was keeping the symphony alive by his cajoling and prodding of Golschmann just to meet ordinary deadlines.

By 1953, Oscar Johnson had been president of the Board twenty years. He

Buffet supper, Kiel Auditorium, January 15, 1955. Left to right: Oscar Johnson (former President of the Society's Board); Edwin J. Spiegel (President of the Society's Board); Mrs. James O'Malley Davies (board member); Gus Haenschen (former St. Louisan, conductor of the "American Album" radio program); Mrs. Oscar Johnson; Mrs. Edwin J. Spiegel; Leigh Gerdine (board member).

had apparently loved the relationship—the Symphony Orchestra and its problems and pleasures had become an integral part of his life. He had also, however, been pulling the fiscal chestnuts out of the fire for twenty years, and the need for money was growing beyond the scope of any single pocketbook.

Morton D. May, chief executive of May Department Stores, was one of those working behind the scenes to try to solve some of the financial problems. May (whose father, Morton J. May, was a member of the Society Board from 1922 until his death in 1968) had been an unpublicized supporter of the Symphony since his own college days. Although he had never been willing to be the head of the Symphony Board, he had been one of the most loyal backers, not only providing financial support through family-held foundations and personal gifts, but working for solutions to other sorts of troubles as they came up. The younger May was the prime prodder in the step which the Symphony Society took in 1953—a step which seemed desperate and at the same time logical. They solicited some hard-nosed outside advice: Civic Progress, that organization made up of the titans of the St. Louis business world, was

Party following a 1955 concert. Seated, left to right: Mrs. Isaac Stern, Gregor Piatigorsky, Isaac Stern, Vladimir Golschmann. Standing: Mrs. J. Eldred Newton and Edwin J. Spiegel.

consulted. Mayor Raymond Tucker was drawn into the effort to save the Orchestra. Tucker announced publicly that the Symphony might be forced to disband before the 1954–1955 season. The executive committee of the Symphony Board had met with him and had informed him that the organization had a minimum budget of $337,000. Tucker's statement, published in the *Globe-Democrat* of July 23, 1954, disclosed that the funds raised to that date would support the Orchestra's season only up to February 1955. Edwin J. Spiegel, president of Gaylord Container Corporation and a member of Civic Progress, was appointed chairman of a special committee to save the Symphony.

Privately, there were two schools of thought. One was to let the Symphony expire—thereby stunning the city with the reality of the emergency—and then revive it. The other side was against this tactic. For one thing, it was argued, this was the equivalent of "crying 'wolf'" in the nth degree, and the Symphony Society had never stooped to that level. And another, if the Symphony were truly disbanded, even though a revival was planned the musicians would scatter and it would be nearly impossible to reassemble an experienced, unified body. Fortunately the second point of view—fight till the end to hold the Orchestra together—prevailed.

The Women's Association endorsed the Citizen's Committee and Mr. Spiegel, and immediately planned a giant fund-raising project—a re-sell-it sale of clothing, to be conducted at Battery A, on South Grand Boulevard. The women also announced a rather bizarre bonanza: they had talked those in charge of the race track at Cahokia Downs into donating the proceeds from the 9th race on a certain evening to the Symphony cause.

By September 1954 the Citizen's Committee had raised the needed funds—$60,000—to guarantee the 1954–1955 season, and so the year proceeded on schedule.

That winter, the Orchestra was again in the news because of an episode which had nothing to do with its financial problems. In February 1955 the Orchestra was on tour—by now in buses instead of trains—when a serious accident occurred. The "B" bus (the group travelled in three buses) skidded on a patch of ice and hit a bridge abutment near Clifton Forge, Virginia. Fourteen members of the orchestra were hurt, three seriously. Robert Gustat (French horn player) and Dominick Sottile (cellist) sustained jaw injuries. Most seriously injured was the harpist Graziella Pampari, who sustained jaw injuries and the loss of some teeth. The orchestra continued on to play the last scheduled concert for the tour in Muncie, Indiana. Face and jaw injuries were extremely critical to the brass players in particular. Those who were not injured were deeply distressed by the event, and only because of an ingrained professionalism and unwillingness to default was the concert in Muncie performed.

Although there had been no publicity regarding specified sources, the funds to salvage the Symphony had come primarily from the corporations and individuals involved in Civic Progress. In coming to the aid of the Symphony, Civic Progress also felt—justifiably, it would seem—that it should insist on certain conditions. One was that a businessman should become president of the Society, one toughened in budget balancing, especially those budgets which, like the Symphony's, might prove impossible to balance. This was in no way a slur at Oscar Johnson. The Symphony could not have survived the 1930's and 1940's without his financial help. His moral support had been just as important. But he had done enough, and if the Orchestra was to continue as a major orchestra, it would have to enter a financial phase which required more than any one benefactor could handle. That was the first condition. The second was that Vladimir Golschmann, who had wrought wonderful things for the Orchestra, had nevertheless reached the point at which he had to be phased out. In an effort to recapture some of Golschmann's former public image and influence on the Orchestra, the executive committee of the Board told Golschmann that he should linger in St. Louis for a while after the season was over to lend his presence in community relations (the Golschmanns invariably left St. Louis immediately following the last concert), and that he should also be around early in the autumn to help promote the upcoming season. Golschmann is reported to have responded that perhaps the Board wanted a new music director. His remark was accepted.

During the last three years of Golschmann's tenure, the search for a new conductor was on, though not officially announced. Edwin Spiegel had been elected president of the Society's Board in 1955. In spite of the upheavals and

Golschmann departing for Paris as soon as the St. Louis season was finished. (Picture taken at "New York International Airport" by Air France, May 3, 1956)

tensions in the rethinking of the Orchestra's future, the concerts proceeded on schedule, enhanced by a good number of visiting artists and a great many visiting conductors.

Occasionally, the concerns of the Orchestra made the papers in rather unusual ways. Golschmann, on Christmas Day 1955, tripped on a throw rug in the Golschmann apartment on Argyle Place and fractured his ankle. Clarence Gesner, ever the resourceful stage manager, designed a rather odd-looking but effective arrangement whereby Golschmann could conduct while sitting on a high stool, the affected foot elevated on a footstool on the podium. And André Kostelanetz (conducting the Orchestra in a special concert) had Don Carver, St. Louis bowling expert, bowling at ten-pins down a special alley, set up onstage in front of the orchestra, to lend realism to Grofé's *Hudson River Suite*.

After the 1955–1956 season, Golschmann became "Conductor Emeritus," so that it was known to all far and near that the Symphony Society was looking for a new conductor. The season beginning in October 1956 projected the usual twenty pairs of concerts, with Golschmann conducting ten only. He handled the concerts featuring the soloists Henri Deering, Glenn Gould, Nathan Milstein, Gary Graffman, Isaac Stern, Rudolph Serkin, Gregor Piatigorsky, and Artur Rubinstein as part of his year's schedule. The rest were led by Harry Farbman, Jascha Horenstein, Edwin McArthur, Georg Solti, Erich Leinsdorf, Igor Markevitch, and Fernando Previtali.

This same season, the Orchestra took part in the four-day Exposition called "Mid-America Jubilee." (Edwin McArthur, music director of the Municipal Opera, conducted the Orchestra for this.) Solti had been engaged to guest conduct three concerts, but asked to be relieved of the last one so that he could take his Frankfurt (Germany) Opera company to Rome. Erich Leinsdorf, who was, at the time, director of the New York City Center Opera company, filled in.

Orchestra musicians were still coming and going—there were twenty new musicians at the opening of the 1956–1957 season. (Two were principals: Carl Lutes, flute, and Alfred Genovese, oboe.) The spectre of money shortage was as present as ever, but with the support of more corporations and some increased support from private foundations, the drive for funds was slightly less frenetic. Of the goal of $225,000, $150,000 had been raised by February. As a matter of fact, the Maintenance Fund for the year before had shown a small surplus—something under $2000.

Golschmann's last season was 1957–1958. Although it was not officially billed as his last season, anyone who was paying any attention to the Saint Louis Symphony Orchestra realized that the end of the line was near. The subscription season scheduled its usual twenty pairs, with Golschmann conducting only seven. Harry Farbman conducted one, which meant that twelve concerts were conducted by guests. There weren't twelve individual guest conductors since two of them conducted more than one concert. One of these was Georg Solti, who directed the Orchestra in four "Beethoven Cycle" concerts, one in the fall and three in January 1958. The other guest who conducted more than one concert was Edouard Van Remoortel, who conducted two concerts in December 1957. Single appearances were made by Pierre Monteux for the opening concert, Paul Strauss, Alexander Hilsberg, Fernando Previtali, and Thomas Schippers. (Schippers played the Mendelssohn D Minor Piano Concerto No. 2 as well as conducting.)

Orrin S. Wightman, Jr., an investment banker, succeeded Spiegel as president of the Society's Board. Sixteen new musicians came into the orchestra. Leslie

Golschmann on the occasion of his twenty-fifth anniversary as Conductor, being honored by Orchestra musicians who had been with him since 1931. Max Steindel, at extreme right, is reading the inscription on a silver plaque. Others in photograph are, left to right, John E. Ferrell (contra bassoon), Graziella Pampari (harp), Victor Hugo (viola), Pasquale De Conto (cello, and husband of Mme. Pampari), Clarence Gesner (clarinet), Louis Etzkow (second violin—his head is behind Golschmann's). Photograph does not include all the veterans.

Parnas, the twenty-five-year-old principal cellist in the Orchestra, won first prize in the Concours Pablo Casals, international competition for violon-cellists, in Paris. All of this happened in October and November of the last Golschmann season.

On December 2, 1957, it was announced that Vladimir Golschmann had resigned. His letter of resignation said that he wished to be relieved of the administrative duties with which he had been burdened as music director. The letter said: "It is impossible to maintain the first-rate standing of the orchestra with the loss in the last three years of 40% personnel. Administrative problems," he said, "in the course of the years have prevented our organization from keeping many outstanding players I had found and brought to our city, with the hope of making the Orchestra a major factor in the musical life of our country."

Five days after this news, the Belgian guest conductor Edouard Van Re-moortel conducted his first concert in St. Louis. Featured on the program was

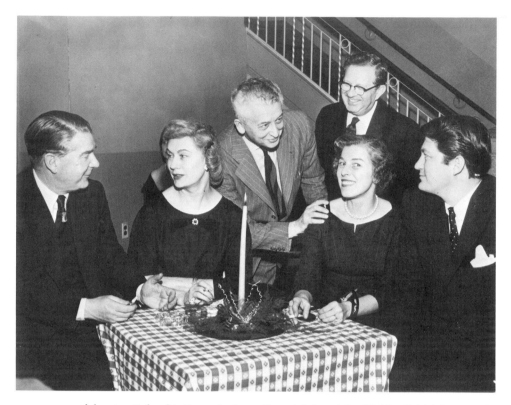

1957 party celebrating Columbia Record release. Seated, left to right: Visiting British impresario Mr. Van Wycke; Mrs. Vladimir Golschmann; Golschmann; Mrs. Morton D. May; Master-works A. and R. Director David Oppenheim. Standing: William Zalken, Manager, Saint Louis Symphony Orchestra. Taken at German House, where recording was made.

the Brahms Double Concerto, with Melvin Ritter playing the violin and Leslie Parnas on the cello. A week later, in the second of Van Remoortel's back-to-back concert appearances, he conducted the Orchestra accompanying Isaac Stern playing Prokofiev's Second Concerto for Violin and Orchestra. Both concerts were met with great acclaim from the critics, the audiences, and the board members. On December 17, Van Remoortel was given a three-year contract as Music Director of the Saint Louis Symphony Orchestra. Whether he had been the executive committee's first choice, or whether his two concerts had been so compellingly dramatic that other candidates seemed less exciting, doesn't matter. The Orchestra had a new conductor signed up for the future and the rest of the season could now proceed without the diversion of speculation.

Arthur Fiedler conducted an enormously successful Pops concert on New Year's Eve at the Chase Hotel. Solti pursued his Beethoven cycle; Eloise Polk, concert pianist, and coincidentally the stepdaughter of Oscar Johnson, was the soloist at a Benefit Concert on April 1. Announcement was made that the Friday matinee concerts would in the future be played in the Khorassan Room of the Chase Hotel. The Maintenance Fund Drive got underway with a goal of

Golschmann with Morton D. May, right, at German House party celebrating record release. (1957)

$250,000, the undertaking being given a boost by the newspapers as usual. A *St. Louis Globe-Democrat* editorial pointed out that whereas the minimum wage for orchestra musicians was $100 a week (for twenty-five weeks), a blacksmith was being paid $144 a week, a plumber $149, and a bricklayer $150.[11] Artur Rubinstein was here in February for what became known as a Rubinstein Festival—three concerts being played with the Symphony Orchestra (though not part of the subscription series) and one program being piano

Orrin S. Wightman, Jr. receiving check for $16,400 following a benefit concert sponsored jointly by the Junior Division of the Women's Association and the St. Louis Junior League. Presenting check are (center) Mrs. Howard L. Bland, Jr. (President of the Junior League), and Mrs. William P. Williams (Chairman, Junior Division). (*St. Louis Post-Dispatch* photograph, May 27, 1958)

only. (It was Rubinstein's seventeenth appearance in St. Louis.) Also during February a series of four special Pops Concerts was played at the Chase Hotel and conducted by Arthur Fiedler. (One of the soloists was Edith Schiller, concert pianist and wife of Harry Farbman, concertmaster.)

Golschmann's last concerts were on April 4 and April 5. KSD-TV and KSD radio broadcast the final concert live. The program presented *Fanfare to Israel* by Paul Ben Haim, Kabalevsky's Second Symphony, Mozart's G Minor Symphony, two *Gymnopedies* by Satie, with orchestration by Debussy, Ravel's *La Valse*, and Wagner's Prelude to *Lohengrin*. Golschmann wore the crimson rosette of the Legion of Honor which had been conferred on him by the French government. At intermission he was interviewed, given a stereophonic tape recorder, and wished well by Orrin Wightman and Kenneth J. Farmer, president of Local #2, American Federation of Musicians. Some twenty orchestra members—those who had been with him all the way, so to speak, from 1931—trouped past him and shook his hand. It was an event rife with emotion.

One more Golschmann occasion took place in St. Louis after the last concert.

On April 19, 1958, a non-musical side of Vladimir Golschmann was made public when a collection of paintings and drawings by the French modern artists—a collection gathered by the Golschmanns through the years—was put on display in Givens Hall at Washington University. The exhibit included paintings and graphics by Matisse, Rouault, and Modigliani, and numerous canvases by Picasso and Braque. In the collection was also a large group of African primitive sculptures. Although this may have been a surprise to the public, Golschmann had been known to many St. Louis art collectors as a connoisseur with a shrewd eye for quality in modern paintings, and an excellent go-between for purchases. His reputation in this field had not been confined to St. Louis: art collectors in towns where the Orchestra played on tour had often asked for Golschmann's advice on various purchases. (In 1950, the City Art Museum had exhibited a small part of Golschmann's collection, including two Renoirs—one drawing and one water color—a Dufy, an Utrillo, and two works by Maurice de Vlaminck. These works of art were ones which Golschmann had removed from his Paris apartment and had brought to the St. Louis apartment when World War II was imminent in 1939.) A kind of farewell reception was held for the Golschmanns in connection with the Washington University exhibit. It was one more reminder of the end of an era.

Whatever conclusions are drawn about the Saint Louis Symphony Orchestra under the baton of Vladimir Golschmann for twenty-seven years, it should be obvious that the earlier part of the era undeniably advanced the Orchestra immeasurably. As a French conductor in a German-dominated field, he was anything but commonplace. In the Golden Years—the 1930's and the early 40's—he was regarded throughout the world of music as a gifted conductor, one with taste, artistry, innovative curiosity, and, above all, "elegance." This was the favorite word used to describe his music by reviewers and cataloguers of American orchestra conductors during the period. He had the highest of standards for his adopted orchestra and he achieved them in many ways. His string section, in the peak years, was considered one of the finest in the United States. That the Orchestra reached a pinnacle and then failed to continue growing cannot undo what *was* accomplished. Golschmann moved the Orchestra ahead. Let that not be forgotten.

THE ST. LOUIS SYMPHONY ORCHESTRA
VLADIMIR GOLSCHMANN, Conductor

EIGHTH SYMPHONY CONCERTS

Saturday Evening, December 8, at 8:30 P. M.

Sunday Afternoon, December 9, at 3:30 P. M.

DIMITRI MITROPOULOS, Guest Conductor

MOZART........................Suite from "Idomeneo" (K. 366)

Overture
The Sacrifice
Festive March

(First performance in St. Louis)

BEETHOVEN............Symphony No. 4 in B Flat Major, Opus 60

Adagio: Allegro vivace
Adagio
Allegro vivace
Allegro ma non troppo

INTERMISSION

KRENEK..Elegy for String Orchestra

(First performance in St. Louis)

DEBUSSY...*La Mer* (The Sea)

From Dawn 'til Midday on the Sea
Sport of the Waves
Dialogue of the Wind and the Sea

The Steinway Is the Official Piano of the St. Louis Symphony Orchestra.

The St. Louis Symphony Orchestra Records Exclusively for RCA Victor.

Golschmann's twenty-first season saw various guest conductors.

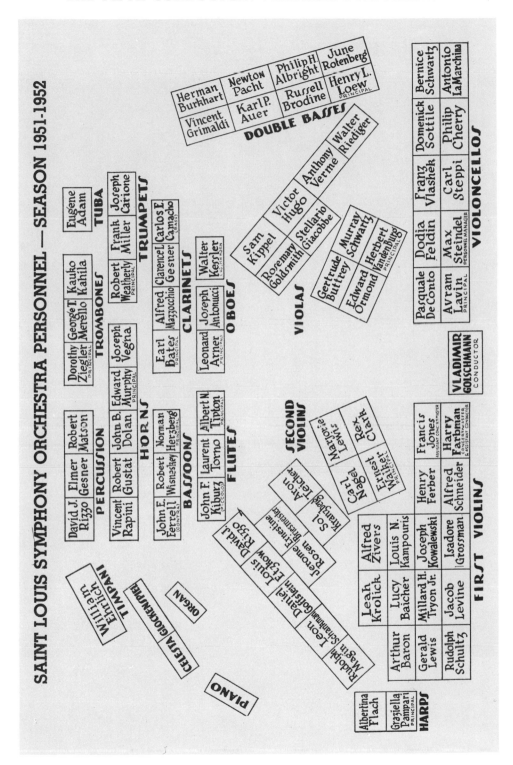

Golschmann's Orchestra in his twenty-first season. Graphic chart of personnel seating was printed for brief period only.

Edouard Van Remoortel

EDOUARD VAN REMOORTEL

The Symphony Years 1958–1962

THE SAINT LOUIS SYMPHONY SOCIETY, with the appointment of its enthusiastic new, youthful Belgian conductor, looked ahead to a bright future for the Orchestra. It envisioned a repeat of the happy years when Vladimir Golschmann had first arrived, with the Orchestra commencing a signal ascendancy. The Van Remoortel appointment was unquestionably a shot in the arm for the public relations department. Van Remoortel was a handsome, dashing young bachelor and the concerts he had conducted as a guest had impressed everyone. This was to be another turning point—an upsurge, after the Orchestra's waning image in the Fifties.

Van Remoortel, whose father was a banker and a member of the Belgian Senate, had studied the cello as well as conducting. He had acquired his higher education at the Conservatory of Brussels and had conducted numerous orchestras in Europe as well as in the United States. In July 1958, in advance of his first season in St. Louis, he flew in to attend a party given to plan the season ticket sales. He charmed guests and reporters alike. He had just come from a conducting engagement in Australia and was to continue his summer activities by conducting in New York, Chicago, and in Europe. He spoke glowingly of his admiration and hopes for the Saint Louis Symphony Orchestra.

During the summer and fall of his first season, Van Remoortel inadvertently shared the limelight, in a way, with Max Steindel, veteran principal cellist and personnel manager of the Orchestra. Steindel had then been with the Orchestra for forty-two years, and was an exceedingly colorful and well-loved member of the organization. He was interviewed and featured in an article by Clarissa Start in the *St. Louis Post Dispatch* in July, [1] an article that discussed his wit, his talents as a raconteur and as a perennial trouble shooter, as well as his being a capital cello player. (He was also very fond of food, particularly soup.) In the fall, Steindel was given the "Page One Civic Award"[2] and referred to as the dean of St. Louis musicians. All of this was subsidiary to what Van Remoortel was involved in, but it was a happy bit of news which served the interests of the Orchestra as well.

The 1958–1959 season started auspiciously. The opening pair of concerts consisted of Wagner's Prelude to *Lohengrin*, Paul Creston's Symphony No. 2, and Beethoven's Symphony No. 7. The Creston work was a world premiere. Reaction to the new maestro was highly favorable, evoking such words as "exciting" and "brilliant." KSD-TV and KSD Radio carried the concert live from Kiel Auditorium.

The second concert won special acclaim, not solely because of Van Remoortel, although he carried his part admirably. The focal point was Van Cliburn, who had won the Tchaikovsky Piano Competition in Moscow the previous April and had been engaged to play with the St. Louis Symphony Orchestra as one of his first concert appearances. An open rehearsal was conducted and 2500 teenagers attended. Van Cliburn complained a little about the tuning of the piano in the treble range, but allowed as how it would be corrected by evening.[3] In fact, the entire season of subscription concerts was impressive, featuring such soloists as Isaac Stern, Eugene Istomin, Robert Casadesus, Glenn Gould, Zino Francescatti, Nathan Milstein, and Marian Anderson.

One aspect of the season's planning which perhaps went unnoticed by the concert-goers, but which startled the Board somewhat, was that the new young conductor insisted at the outset that he have the month of January off. The Board accepted this and the January concerts were handled by Aaron Copland, Eleazar De Carvalho, Joseph Krips, and Harry Farbman.

Although the reaction to the podium performances and resulting concerts continued to be complimentary, backstage trouble began brewing before the first season was over. There were subtle signs of musical immaturity and very pronounced signs of lack of rapport and of mutual respect between conductor and musicians.

To deal first with the musical immaturity, let it be said that, to Van Remoortel's credit, he was generally conscientious and determined to deliver a good performance. He was evidently not, however, a conductor totally at home with a score. His approach was to memorize every score. Granted many conductors carry a piece of music through without a score in front of them. Also granted, many have, in effect, memorized the score and have the music in front of them only as a kind of insurance. With Van Remoortel, it was apparently *essential* that he memorize and that he do all of his thinking ahead of time, a condition that did not allow for the customary hairline adaptations which make every performance slightly different from every other. Total familiarity with the musical score is obviously necessary. Total memorization of every piece to be presented is somewhat unusual. Perhaps the fact that he felt the need to memorize every score is neither here nor there. What was more significant were the warning signals about his relationships with and regard for the Orchestra as a whole.

It is an accepted tradition that a new conductor have ambitious ideas of improving the quality of the orchestra which he has acquired. The "new broom" syndrome is nothing new. It is usually undertaken with a certain amount of restraint and tact. With Van Remoortel, this was not the case.

Van Remoortel rehearsing Orchestra.

Perhaps because of his youth and because he was not nearly as experienced a leader as the Board had assumed, he got into serious trouble early in the season. By March, his trouble was public knowledge, emblazoned in the newspapers. He had originally intended to fire forty-two of the eighty-five musicians of the orchestra. He narrowed it down to between fifteen and seventeen. The tension increased to the point that the Orchestra refused to play at a rehearsal on

Van Remoortel in special chair which he had installed for himself on the bus tours. Edward Murphy, Assistant Conductor, immediately behind Van Remoortel. (*St. Louis Post-Dispatch* photograph by Art Witman, March 25, 1962)

March 2. The crisis had built up to explosive proportions. Van Remoortel had given notification to the Symphony Committee (the group representing the musicians in their dealings with the Society) that fifteen musicians were to be let go. Manager Zalken reported that the men had not appealed to the Dismissal Committee, which consisted of four members of the Orchestra and four from the Society. Henry Loew, principal bass player and a member of the Orchestra Committee, told a *St. Louis Post Dispatch* reporter that "the Symphony Orchestra should not be made up of transient members out of musical schools"[3] which would happen if the neophyte music director fired so many musicians. At the March 2 rehearsal, George Hussey, English horn player and chairman of the Orchestra Committee, informed Van Remoortel that the Orchestra had voted not to play for him. Van Remoortel refused to discuss the issues at that moment and asked if this were a strike. Loew responded that it was not a strike, that the orchestra members would not go back on their contracts, that they were ready to play, but would not play for Van Remoortel until he had settled the matter at hand. Van Remoortel stalked off to his dressing room. Loew and Hussey, with Zalken, Edward Ormond (viola), and Earl Bates (clarinet), pow-wowed with the maestro in his dressing room. They came to an agreement of sorts, that the matter would be handled through the Dismissal Committee. The rehearsal and subsequent concert went on, but not without the newspapers having gotten hold of the story that the concert had been played "under protest."[4] The Orchestra left on tour immediately following the incident, and by the end of March, public announcement was made of the agreement to settle the dispute. Of the seventeen players whose jobs Van Remoortel had threatened, two resigned to go to Cleveland where the pay was higher and the season was for thirty-three weeks, compared to twenty-five in St. Louis. (These two were Alfred Genovese, principal oboe, and Edward Ormond, assistant principal viola.) Of the remaining fifteen, eight were to get further consideration and auditions, three were to be retired on half-pay minimum wage, two were put on probation or trial for one year, and two were to be retained. The fact remained, however, that Van Remoortel's abysmal lack of friendly relationships with the musicians was now public knowledge, and that he was, in the eyes of the Orchestra, "overbearing and intolerant."[5]

In spite of these "in-house" rumblings the Orchestra continued to play its well-set-up programs. The 1959–1960 season (subscription concerts) featured, among others, Malcolm Frager, Byron Janis, Yehudi Menuhin, Geza Anda, Artur Rubinstein, Isaac Stern, Eloise Polk, and John Browning. Van Remoortel conducted all but four of these concerts, those four being led by Harry Farbman, Paul Kletzki, Sir John Barbirolli, and the familiar Vladimir Golschmann. The Orchestra played sixteen concerts on tour and ten "special concerts" in and around St. Louis, one of which featured Jack Benny and another conducted by Rudolph Ganz. The Metropolitan Opera performed *La Traviata* with the Orchestra in May, after the regular season was over.

In his third season as Music Director (1960–1961) Van Remoortel's image was improved a little by some favorable publicity. In October, Van Remoortel was given the Order of King Leopold II (Belgium's highest award) by Prince Albert of Belgium, here in St. Louis with a delegation of Belgian businessmen in attendance. In November, the *St. Louis Globe Democrat* carried a feature article on Van Remoortel's avocation as a chef—it published his recipe for Russian Golubtsi, a meat-filled cabbage dish.[6]

The season's opening concert included a new work by American George Rochberg, *Time Span*. Soloists during the first half of the year included Isaac

Stern, Robert Casadesus, and Edith Schiller. Van Remoortel was, as usual, away from St. Louis for four weeks in mid-season and the January concerts were conducted by Harry Farbman, Irwin Hoffman, and Georg Solti (then Director of the Los Angeles Philharmonic).

A $300,000 goal had been set for the Maintenance Fund. Wightman, still president of the Symphony Society, announced that the Society had extended unemployment compensation, set up a retirement fund, and made a substantial increase in minimum pay for orchestra musicians. Civic Progress's president, David Calhoun, stated publicly that "the members are convinced of the importance of the Saint Louis Symphony Orchestra . . . [as] a vital civic asset." The plight of symphony orchestras was a growing topic of conversation in all of the larger cities in America. Orchestras everywhere were caught, to varying degrees, in the financial vise. This was, of course, before the inception of the National Endowment for the Arts.

In the same season (Van Remoortel's third), André Previn conducted a benefit concert (a "Beer and Pretzels" Pops concert) in the Convention Hall of Kiel Auditorium. Six thousand people attended.

In the spring, the Orchestra had twenty-four concerts on tour. Van Remoortel indulged in a creature-comfort luxury on the tours, one which did not endear him to his personnel. He disliked long rides in the ordinary bus seat and thus had the front seats of his bus removed and a large lounge chair installed for himself. The tour of that particular year ended on another rather sour note: three of the musicians made a formal complaint to Van Remoortel protesting his conduct during one of the tour concerts. He, in turn, filed charges against them, threatening to fire them. Countercharges flew back and forth, until, finally, the matter simmered down and no one was dismissed.

Van Remoortel did have his lighter side and he enjoyed cordial relationships with a few of the orchestra members on whom he depended heavily. Some of the first chair players were on good terms with him. Herbert Van den Burg, principal violist, recalls one time on tour when the insouciance of the Maestro's youth created an emergency and then enabled him to cope with the emergency with notable aplomb. The circumstances were that a reporter, joining the tour, wanted his automobile, but didn't want to drive it cross-country. He asked Van den Burg to ferry the car for him. Van Remoortel, always attracted to good cars and fast driving, proposed to Van den Burg that he ride along while the conductor did the actual driving. Van Remoortel, to enhance the excitement, avoided the major highways and took to the back roads. Van den Burg recalls the episode as reminiscent of Tam O'Shanter's ride, barrelling along the curving and twisted country lanes at terrifying speeds. The car very suddenly broke down in a remote area. While the two men were speculating about how to get to the next concert on time, a farmer with a flat-bed truck, loaded with a "natural fertilizer," came along. He hooked the car up with a tow chain and pulled the two men in the vehicle to the closest repair station while the contents of the truck-back periodically flew over the disabled car. The repairs took several hours, and when finally Van Remoortel and Van den Burg got going

The Order of King Leopold II, Belgium's highest award, is bestowed on Van Remoortel by Prince Albert of Belgium, in a ceremony in the Crystal Room of the Sheraton-Jefferson Hotel. Looking on is Princess Paola. (*St. Louis Globe-Democrat* photograph, October 13, 1960)

again, they had very little time left in order to arrive for the scheduled concert. When they reached their destination, the Orchestra was already onstage. Looking only a little flustered, the conductor and the principal violist took their places and the concert proceeded, no more than a few minutes late.[7]

Harry Farbman, concertmaster since 1942, and assistant conductor *par excellence* of hundreds of concerts with the Orchestra, resigned at the end of the 1960–1961 season to accept a post at the University of Indiana at Bloomington. Edward Murphy, principal horn player, succeeded Farbman as assistant conductor.

Whether it had been apparent to the concert-going public or not, the executive committee of the Society Board had become increasingly uneasy, to say the least, about Van Remoortel as Music Director. As has been pointed out, his relationships with Orchestra personnel were (with few exceptions) poor, to understate the case. As to performance, he was conscientious in his preparations, but not essentially well-grounded in a broad base of repertoire. His contract was for three years, and no successor had been lined up. At the end of his third year, it was announced that he had been engaged to conduct only ten programs the next season. This was not a customary arrangement. On top of this, the upcoming budget was announced to be $500,000, the largest ever. (One unexpected and offbeat boost came when the Hawks Basketball Team owner, Ben Kerner, gave a check to the Orchestra for $2,500, in return for which a concert was to be played after a basketball game.)

As it turned out, Van Remoortel conducted only seven of the 1961–1962 concerts, not ten as had been announced. The thirteen other concerts were handled by Leopold Stokowski, Christoph Von Dohnanyi (two concerts), Kenneth Schermerhorn, Zubin Mehta (two concerts), Werner Torkanowsky (two concerts), Laszlo Somogyi, Eugen Jochum, Franz Waxman, and Jean Martinon (two concerts). Aram Khachaturian had been scheduled to conduct in February, but had cancelled his American tour.

Although very little attention was called to the fact, the 1962–1963 season passed with no Music Director or Permanent Conductor. (Over the years, these titles became interchangeable, or up to the choice of the maestro.) Assistant Conductor Murphy handled whatever wasn't conducted by a guest. The guest conductor for the opening pair of concerts was Eleazar De Carvalho, the Brazilian maestro who had first appeared with the Saint Louis Symphony Orchestra during the 1950–1951 season. (Since De Carvalho's association with the Orchestra is discussed in detail in the following chapter, no further comment is needed here.) During the "conductorless" season, Van Remoortel was an invited guest conductor in early November, and Golschmann was on the podium in February. In March 1963, it was announced that the forty-seven-year-old De Carvalho had been appointed as new Music Director.

80th Anniversary Season

THE ST. LOUIS SYMPHONY ORCHESTRA

EDOUARD VAN REMOORTEL, *Conductor and Musical Director*

FIRST SYMPHONY CONCERTS

Opera House — Kiel Auditorium

SATURDAY EVENING, OCTOBER 24, *at* 8:40 *o'clock*

SUNDAY AFTERNOON, OCTOBER 25, *at* 3:00 *o'clock*

MALCOLM FRAGER, Pianist

Symphony No. 5 in C Minor, Opus 67   Beethoven
>   Allegro con brio
>   Andante con moto
>   Allegro
>   *Finale*: Allegro

INTERMISSION

Seventh Symphony (*Liturgical*), Opus 80   Vincent Persichetti
>   (Commissioned by the Junior Division of the Women's Association
>   of the St. Louis Symphony Society, in honor of the 80th Anniver-
>   sary of the St. Louis Symphony Orchestra)
>   Lento
>   Allegro
>   Andante
>   Vivace
>   Adagio

(First performances anywhere)

Concerto No. 2 in G Minor, Opus 16, for   Prokofieff
>   Piano and Orchestra
>   Andantino—Allegretto—Andantino
>   Scherzo
>   Intermezzo
>   Finale

(First performances in this concert series)

MALCOLM FRAGER, Pianist

•

Mr. Frager plays the Steinway

Columbia Records   **Capitol Records**

Opening concert, Van Remoortel's second season.

ST. LOUIS SYMPHONY ORCHESTRA PERSONNEL
Season 1959-1960

EDOUARD VAN REMOORTEL, Conductor

Harry Farbman, Assistant Conductor

FIRST VIOLINS
Harry Farbman
  Concertmaster
Melvin Ritter
  Assistant Concertmaster
Teruko Akagi
Robert Gimprich
Isadore Grossman
Andreas Makris
Jacob Levine
Robert Menga
Victor S. Mucci
Benjamin Picone
Gerard Rosa, Jr.
Berton Siegel
Joan Howie Siegel
Eleanor Siranossian
William Steck
Hellmut Stern

SECOND VIOLINS
Ernest Walker
  Principal
Sol Kranzberg
David E. Bakalor
Margaret Bates
Charles Boyle
Joseph Gluck
A. James Krohn
Morris Neiberg
Jerome D. Rosen
Leon Schankman
Robert Velten
Bette Hope Waddington
Fred J. Wild

VIOLAS
Herbert Van den Berg
  Principal
Sally Burnau
Louis Druzinsky
Joseph Elson
Stellario Giacobbe
Rosemary Goldsmith
Arthur H. Knebel, Jr.
William Magers
Walter Riediger
Anthony Verme

VIOLONCELLOS
Leslie Parnas
  Principal
Gerald Kagan
Marilyn Beabout
Pasquale DeConto
Celia Koch
Ken Pinckney
Domenick Sottile
Max Steindel
Carl Steppi
Olga Zilboorg

DOUBLE BASSES
Henry L. Loew
  Principal
Russell V. Brodine
H. Stevens Brewster, Jr.
Martin Sklar
Joseph C. Kleeman
Ralph R. Maisel
Janice A. Roberts
Thomas S. Monohan, Jr.

HARP
Graziella Pampari

FLUTES
Israel Borouchoff
  Principal
Janet Sillars
John F. Kiburz

PICCOLO
John F. Kiburz

OBOES
George A. Hussey, Jr.
  Principal
Claude Worrell
Peter Angelo

ENGLISH HORN
Peter Angelo

CLARINETS
Earl O. Bates
  Principal
Michael E. Burgio
Leslie Scott

BASS CLARINET
Leslie Scott

BASSOONS
Lester Cantor
  Principal
Robert J. Wisneskey
Sam Gravell

CONTRA BASSOON
Sam Gravell

HORNS
Edward Murphy
  Principal
Henry Sigismonti
Albert W. Schmitter
Kenneth W. Schultz
Robert L. Gustat

TRUMPETS
Robert Weatherly
  Principal
Donald R. Stolz
Frank Miller

TROMBONES
Bernard Schneider
  Principal
Dorothy Ziegler
Mel Jernigan

TUBA
James Emde

TYMPANI
Edward L. Friedlander

PERCUSSION
Richard L. O'Donnell
William Ehrlich
David J. Rizzo

PIANO
Walter Steindel

CELESTA and PIANO
Dorothy Ziegler

LIBRARIANS
Elmer Gesner
Rudolph Magin

PERSONNEL MANAGER
Max Steindel

STAGE MANAGER
George Buermann

Van Remoortel's Orchestra during his second season. Fourteen members of 1979–1980 Orchestra in the roster.

ST. LOUIS SYMPHONY ORCHESTRA

THIRD SYMPHONY CONCERTS
Opera House — Kiel Auditorium

SATURDAY EVENING, NOVEMBER 3, AT 8:40 O'CLOCK
SUNDAY AFTERNOON, NOVEMBER 4, AT 2:30 O'CLOCK

EDOUARD VAN REMOORTEL, Guest Conductor
VAN CLIBURN, Pianist

Adagio for String Orchestra, Opus 11   Barber

Saturday Evening

Concerto No. 2 in B Flat Major, Opus 83,   Brahms
    for Piano and Orchestra

        Allegro non troppo
        Andante appassionato
        Andante
        Allegretto grazioso

        VAN CLIBURN, Pianist

Sunday Afternoon

Concerto No. 2 in C Minor, Opus 18,   Rachmaninoff
    for Piano and Orchestra

        Moderato
        Adagio sostenuto
        Allegro scherzando

        VAN CLIBURN, Pianist

INTERMISSION

Symphony No. 9 in C Major   Schubert
        Andante: Allegro ma non troppo
        Andante con moto
        Scherzo: Allegro vivace: Trio
        Finale: Allegro vivace

Mr. Cliburn Plays the Steinway

**The Steinway is the Official Piano of the St. Louis Symphony Orchestra
Columbia Records**

SATURDAY EVENING PATRONS

For your convenience special shuttle bus service is available from the Union Station
Parking Lot, 20th and Market Streets, to Kiel Opera House and return. We urge
you to take advantage of this special service. Parking lot fee only $1 per car. Bus
service free.

Van Remoortel listed as Guest Conductor, in the year after his tenure in St. Louis ended. The
Orchestra had no Music Director or Principal Conductor this year. Note that Cliburn played
different concerti in the pair of concerts.

Eleazar De Carvalho

ELEAZAR DE CARVALHO

The Symphony Years 1963–1968

EVEN by the time that Eleazar De Carvalho had first appeared as guest conductor of the Saint Louis Symphony Orchestra in the 1950–1951 season, he had made quite a mark for himself in the world of concert music. While serving in the Brazilian Navy, the young De Carvalho had realized that he wanted to devote his life to music. By the time he received his Honorable Discharge from the Navy, in 1956, he had managed to acquire music degrees from both the Music School of the University of Brazil, in Rio de Janeiro, and the Institute Rio Branca. Four years later, he earned a doctor's degree in music and a diploma as a conductor-composer from the University of Brazil. In 1956, he came to the United States where he was an assistant to Koussevitsky in the training class for conductors at the Berkshire Music Festival. (Another assistant to Koussevitsky during this period was Leonard Bernstein.) While working with the Berkshire group, De Carvalho was invited to conduct the Boston Symphony Orchestra, and later the Chicago and Cleveland Orchestras. In 1951, he became Music Director of the Brazilian Symphony Orchestra. He had accumulated a wide background of experience, from conducting of Beethoven cycles to directing opera. By the time he came to St. Louis to stay, in 1963, he had made innumerable guest appearances not only in this country but in England, France, Belgium, and Germany. There were no doubts about his practical experience or his ability to deal effectively with an orchestra as a music director. The Orchestra had faith in him. The musicians had been polled before the decision was final. De Carvalho had been their choice as well as the Board's.

The new conductor was immediately recognized as a man of limitless energies and an almost animal dynamism. Not being a scholar in the conservative sense of the word, not steeped in the revered European tradition, he dealt only with music which he felt he could thoroughly master. He had respect for his musicians and, although he recruited significant new members for the Orchestra, he made no effort to dismiss ruthlessly. Professionalism began to color rehearsals—no coffee, no smoking, everything on stage in perfect readiness before the rehearsals began.

The opening concert consisted of Beethoven's First Symphony, a new work by Gordon Binkerd (commissioned by the Junior Division of the Women's Symphony Association)[1] and the first performance in St. Louis of Stravinsky's *Rite of Spring*.

As the season progressed, it became apparent to the concert-goers that the new Director had a hearty interest in presenting new and innovative works. The first season, De Carvalho conducted (mixed in with some of the more standard repertoire) William Schuman's *Symphony for Strings*, Schoenberg's *A Survivor from Warsaw* (for Narrator and Chorus), Peter Mennin's *Canto for Orchestra*, Victor Legley's *La Cathedrale d'Acier*, *Five Pieces for Orchestra* by Anton Von Webern, *Nones* by Luciana Berio, *Rimes* by Henri Pousseur, Aaron Copland's Symphony No. 3, and *Momoprecoce ("The Children's Carnival")*, a Fantasia for Piano and Orchestra by Villa-Lobos.

The pianist who played the Villa-Lobos music was another new personality in the concert-music world of St. Louis. She was Jocy de Oliveira, a Brazilian soloist who had had an early career as a child prodigy in Brazil. She had gone on to study in Paris, had performed in Europe, and had made her American debut with the Boston Symphony Orchestra at the Berkshire Festival in 1956. She was a journalist, a playwright, and a composer (of several sambas) with special interest in the evolution of Brazilian popular music. She was also the wife of De Carvalho. De Carvalho had waited until he was thirty-six to marry, and Jocy was eighteen years his junior. That she was a qualified pianist, there was no doubt. There was also no doubt that she espoused the world of avant garde music even more determinedly than did her husband.

People began to talk about the Saint Louis Symphony Orchestra. Tongues wagged particularly vigorously after the Friday afternoon matinees, as the audience streamed out of Kiel Auditorium. Of course, the talk wasn't all negative—far from it. The Orchestra was becoming known as one of the few orchestras of rank giving major exposure to new works. The more conservative season-ticket holders were somewhat critical of the programming, but the maestro would mollify them with a fine rendition of one of the familiar standards, and they would try harder to tolerate the alien sounds of the new. At the conclusion of a piece which had not been to the exact taste of the less venturesome listeners, the applause would be routinely polite. But when De Carvalho returned to the stage for his curtain calls, the applause would grow. The audience was applauding the man, the individual with his tremendous enthusiasm and vigor of performance, whether they liked the music or not.

During the next few years, an extraordinary number of new works were programmed into the concerts. There were works by Stockhausen, more Webern, more Schoenberg, Pisk, Berg, Elliott Carter, and Penderecki, to mention a few. Lukas Foss, Conductor of the Buffalo Philharmonic, was the other outstanding proponent of avant garde music in the United States at the time. He guest-conducted the Saint Louis Symphony Orchestra in his own composition *Elytres* in the 1966–1967 season. It was also during this period that the works of Robert Wykes,[2] Composer-in-Residence at Washington University, began to be performed. His work, *The Shape of Time*, had been introduced by the Orchestra in the spring of 1965. De Carvalho had requested the composition. The program notes referred to it as the most interesting work introduced that season.[3] The following season, De Carvalho presented another new Wykes work, *Letter to an Alto Man*, based on a poem by Donald Finkel, Poet-in-Residence at Washington University. The music was written for a chamber chorus of sixteen voices, solo harp, solo piano, percussion, and orchestra. (Incidentally, Rosalyn Wykes, wife of the composer, appeared as soprano soloist frequently during the 1960's—three times during the 1966–1967 season alone.)

The Orchestra made the national news after a performance of a work by the Greek expatriate composer, Iannis Xenakis, then living in Paris. The work *Strategie* was in the form of a competition or battle between two orchestras, using an electronic score board. The music required two conductors. De Carvalho conducted one group, Edward Murphy the other. The fact that some practical joker among the musicians had changed all the electrical connections in the score board made no difference to most of the members of the audience. They were confused anyway.

De Carvalho and the Orchestra were more than capable of attracting stellar celebrities. Igor Stravinsky was a guest conductor during De Carvalho's second season. It was Stravinsky's last tour. Mstislav Rostropovich, at that time still living in Russia and teaching at the Moscow and Leningrad Conservatories, appeared during the 1966–1967 season. He played the Prokofiev Sinfonia Concertante for Cello and Orchestra and the Dvorak Cello Concerto in B Minor.

De Carvalho was possessed with ambition to make a name for the Saint Louis Symphony Orchestra. In conversations with individual musicians he would say words to the effect that *anyone* could present Beethoven, Brahms, Tchaikovsky, *et. al.* However, when he would invite orchestra members to his apartment in the Central West End, the visitors would observe that the Maestro's own record collection was replete with music of the classic and romantic stripe. He was well acquainted with the music of the solid concert repertoire; he simply didn't want to weave great amounts of it into his programs. He felt that it was essential to make the Middle West, in general, and St. Louis, in particular, a major center of culture and that this involved deep awareness of the culture of our times, not of the past. Robert Wykes, interviewing him in connection with a contemporary music program at the University of Illinois at Urbana, asked him if he had come to the midwest with a sense of pioneering and with the idea of making the area a center of international music. His answer was, "I did not come here with the idea of becoming a 'messiah.' You already had, right in this region, the wonderful music departments at Washington University and at Urbana. My duty was to keep it alive."[4] This interview, or dialogue, between two professional musicians brought to light many aspects of De Carvalho's programming which may have escaped the average season-ticket holder. De Carvalho expressed his fascination for historical continuity in music. He explained that when he programmed, say, Mahler's Symphony No. 6 on the same program with Berg's *Pieces for Orchestra*, he was hoping to show the influence of the older work on the newer. A similar revelation was intended in the case of a joint presentation of Debussy's *Jeux* and Lutoslowski's *Jeux*. He wanted to show the same "subject" treated by different generations. He felt that the young musicians of today (as well as the concert-goers) should not cherish the delusion that all great music is from the past; he felt that good contemporary compositions *must* be performed, and that understanding of music, to be comprehensive, should range from Palestrina to John Cage.[5]

During De Carvalho's regime, two enormously significant events transpired, neither of which were caused nor controlled by him. One of these events threatened the existence of the Orchestra while the other opened up a whole new future, full of promise. The first was the musicians' strike of 1965—the first such strike in the history of the Orchestra. The second was the acquisition of and moving into Powell Symphony Hall, the first permanent home of the Orchestra. Since these two happenings are so closely wound together in time and the people involved, it is necessary that they be recounted together.

As for the men deeply involved in both, the one who held the most authority was Stanley Goodman, May Department Store executive, who had succeeded Orrin Wightman as president of the Symphony Society. Goodman took office at the start of the 1964–1965 season. William Zalken, the long-time entrepreneur, booking manager, and general manager of the Orchestra wanted to leave, in the spring of 1965, in order to devote full time to the Municipal Opera. Goodman persuaded Dr. Leigh Gerdine, then the head of the Music Department at Washington University, to act as temporary manager. Dr. Gerdine was already writing the program notes for the concerts, holding down his post at Washington University, and involved in a host of responsibilities to the academic and music world of St. Louis. He agreed to help out on an interim basis.

Both Goodman and Dr. Gerdine almost immediately found themselves in the middle of a rather drastic situation which came to a head in the fall of 1965. The musicians were increasingly resentful of non-rising pay checks in the face of rising costs of living. Other orchestras had managed to build up substantial endowment funds, had been able to increase the stipend to orchestra members, and had been able to extend their seasons. The Saint Louis Symphony Orchestra ranked far down the national scale in payroll. Before the season opened, the Musicians' Union called a strike.

Public sentiment during the strike was vociferous and ongoing. There were those who felt that the musicians should behave like artists and that they had no business crassly demanding more money. There were many others who realized the musicians' plight, but didn't see any solution. There was much feeling that the situation was, indeed, desperate and might mean the end of the Orchestra. A group of citizens organized under the acronym "S.O.S." ("Save Our Symphony"). These supporters and their concern for the future were in the news daily but, as is usually the case in such situations, they were unable to stir up, on

Eleazar De Carvalho and his wife Jocie Oliveira. Miss Oliveira made occasional appearances as piano soloist with the Saint Louis Symphony Orchestra. (*St. Louis Post-Dispatch* photograph, 1967)

their own hook, the kind of money that was needed to solve the crisis. The people involved behind the scenes were new at mediation and much too much personality projection encumbered the sessions. There were near-settlements, then rejections. The situation became so tangled that the Board announced that the season was to be cancelled. The Arts and Education Fund of St. Louis (founded in the spring of 1963) had begun to augment the funds needed to operate the Orchestra, and so it became logical for that organization to enter the negotiations. W. MacLean Johnson, head of Webster Publishing Company and senior vice-president of McGraw-Hill, was the head of the Arts and Education Fund. He stepped into the middle of the tangle, and, as an "outsider" with patience and objectivity, was able to work out some of the knots and thus bring a conciliatory atmosphere to the negotiations. Working with him were Merrimon Cuninggim and Homer Sayad. The season's start having been delayed some four weeks, the problems were finally worked out and a three-year contract was signed.

The conditions agreed upon were that the minimum weekly pay would be $145, $150, and $155, in the three upcoming years. In addition, there was to be an $11 additional weekly payment which had been made possible by a newly-formed group of citizens calling themselves the St. Louis Ambassadors. This organization was spearheaded by the Mayor at the time, A. J. Cervantes, and pledged itself to raise $100,000 for the Symphony. Additional funds were to come from benefit games played by the St. Louis Football Cardinals. It was agreed that the season covered by the contract should be twenty-eight weeks in length, thirty-five the second year, and thirty-six the third.

The Women's Association immediately started a *Blitzkrieg* on ticket sales, and the Orchestra commenced the season in November. In spite of the delayed start, the season's concerts were as numerous as ever and the touring was actually more extensive than usual. In addition to a five-day tour of concerts in Missouri alone, the Orchestra played another thirty concerts within a thirty-four day period from February 28 to April 2. This long safari went all the way to the west coast where the Orchestra played in San Francisco, Sacramento, Fresno, and Los Angeles. The Los Angeles engagement was an extremely frustrating one, for when they arrived in that city, a Teamsters' Union strike was in effect, and it was impossible to get the instruments moved to the concert location. The scheduled soloist was Tamas Vasary, a thirty-two year-old Hungarian pianist, who saved the day by playing an entire program of solo piano music before an audience of some 2700 persons.

With the St. Louis strike in the past and the season progressing, finally, Dr. Gerdine—acting as manager—found himself faced with various responsibilities not usually part of a typical year's agenda. The first of these was, of course, to preside over the healing of the wounds after the strike. The second was to start negotiating for a grant from the Ford Foundation. (Also hovering in the future was the possibility of financial aid from the National Endowment for the Arts and Humanities, established officially in October 1965.) On top of these, he had a third challenging job, which was to work with Goodman to explore the possibilities of a permanent hall for the Saint Louis Symphony Orchestra.

This endeavor was the result of a gift of $500,000 from Oscar Johnson—a gift to be used specifically for the purchase of a building for the Orchestra before January 1, 1967. If not used as specified, the gift was to revert to Washington University's Medical School. And time was running out.

Photograph taken for S.L.S.O. Rotogravure, 1964. Left to right: William Zalken; Stanley J. Goodman (newly elected President of the Society's Board); and Orrin S. Wightman, Jr. (preceding President of the Board).

As is often the case, happenstance played an unexpected role in what was to happen. The Orchestra was still playing in Kiel Auditorium, which necessitated routine scheduling and leasing of the Auditorium for the season's concerts. Because of the strike, there had been a delay in confirming all necessary dates for the 1965–1966 season, and the Orchestra found itself facing one concert date with no hall in which to play. The St. Louis Theater, one of the city's old movie houses (at the time showing, appropriately, "The Sound of Music") was available for leasing. Without much time for anyone to think about it as anything more than an emergency stop-gap, the St. Louis Theater was leased for the concert. The acoustics in the building, exactly as it stood, proved to be astonishingly good, perhaps because of the acoustical needs of the vanishing vaudevillians. Those in charge of the affairs of the Symphony Society—that is to say, Goodman, Dr. Gerdine, the executive committee, the Music Director and the Orchestra Committee—began to realize surprising possibilities.

During all this, Dr. Gerdine, who had agreed to help only on a purely temporary basis, was eager to have the interim assignment end so that he could catch his breath and return to his other responsibilities. It was at this time that a new significant personality came into the picture in the person of Peter Pastreich. Goodman had been scouting for a full-time permanent manager. The job of manager of a major orchestra had grown enormously demanding. Someone was needed who could not only handle the routine bookings, arrangements for tours, dealings with the artists' agents, and many other details, but who was also a seasoned fund-raiser. The job was comparable to that of a university president, and required a person fired with a visionary approach to future growth. Pastreich was managing the Kansas City Philharmonic when, in March 1966, through an organizational dispute, he found himself jobless. Pastreich was known to Goodman as a young man with a great deal of competence and drive. The moment Goodman heard that he had been fired in Kansas City, he hired him for St. Louis. (Pastreich was hired as Assistant Manager to Dr. Gerdine. After Dr. Gerdine left, he became Manager but the job was growing so rapidly that the title was soon changed: in 1970, Pastreich became Executive Director, and his assistant, James N. Cain, engaged in 1968, became Manager.)

In April 1966, the Symphony Society's Board of Directors voted to proceed with the acquisition of the St. Louis Theater. The building, located at the southeast corner of Grand and Delmar Boulevards, was part of a chain of movie theaters owned by a company named Arthur Enterprises. Constructed in 1925, the theater had been designed by a Chicago firm, Rapp and Rapp. It was not typical of large motion picture palaces of the period. Its design was not a product of Art Nouveau, Art Deco, or even Hollywood's idea of "Cleopatra Classic." This building was different. Its architects had been inspired by no less than the chapel at Versailles, and had designed their foyer with that ambience in mind. The theater proper was not oblong like the classic concert hall, but, having been planned to carry live voices from the stage to the audience, its acoustic design was surprisingly successful.

Buying a motion picture theater for conversion and use as a symphony hall was in many ways quite a daring prospect. This was a period when the thing to do was to build a brand new "cultural center." Examples of this philosophy were constructed and in use in many major American cities. The functional appearance of such structures had become accepted, but the acoustics were not always proving to be as excellent as advertised. With these disappointments serving as hindsight, the Saint Louis Symphony Society judiciously took the innovative route of purchasing and refurbishing the old St. Louis Theater, instead of starting from scratch.

Two acoustics experts were summoned for advice. They were Paul Veneklasen and Heinrich Keilholz. Keilholz, who had been engaged by George Szell to "do over" Severance Hall in Cleveland, moved around in the hall with his tape recorder while a blank pistol was fired on the stage. He pronounced the acoustics very good just as they were, but recommended a canopy over the stage to make them even better. This idea was rejected, as were various other suggestions, as being too radical in appearance and not really guaranteed to be completely successful. The man who finally came up with the plan that was adopted was Cyril Harris, a professor of Architecture and Acoustics at Columbia University. His theory was to avoid the escape of sound through any avenue whatsoever. The interior of the theater was revamped according to his plans. Thicknesses of plaster were added here and there, a heavy wall was built at the back of the stage, apertures around doors and lights were sealed, and so on. Where other acoustical planners had suggested scrim, he used solids. It worked.

Although the mechanics of transmitting the music to the audience was of paramount importance, the general esthetic renovation of the building followed as a close second. The foyer was fitted with the lush red draperies and the stair carpeting; sconces and existing chandeliers were cleaned, refinished, and adorned with crystal; new seats in the theater carried out the royal red look. Perhaps the most demanding work—and the most effective—was the restoration of the plaster ceilings and walls to off-white, high-lighted with gold leaf on the mouldings. Craftsmen capable of applying the gold leaf were found, but the square inches to be covered vastly exceeded the original estimate, and the project exhausted all available sources of gold leaf before it was completed. More was flown in from Germany.

Money, and more money, had to be raised to make this dream come true. The Johnson gift had been the start. In July 1966, the Ford Foundation had given the Saint Louis Symphony Orchestra $500,000 as an unconditional gift with the promise of another $2,000,000 provided a matching amount could be raised locally. Mrs. Walter Powell, a long-time concert-goer, gave a one-million-dollar, lifetime interest contribution to the Saint Louis Symphony Society, which made the Ford Foundation challenge grant accessible. Mrs. Powell's husband, for whom the Hall is named, had been an executive with the Brown Shoe Company and a dedicated amateur figure skater. An international judge of figure skating, he was accompanying the United States Olympic Team in 1961 when the plane in which they were travelling crashed in Amsterdam, Holland, killing all aboard.

The Orchestra did not move into Powell Symphony Hall until January 1968. In April 1967, De Carvalho announced that he would resign at the conclusion of his contract term—the end of the next season. It seemed ironic that the man who had poured so much vitality and personal energies into the Orchestra for four years would not be basking in the pleasures and pride of the Orchestra permanently established in its first home. The reasons for his resignation were fairly obvious to anyone who had followed the concerts and the general reactions to them. Although there had been an element in the audiences which had been exhilarated and stimulated by the presentations of so many new compositions, the majority was critical. Despite De Carvalho's careful programming of the old and new in juxtaposition to demonstrate musical influence and development, the average listener failed to grasp the lesson—or perhaps did not wish to be educated. The sale of single tickets to the concerts had begun to dwindle badly. De Carvalho felt that the Board was trying to curtail his programming of avant garde music which he believed was the essential element of orchestral repertoire. So much for a classic confrontation between the

The De Carvalhos are taken to their first baseball game—the St. Louis Cardinals versus the Phillies. August A. Busch, Jr., their host, in center, points out some of the action. (*St. Louis Post-Dispatch* photograph, April 14, 1963)

certain and the somewhat experimental; it is not unusual in the relationship between symphony boards and their music directors. De Carvalho had infused fresh vitality into the Orchestra, had increased the number of players to ninety, and had taken the Orchestra back to the East Coast for the first time in fifteen years. Much good had been wrought. The concert schedule had been heavy and he had personally carried a tremendous work load. With the increased number of concerts, an Associate Conductor, a man who was not part of the Orchestra, was appointed for the first time. This was George Cleve, engaged to start the 1967–1968 season (De Carvalho's last). Edward Murphy, who had been the Associate Conductor in addition to playing the French horn was stepping down, after more than thirty years on the roster, and the operation now needed a number-two conductor who did nothing but conduct. (As it turned out, not only did Murphy bow out at the end of the 1967–1968 season, but Cleve also resigned at that time to accept a post as conductor of the Winnipeg Symphony Orchestra.)

During De Carvalho's last season in St. Louis, his appointment as conductor of the Pro Arte Symphony of Hofstra University, in Hempstead, Long Island, was announced. Later in this season, the Symphony Society announced the appointment of Walter Susskind as future Music Director of the Saint Louis Symphony Orchestra. An ironic coincidence had been that, during the previous year, De Carvalho had guest conducted the Pro Arte Symphony at the same time that Susskind was guest conductor in St. Louis. Each visitor had been warmly endorsed by the community he was visiting—De Carvalho for his almost brutal energies and forcefulness and Susskind for his refinement and subtlety.

Although the conductor-elect was to be welcomed royally in his new post, the departure of De Carvalho was regarded with mixed emotions. Clark Mitze, music critic for the *St. Louis Globe-Democrat*, wrote: "Before De Carvalho came to town St. Louis was becoming known for its placid, cold audiences. The energetic Brazilian changed that. Vigorous demonstrations of enthusiasm— occasionally of rejection—have added excitement and enjoyment to the concerts on a scale which would have been regarded as impossible five years ago."[6]

During De Carvalho's last season, Susskind was scheduled to conduct four subscription pairs. De Carvalho conducted thirteen and the remainder were handled by miscellaneous guests. The incumbent Brazilian maestro conducted the final concert in Kiel Auditorium, the special gala inaugural program in Powell Symphony Hall, and the first regular subscription concerts in the new home.

The final concert to be played in Kiel Auditorium, after thirty-four years there, concluded with Haydn's Symphony No. 45, informally called the *Farewell* Symphony. The last movement of this piece ends with the instruments dropping out one by one until there are only two violins to sound the last notes. Generally this part of the music is handled with no physical actions on the part of the musicians. For this performance, De Carvalho went all the way, so to speak, and had the musicians turn off the lights on their music stands and leave the stage as each instrument's part was finished. It was dramatic, to say the least.

On January 24, 1968, De Carvalho conducted the concert to inaugurate Powell Symphony Hall. The program started out with Gunther Schuller's *Fanfare for St. Louis*, a piece written especially for the occasion. Schuller was present. The second selection was the American premiere of Benjamin Britten's *The Building of the House*. The third work on the program was Stravinsky's Suite from the Ballet *Petrouchka*. The hall was filled, the patrons were bedecked in formal dress, the chandeliers in the foyer glittered, and after the nine o'clock concert was over, champagne flowed.

The first subscription concert in the new Hall featured Isaac Stern playing the Lalo *Symphonie Espagnole* in D minor. The house was a sellout, as it continued to be for the rest of the season. De Carvalho conducted the last two concerts of the season. The others were conducted by guests, two under the baton of Susskind. Before the end of the season there was a very special concert when the Boston Symphony Orchestra, under Erich Leinsdorf, played in Powell Symphony Hall. It was their first appearance in St. Louis since 1915, when they had played at the Odeon, conducted by Karl Muck. Undoubtedly the earlier concert had been arranged in part by Max Zach, who had been a member of the Boston Symphony Orchestra before becoming the Saint Louis conductor in 1914.

A colorful five-year period in the Saint Louis Symphony Orchestra's history had come to an end, leaving the Orchestra larger, better in quality, and certainly more visible in the world of American orchestras.

SEASON 1963-1964

ST. LOUIS SYMPHONY ORCHESTRA

ELEAZAR DE CARVALHO, Conductor and Music Director

EDWARD MURPHY, Assistant Conductor

Future Concert Dates and Guest Artists

Saturday-Sunday, January 18-19
 ROSALYN TURECK, Pianist
Friday-Saturday, January 24-25
 MELVIN RITTER, Violinist
Saturday-Sunday, February 1-2
 VINCENT PRICE, Narrator
 Sumner High School A Capella Choir
 and Sumner Alumni Choir
 KENNETH BILLUPS, Director
Friday-Saturday, February 7-8
 CLAUDIO ARRAU, Pianist
Friday-Saturday, February 21-22
 ANDRE PREVIN
 Guest Conductor
 HENRYK SZERYNG, Violinist
Saturday-Sunday, February 29-March 1
 Wagner Festival
 SANDOR KONYA, Tenor

Saturday-Sunday, March 21-22
 ALDO PARISOT, Violoncellist
 All-Suburban Choir
Saturday-Sunday, March 28-29
 St. Louis University Chorale
 FATHER FRANCIS J. GUENTNER, S.J.,
 Director
 (Soloists to be announced)
Friday-Saturday, April 3-4
 Tschaikowsky Festival
Saturday-Sunday, April 11-12
 Beethoven Symphony No. 9
 MARTINA ARROYO, Soprano
 HELEN VANNI, Mezzo-Soprano
 JOHN McCOLLUM, Tenor
 YI-KWEI SZE, Bass-Baritone
 Cosmopolitan Singers
 HELEN LOUISE GRAVES, Director

All Saturday-Sunday concerts at Opera House, Kiel Auditorium. All Friday
concerts at Khorassan Room, Hotel Chase-Park Plaza, with exception of October 18
and November 29, which will be at KIEL OPERA HOUSE. Saturday concerts begin at
8:40 p.m., Sunday concerts at 2:30 p.m., and Friday concerts at 1:45 p.m.

Ticket prices: SATURDAY EVENINGS AND SUNDAY AFTERNOONS. Box Seats—
$4.40; Mezzanine—$3.85; Orchestra—$3.50; Lower Balcony—$2.75; $2.25; Upper
Balcony—$1.75; $1.10. Ticket Prices: FRIDAY AFTERNOON CONCERTS. All Seats
$3.50 Each. Tickets on sale Aeolian Ticket Office, 1004 Olive St., and Kiel Auditorium.
Mail orders are filled on receipt. Send remittance and stamped, self-addressed
envelope for ticket return to the Aeolian Ticket Office, 1004 Olive St., St. Louis 1, Mo.

Season 1963-1964

ST. LOUIS SYMPHONY ORCHESTRA PERSONNEL

ELEAZAR DE CARVALHO, Conductor and Music Director

EDWARD MURPHY, Assistant Conductor

VIOLINS
Melvin Ritter
 Concertmaster
Alvaro O. De Granda
 Assistant
 Concertmaster
Robert Gimprich
Isadore Grossman
A. James Krohn
William L. Legate
Jacob Levine
John Lippi
Rudolfs O. Mikelsons
Thomas Pettigrew
Walter Steindel
Robert Swain
James E. Swindells
Carol W. Tatian
Richard Voldrich
Bette Hope Waddington

SECOND VIOLINS
Ernest Walker
 Principal
Sol Kranzberg
Carmine Ficocelli
M. Louise Grossheider
Oleg Kovalenko
Michael G. Logan
Frank Mader
Aaron Nieman
Ben Pocost
Judith Riediger
Beverly Beasley Robbins
Jerome D. Rosen
Leon Schankman
Paul Schreiber

VIOLAS
Herbert Van den Burg
 Principal
Rosemary Goldsmith
Nelda Evans
Stellario Giacobbe
Lee Gronemeyer
Arthur Knebel, Jr.
Robert Lowenthal
Walter Riediger
Sally Trembly
Anthony Verme

VIOLONCELLOS
Douglas Davis
 Principal
Hrant N. Tatian
C. Marilyn Beabout
LaVara Farmer Jones
Celia Knebel
K. A. Lydzinski
Sallie Lydzinski
Ken Pinckney
Domenick Sottile
Carl Steppi

DOUBLE BASSES
Henry L. Loew
 Principal
Russell V. Brodine
Warren L. Claunch
Terry M. Kippenberger
Joseph C. Kleeman
Ralph R. Maisel
Donald R. Martin
Janice A. Roberts

HARP
Maria Muribus
Laura Marriott

FLUTES
Israel Borouchoff
 Principal
Janet Scott
John F. Kiburz

PICCOLO
John F. Kiburz

OBOES
Carl P. Sonik
 Principal
David H. Crowley
Colin G. Smith

ENGLISH HORN
Colin G. Smith

CLARINETS
Andrew J. Crisanti
 Principal
Robert L. Coleman
Leslie Scott

BASS CLARINET
Leslie Scott

BASSOONS
George E. Berry, Jr.
 Principal
Robert J. Wisneskey
Sam Z. Gravell

CONTRA BASSOON
Sam Z. Gravell

HORNS
Edward Murphy
Kaid Friedel
 Principals
Carl Schiebler
Kenneth W. Schultz
Robert L. Gustat

TRUMPETS
Donald R. Stolz
 Principal
Roger M. Grossheider
Frank Miller

TROMBONES
Bernard Schneider
 Principal
Dorothy Ziegler

BASS TROMBONE
Melvyn L. Jernigan

TUBA
John MacEnulty, III

TYMPANI
J. Massie Johnson

PERCUSSION
Richard L. O'Donnell
William G. Clark
David J. Rizzo

CELESTA
Dorothy Ziegler

PIANO
Jane Allen

LIBRARIAN
Elmer Gesner

PERSONNEL MANAGER
Edw. Murphy

STAGE MANAGER
George Buermann

MENDLE PRESS, INC., ST. LOUIS, MO. 63144

De Carvalho's Orchestra his first season, plus the projected guests for the second half of the
season.

THE ST. LOUIS SYMPHONY ORCHESTRA

SEVENTH SYMPHONY CONCERTS

FRIDAY AFTERNOON, NOVEMBER 29, *at 1:45 p.m.*
SATURDAY EVENING, NOVEMBER 30, *at 8:40 p.m.*
Both Concerts—Kiel Opera House

Soloist: JENNIE TOUREL, Mezzo-Soprano

Symphony No. 6   Claudio Santoro
  Allegro giocoso e vivo
  Andante molto
  Allegro vivo
  Finale: Allegro deciso
          (First performances anywhere)

Lieder eines fahrenden Gesellen   Mahler
  (Songs of a Wayfarer)
    Wenn mein' Schatz Hochzeit macht
    Ging beut' Morgen über's Feld
    Ich hab' ein glühend' Messer
    Die zwei blauen Augen
          JENNIE TOUREL, Mezzo-Soprano

INTERMISSION

Scheherazade, Three Songs for Voice   Ravel
  and Orchestra, on poems by Tristan Klingsor
    Asie
    La Flûte Enchantée
    L'Indifférent
          JENNIE TOUREL, Mezzo-Soprano

Rapsodie Espagnole   Ravel
    Prélude à la Nuit
    Malaguena
    Habanera
    Feria

The Steinway is the Official Piano of the St. Louis Symphony Orchestra

---

SATURDAY EVENING PATRONS

For your convenience special shuttle bus service is available from the Union Station Parking Lot, 20th and Market Streets, to Kiel Opera House and return. We urge you to take advantage of this special service. Parking lot fee only $1 per car. Bus service free.

First season of De Carvalho, although for some reason his name is not listed. World première of the Santoro work.

THE ST. LOUIS SYMPHONY ORCHESTRA

NINETEENTH SYMPHONY CONCERTS

SATURDAY EVENING, MARCH 21, *at 8:40 p.m.*
SUNDAY AFTERNOON, MARCH 22, *at 2:30 p.m.*

Opera House—Kiel Auditorium

Soloist: ALDO PARISOT, Violoncellist

La Cathedrale d'Acier, Opus 52   Victor Legley
(first performances in the United States)

Concerto for Violoncello and Orchestra in   Schumann
  A Minor, Opus 129

   { Nicht zu schnell
   { Langsam
   { Sehr lebhaft

ALDO PARISOT, Violoncellist

INTERMISSION

Five Pieces for Orchestra, Opus 10 (1913)   Webern
(first performances in this concert series)

Choros No. 10, *"Rasga o coracao,"* for   Villa-Lobos
  Chorus and Orchestra

ALL-SUBURBAN CHOIR

Miss Jerry Galloway   B. C. Bundy   Ronald Phillips
Directors of the Choir

The Steinway is the Official Piano of the St. Louis Symphony Orchestra

---

SORRY!

The Fire Marshal has issued a ruling that visitors will not be allowed Back Stage
at Kiel Opera House before the Concert or at Intermission.

SATURDAY EVENING PATRONS

For your convenience special shuttle bus service is available from the Union Station
Parking Lot, 20th and Market Streets, to Kiel Opera House and return. We urge
you to take advantage of this special service. Parking lot fee only $1 per car. Bus
service free.

De Carvalho's first season.

Walter Susskind

WALTER SUSSKIND

The Symphony Years 1968–1975

WALTER SUSSKIND was the most musically sophisticated and internationally experienced conductor ever to be director of the Orchestra. He had acquired more concert expertise in knowledge of repertoire and in conducting skills than any of the previous conductors. Zach's background, solid as it was, was built primarily through performance and conducting in one place with one orchestra—Boston. Ganz was more truly a piano soloist than he was a conductor. Golschmann was in his thirties when he came to St. Louis, and his long stay here limited to some extent his continuing experiences. Van Remoortel, too, was young and had neither the foundation nor the staying power to foster growth to any substantial degree. De Carvalho, for all his force and drive, was so wedded to the music of the day that he tended to overemphasize it.

Walter Susskind was fifty-five years old when he became Music Director of the Saint Louis Symphony Orchestra. At age twenty, he had been made assistant conductor of the Prague German Opera House, in his native city. Even in those early days of his career he was known as a piano soloist of considerable skill as well as a talented young conductor. He was, moreover, already a prolific composer. While associated with the Opera House, he wrote song cycles, string quartets, cantatas, operas, transcriptions, film scores, and other works, many of which were introduced in various European countries. The German Opera in Prague closed down in 1938, and Susskind spent the next two years touring. He appeared in twenty-six European countries as a soloist and as a conductor. When Czechoslovakia was invaded and occupied by the Nazis, he chose England as his home base. There he continued to tour and also conducted at the Strand Theater and at the Royal Carl Rosa Opera Company. He appeared as a guest conductor of the Sadlers Wells Opera Company and the Glyndebourne Opera Company. In 1945, he made his English debut as a symphony conductor with the Liverpool Philharmonic, an appearance followed immediately by engagements with the London Symphony, the London Philharmonic, and the BBC Orchestras. In 1945, he became conductor of the Scottish Orchestra, continuing to make guest appearances with other major European orchestras.

His travels took him as far afield as Australia and North America. In 1955, he was named Music Director of the Toronto Symphony. From 1962 until the time he came to St. Louis, he was Music Director and Conductor of the Aspen Music Festival and Music School in Colorado.

An articulate speaker, and an individual of great charm and not a little wit, Susskind immediately appealed to St. Louis audiences wherever he put in a public appearance. Musical St. Louis was delighted to have him in town and congratulated itself justifiably in private and in public. One piece of news that was mentioned almost casually at first was that with Walter Susskind had come a young apprentice conductor, Leonard Slatkin, then twenty-four years old, who was to assume the responsibility of some of the subsidiary concerts such as the various Pops performances. Precedent had been set the previous year: there was now the need for a full-time assistant conductor. It was not realistic to count on the concertmaster or some section principal to double his role. Susskind's assistant was his own protégé, one who had been in Aspen studying conducting with him.

Susskind began making his changes in Orchestra personnel before the season began. His *modus operandi* was not to engage in mass replacements, but rather to augment. He built the woodwind sections up to four each in number, a format practiced by all of the top orchestras. He also increased the number of string players.

He "inherited" his concertmaster, Max Rabinovitsj, who had joined the Orchestra in 1965 when Melvin Ritter left. Rabinovitsj was a superb violinist and a highly competent leader. In Susskind's first season, there was a new principal viola player, Guillermo Perich, and a new principal cellist, John Sant'Ambrogio. The second violin section was to have a new principal—Fryderyk Sadowski, concertmaster of the Warsaw Philharmonic—but his arrival was delayed because of the Iron Curtain. He had been sent the word that if he could get out and get to St. Louis, the Saint Louis Symphony Orchestra wanted him. He managed to get here before the season ended. Of the ninety-one musicians, nineteen were women. Golschmann's orchestra had had usually no more than a small handful of women—the harpist, and two or three string players. The professional women musicians were finally coming into their own.

The schedule for the season included ten Sunday concerts to be conducted by Leonard Slatkin. The Orchestra's eighty-ninth year was to be the first entire season to be played in Powell Symphony Hall. It was a building that pleased everybody—audiences and players alike. The public enjoyed fine acoustics and beautiful surroundings. The musicians had those and more—their own lounge, complete with pool table, in the backstage area.

With the new hall, the new Music Director, and, in general, the new look for the future, everything might have been smooth as the proverbial silk had it not been for the usual and proverbial fly-in-the-ointment—money. The Orchestra had been negotiating with management during the summer months for a new contract. By fall, no agreement had been reached. The Orchestra agreed to start the season, playing without a contract, while discussions continued.

Susskind's opening concert, in September 1968, admirably displayed his talents. The program started with Beethoven's Overture, *Consecration of the House*, followed by Mozart's A Major Piano Concerto, K. 488, in which Susskind performed as the soloist as well as the conductor. The final piece was Shostakovich's Symphony No. 10 in E Minor, performed for the first time by the Saint Louis Symphony Orchestra. The program was well designed to display the multifaceted abilities of the new Music Director. Those who had not realized he was a superb pianist were enlightened. Those who had not realized he was one of the great interpreters of Mozart were also enlightened. And finally, his ability to mould and shape and present a vast symphonic work was also impressively on display. It was a season's opener to delight the hearts of management and musicians alike.

In the third program of this "contractless" autumn, yet another of Walter Susskind's musical talents was demonstrated—his talent as a composer, actually in this case, as "orchestrator." The music which brought this to the audiences was Prokofiev's *Visions Fugitives*, a composition written in 1917 for piano which Susskind had scored for full orchestra. Susskind had met Prokofiev, through his (Susskind's) composition teacher, Josef Suk, in Prague. Prokofiev had stated that these twenty miniatures were among his own favorites of his work. He had also said that some day he intended to orchestrate them. After Prokofiev's death in 1953, Susskind undertook the project on his own. This was the first performance of the Prokofiev-Susskind work in the Saint Louis Symphony Orchestra's programs.

The Symphony Orchestra was basking in a good deal of limelight by 1968, because of the new conductors and their new programs. It was also coming to the attention of other city orchestra leaders because of its Kinder Konzerts. These concerts, given for children from four to eight years old, had been instituted by the Women's Association in 1966, and played on the stage of the Loretto Hilton Theater. They were now scheduled to be played in Powell Symphony Hall to audiences of 2500. The programs, first using Clif St. James (the "Corky, the Clown" of KSD-TV) as narrator, had captured the fancy of orchestras and their programmers in other cities, and the project, monitored by the Junior Division of the Women's Association, had become an enviable "staple" in the regular symphony season.[1]

In September 1968, Thomas Sherman, music critic of the *St. Louis Post-Dispatch*, died. He had been a friend, albeit occasionally an argumentative friend, of the Saint Louis Symphony for forty years. His reviews, favorable or otherwise, had always offered a penetrating and knowledgeable analysis; he had never skimmed the surface.

After playing four weeks without a contract and having come to no agreement with the Symphony Society during that time, the musicians went on strike, and the season ground to a halt. The orchestra members picketed in front of Powell Symphony Hall in their formal black concert clothes. As had been true of the strike of 1965, it appeared that the Society and the Musicians' Union were irrevocably split on acceptable figures. Again, the Save Our Symphony (S.O.S.) organization offered to help. Their plan was a proposal to sell stock to businesses, labor groups, and individuals at $1000 a share, and thereby raise $100,000 annually. This plan was not adopted; the negotiations continued. Concert dates were cancelled, one by one. Frank Peters, the successor to the *St. Louis Post-Dispatch*'s Thomas Sherman, looked at both sides when he pointed out that, "pensions, decent pay, health insurance, and protection against capricious firings all came to the musicians much later than they did to bricklayers and bus drivers. . . . The Symphony Society is in a deficit operation, and so are all professional orchestras. The more fortunate symphonies are the ones that have built up endowment backing over many years. . . . The Symphony here was a little late in confronting the harsh terms of survival, and is trying to catch up. These survival conditions are harsher than most people realize, and symphony deficits are getting inexorably bigger. The underlying reason is the fixed productivity of performing artists. Factories meet their rising labor costs by automating and increasing each worker's productivity, but the Minute Waltz cannot be played in thirty seconds."[2]

The strike was finally settled in time for the concerts to resume on November 21. A three-year contract was signed, the terms of which called for an escalating minimum salary of $8,500, $9,400, and $10,045 for the three years, an increase in the *per diem* for the touring periods, and provision for insurance on musicians and their instruments.

These conditions were made possible in large part by the creation of a six-weeks' summer season, to be called the Mississippi River Festival, on the campus of Southern Illinois University at Edwardsville, Illinois, just across the river from St. Louis. The new Festival was announced by Dr. Delyte W. Morris, president of S.I.U., and Stanley Goodman. An MRF Board was formed, made up of individuals representing S.I.U. and the Symphony Society. The site for the concerts was a vast natural amphitheater at the base of which was constructed a tent large enough to accommodate 1850 canvas chairs. There was room for an additional 10,000 spectators on the sprawling slopes of the bowl—spectators who would have an unobstructed view of the concert stage. Obviously, there was not the wildest hope that 10,000 persons would attend the regular weekend symphony concerts. The gigantic audiences were expected at the various rock, pop, and country music concerts which were to be interspersed with those of the Saint Louis Symphony Orchestra. Parking space for 4000 cars was established around the amphitheater. The Symphony Orchestra would play concerts on six weekends.

The musicians' new contract guaranteed thirty-eight weeks the first year, forty-one the second year, and forty-four the third year, and an additional six weeks at the Mississippi River Festival each of the three following years, although this latter was not actually part of the contract. The Society was well on its way to being able to furnish a full year's employment to the musicians.

In spite of time lost during the strike, twenty pairs of concerts were played during Susskind's first season. He conducted fifteen. The other five were conducted by Peter Eros, Reinhard Peters, Ferdinand Leitner (two), and Elea-

Peter Pastreich, Executive Director (left) and Edmonstone F. Thompson, member of the Society's Board since 1947.

zar De Carvalho. The visiting soloists included Gina Bachauer, Zara Nelsova, Charles Rosen, Malcolm Frager, Mstislav Rostropovich, Jeffrey Siegel, Henryk Szeryng, Rudolph Firkusny, and André Watts. The soloists from the Orchestra included Max Rabinovitsj (the concertmaster) and six other section principals. Walter Susskind appeared as piano soloist twice—in the opening concert and again in January. Leonard Slatkin made his St. Louis piano debut in a February concert, playing in Frank Martin's Petite Symphonie Concertante for Harp, Harpsichord, Piano and Two String Orchestras.

In April 1969, the Philadelphia Orchestra, Eugene Ormandy conducting, made its first St. Louis appearance, playing a concert in Powell Symphony Hall. The program presented Bach's Passacaglia and Fugue in C Minor (transcribed for orchestra by Ormandy), the Brahms Symphony No. 2 in D Major, and two selections of Debussy: Prelude to *The Afternoon of a Faun* and *La Mer*.

As for the Mississippi River Festival, all bookings and engagements were to be handled through the professional management of the Saint Louis Symphony Society. Contact with folk, pop, and rock performers was an innovation for the Powell Symphony Hall offices. Fortunately, the new assistant conductor, Slatkin, managed to keep aware of all kinds of music and occasionally passed on some suggestions to his elders. The list of non-Symphony performers at MRF,

The tent and outdoor audience at a concert at the Mississippi River Summer Festival, Southern Illinois University at Edwardsville.

during the eight years in which the Saint Louis Symphony Orchestra remained involved, included such names as Kris Kristofferson, John Denver, Mary Travers, David Cassidy, Blood, Sweat and Tears, the Beach Boys, Cannonball Adderly, the New Christy Minstrels, the Grateful Dead, the King Family, and the Tribal Dancers of Zambia.

Walter Susskind was not fond of his role in the new summer season, but carried on with his usual high standards despite the hot midwest nights, the frequent violent thunderstorms, and the less-than-luxurious dressing rooms provided for conductor and visiting artists alike. He accepted these conditions as necessary evils of a summer outdoor festival and presented the same professional appearance to the audiences as he did in the formal winter splendor of Powell Symphony Hall. The well-tailored summer evening jacket was never doffed, no matter what the thermometer read.

The good news at the end of Susskind's first season was that the earned income (as opposed to contributions) had increased by 98% over the previous three years. However, total expenditures had more than doubled. The functions and services of the Orchestra were growing with the times and the budget was growing along with the Orchestra. The interest in the Orchestra at this time—stimulated by the Powell Symphony Hall concerts, the newly instituted open air concerts, and by the bi-state alliance generated by the summer festival concerts—had grown to the highest level ever. The operation had burgeoned to gigantic proportions, but the team of individuals "running the show" was equal to the increased activities and problems.

This team had begun to come together during De Carvalho's tenure. There was Stanley Goodman, of course—still president of the Society's Board. There was Peter Pastreich, who had come as Assistant Manager in 1966 and was, by 1970, Executive Director. There was Jim Cain, who had come in 1968 as Assistant Manager and in 1970 was named Manager. His job was distinct from Pastreich's, in that Cain was the contact between the artists and their agents, and the man in charge of scheduling all concerts including those for MRF. Pastreich kept his finger on everything, but concentrated on the securing of grants, the enhancement of the Endowment Fund (which was less than $100,000 when he came to St. Louis), and policing the budget. Walter Susskind and Leonard Slatkin, in joining Jim Cain in St. Louis, were actually reuniting, since all three had been part of the Aspen Festival during the same period and were already fast friends who worked together smoothly. Rabinovitsj, concert-master, fitted into this scheme well, and the Orchestra enjoyed an upsurge in quality such as it had not experienced since early in the 1930's.

The lion's share of credit for the level of the Orchestra during this period of ascendancy goes to Susskind. In making this claim, two factors predominant in Susskind's make-up come to mind. One is his consummate skill as an orchestra builder. The second is his abiding faith in youth—his ability to recognize talent almost before it had been proven. Wherever he had spent a period of several years, he had strengthened and elevated the orchestra entrusted to him. He had done it with the Scottish National Orchestra and later, with the Toronto Orchestra. He had enormously strengthened the Aspen Festival.

To use a simplistic term, he was the most complete musician the Saint Louis Symphony Orchestra had ever had as its conductor. Moreover, he was an instinctive teacher, an educator, and particularly superb as a teacher of conducting. During his tenure in St. Louis, he was director of a session of the American Institute of Orchestra Conductors, a five weeks' training program supported by the National Endowment for the Arts and the Martha Baird Rockefeller Fund for Music. Conductors assembled in St. Louis to learn by observation, explanation, and practical experience in performance.

Susskind's extraordinary familiarity with concert repertoire surfaced frequently during these A.I.O.C. sessions. One of the orchestra members recalls a time when a conducting student was attempting to conduct a selection of his own choice—a segment of the César Franck D Minor Symphony. Susskind, who perhaps had not even thought of this symphony for some time, took over—to show the student how it should be done. The maestro led the orchestra through a passage of the symphony with such brilliance, such refined familiarity with the proper interpretation that, according to those present, it would have stood up as a recording.[3]

Susskind was a master of Mozart and of the music of Central Europe, which includes, of course, the music of his native Czechoslovakia. He was also expert in presenting the music of the English composers. The programming during his tenure, although considered rather conservative—especially in contrast to that of his predecessor, De Carvalho—did not bypass contemporary music. Such pieces as Karlheinz Stockhausen's *Kontra-Punkte*, Oscar Morawetz' Concerto No. 1 for Piano and Orchestra (Anton Kuerti at the piano), William Schumann's *Credendum*, Michael Colgrass' *As Quiet As*, Bernhard Heiden's Concerto for Horn and Orchestra, Richard Rodney Bennett's Concerto for Piano and Orchestra, *Lontano* by Gyorgy Ligeti, and Witold Lutoslawski's *Musique Funèbre* appeared in Susskind's programming, and were well accepted by the audiences as part of a balanced diet. One of the new pieces in 1972 was the world premiere of another Wykes composition, *Toward Time's Receding*. Many of these works were conducted by Slatkin, rather than Susskind himself. The contemporary music is mentioned here to give proper dimension to a reflection on the Susskind years.

Whatever kind of music, old or new, the sound of the Orchestra was better than it had ever been. It might be added that this was true no matter where the concerts were played, for, with the extended season, the concerts were growing in number and being played in a variety of locations. In addition to the subscription concerts and the Sunday series played in Powell Symphony Hall, there were the summer concerts played in the tent at S.I.U., the out-of-town tours and—begun during Susskind's regime—a Monday night series called "A Musical Offering." (In 1973, when this series opened, it was performed in the Edison Theatre on the campus of Washington University. It was later transferred to the auditorium of the Ethical Society.) The Baroque Series, a sequence of two to four concerts not part of the subscription series, was introduced. Although this series was not conducted by Susskind (Alexander Schneider was the conductor) it was Susskind's orchestra who delivered the superb music under Schneider's baton. Christmas programs became more numerous—the *Messiah* and *The Nutcracker* were regular December features.

The Saint Louis Symphony Youth Orchestra with Leonard Slatkin as music director, was founded in 1970. Sponsored by the Women's Association, this orchestra rose to excellence so rapidly that it was invited to participate in the International Youth and Music Festival in Vienna only six years after its formation. It was the first American Youth Orchestra to be invited to this summer conclave. Slatkin continued to conduct almost all of the Sunday concerts presenting all kinds of music from Vivaldi to Gershwin. Two of Slatkin's compositions were performed in the Sunday Series: a musical setting to Edgar Allan Poe's *The Raven*, narrated by Vincent Price (1972–1973 season), and *Dialogue for Two Cellos and Orchestra* (1974–1975 season.) The two cellists featured in this latter work were Eleanor Aller Slatkin and Fred Slatkin, mother and brother of Leonard Slatkin.

In 1974, the work load of Susskind and Slatkin was eased somewhat by the arrival of a new assistant conductor, Gerhardt Zimmermann. Now, for the first

September 22, 1974, before the opening concert of the season. Leonard Slatkin, Gerhardt Zimmermann, and Walter Susskind, in Susskind's sixth-floor room in Powell Symphony Hall. (*St. Louis Post-Dispatch* photograph)

time in its history, the Saint Louis Symphony Orchestra had three full-time conductors.

Slatkin was elevated to the position of Associate Conductor. As such, Slatkin was not only being entrusted with the job of conducting some of the subscription concerts in St. Louis, he was also getting busier and busier as guest conductor of some very eminent orchestras. He had made appearances with the New York Philharmonic, the Chicago Symphony, and had been principal conductor of the Grant Park Symphony Orchestra in Chicago. He had been summoned, on very short notice, to fill in for an ailing Sir Adrian Boult of the London Symphony. The music for this concert had already been scheduled, and the young substitute conductor had to step in and take over. The program was Sir William Walton's *Portsmouth Point* Overture, the Delius Violin Concerto (with Wanda Wilkomirska as soloist) and Vaughan-Williams' Symphony No. 6. Slatkin was immediately invited back.

That this account of Walter Susskind's relationship with the Saint Louis Symphony Orchestra is liberally sprinkled with mention of Leonard Slatkin is no accident. The activities of the two men were blended into an association which benefitted the Orchestra mightily. Susskind, a genuine master of interpretation, of conducting, and of teaching, was shaping, moulding, and guiding the Orchestra into a whole new sound. At the same time, he had an abiding confidence in the talents and abilities of his young associate and assigned an

Henry Loew (principal bass) and Jim Cain (Manager) look at time sheet for recording session. Twelve-hour Gershwin recording session (Slatkin conducting) finished with 12 seconds to spare. (*St. Louis Post-Dispatch* photograph, October 7, 1974)

Playback during recording of Gershwin, October, 1974. Slatkin holding score as musicians listen in Green Room. (*St. Louis Post-Dispatch* photograph, October 7, 1974)

inordinately large number of concerts to him from the start. The experience was invaluable; the apprentice absorbed his lessons and rapidly began to develop his own style, his own confidence, his own control from the podium. The association engendered benefits of all sorts.

Meanwhile, there was a change in the Symphony Society's leadership. In 1970, Stanley Goodman let the Board know that he wanted to resign as president because of pressing duties to do with his own business affairs. The man who succeeded him was Ben H. Wells, president of the Seven Up Company. Goodman's skills as a gifted amateur violinist had been widely recognized—he had played chamber music informally with the Orchestra members for years. Wells was not a musician and made sure the Board realized this. Assured that neither musicianship nor critical judgment of repertoire was necessary, Wells accepted and became president of the Board in 1970, succeeding Goodman.

Wells entrusted the music decisions to the Music Committee (of Board members), Susskind, Pastreich, and Cain, and busied himself with stabilizing the financial affairs. These had altered radically—in step with inflation— during Goodman's presidency. The amount spent on Orchestra salaries in 1964 had been $418,000. By 1970, the figure was $1,185,800. The same six-year span had seen the number of concerts jump from 122 to 195, the number of season-ticket holders increase from about 3500 to almost 7500, and the total annual budget more than triple—growing from $723,000 to $2,374,000. It was up to Wells to keep the Society attuned to and in control of a rising budget. More sources of income had to be tapped. With the increasing number of concerts, more St. Louisans were being reached by the performances. The Orchestra had always been considered a civic asset by City Hall and the Chamber of Commerce, but it came to be regarded as even more so as the music touched more and more diverse audiences. Thus, in the 1971–1972 season, the Convention and Tourism Bureau appropriated $50,000 for the Saint Louis Symphony Orchestra. Similar appropriations were made for the next two years, and in 1974–1975, the amount was increased to $75,000. For the season 1977–1978, the Bureau allotted the Symphony $100,000.

A solicitation of private individuals and private foundations named "The Quality Maintenance Fund" had been undertaken in the 1971–1972 season. Under the aegis of the Wells Board, the Symphony Society asked and received permission from the Arts and Education Fund to extend this Fund into an annual giving program which became known as the Green Room Association. The Green Room Association comprised those donors contributing $1000 or more annually. There were slightly more than fifty names in the first listing during the 1972–1973 season. Of these, ten or so were private foundations or companies. The remainder were individuals. This "Association" has persisted and increased each year, providing a substantial boost to meeting the operating expenses.

Another source of income which developed during the early Seventies was an annual appropriation voted on by the Missouri State Legislature. A special committee began to travel to Jefferson City to present the cause to the legislators. This committee, not actually a part of either the Society or of management, brought about spectacular benefits for the budget. The following is a very brief account of how it managed to do this. After the forming of the National Endowment for the Arts in 1965, Missouri was one of the first states to create its own State Council for the Arts. The National body allocated $100,000 to each state which could raise matching funds. Beginning in 1965, $200,000 was made available to Missouri Art Agencies, which included the Saint Louis Symphony Orchestra. In 1970, a Committee was formed to present to the State legislators the need for increased moneys. Walter King, a St. Louis clothing company executive, was made chairman of the committee, originally called the Committee for Symphony Orchestras in Missouri. By 1975, the amount appropriated by the State of Missouri in response to this committee, by then called the Committee for the Arts in Missouri, was $1,151,100. By the 1978–1979 season it had increased to over $2,000,000. The concept of bringing the awareness of a need for the arts to the state lawmakers was primarily Peter Pastreich's idea. Credit for making the idea a reality belongs in large part to Walter King.

By the summer of 1974, the Orchestra was playing sixteen free outdoor concerts—five under the Gateway Arch at the riverfront, two at the County Government Center in Clayton, and the remainder in various parks and "squares" around the city. All were played at eight o'clock in the evening, except for the County Government Center programs which were played at high

Susskind conducting a rehearsal with Mstislav Rostropovich prior to a special concert gala in Powell Symphony Hall January 17, 1975. (*St. Louis Post-Dispatch* photograph, January 18, 1975)

noon, during the lunch hour. The repertoire encompassed a variety of music from Beethoven to Sousa. These free outdoor concerts were "extras," over and above the Mississippi River Festival Concerts and the Little Symphony Concerts. The fact that some of the musicians seemed to play in *all* of the various concerts was a miracle of logistics that only management and the head of personnel could explain. Suffice it to say that the Orchestra had come a very long way from the days when performances were not numerous enough to provide full employment for the musicians.

On January 15, 1974, Walter Susskind announced that he would leave St. Louis at the end of the 1974–1975 season. The news came as a lightning bolt to many concert-goers. The Orchestra had come into such flower under Susskind's cultivation that many symphony patrons had assumed that the association could and would continue indefinitely. The fact was that Susskind is, by nature, a restless being constantly searching for new challenges. Moreover, his duties with the Saint Louis Symphony Orchestra, embracing—as they did—a summer session as well as the winter season, had been extremely demanding of his time. Not only is Susskind a man who likes mobility and change, he is also a composer, and his St. Louis regimen left him little time for this creative pursuit. By 1975, he would have been in St. Louis seven years, which—for him—was a pretty long stop in one place. The announcement of his future resignation immediately started speculation about Leonard Slatkin as his successor, but before the talk got very far, Slatkin removed himself from the guessing game. He announced that even if he were asked, he would refuse. He issued a statement saying that he needed more time, more circulating, more experience, before he would want to be *any* orchestra's Music Director. The matter was thus wide open as to Susskind's successor, but in March it was announced that Georg (later spelled "Jerzy") Semkow, the Polish conductor (who had appeared as guest every year but once since 1969) had been engaged.

There is, when any Music Director announces his forthcoming resignation, usually a feeling among the concert audiences that perhaps the time has come, a feeling of "off with the old, on with the new." This is often an almost immediate turning of backs on the incumbent and focus of attentions on the future. Susskind's case was the exception. His resignation served to bring into focus the spectacular advances the Orchestra had made because of him, and to spread an awareness of his influence on the growth of the Orchestra. The Orchestra roster of some one hundred names included over forty engaged by him.

Ten principals and two associate principals were brought in by Susskind. The principals were Fryderyk Sadowski (second violin), Guillermo Perich (viola), John Sant'Ambrogio (cello), Jacob Berg (flute), Richard Woodhams (oboe), George Silfies (clarinet), Susan Slaughter (trumpet), Frances Woodhams (harp), Barbara Liberman (keyboard), and Richard Holmes (timpani). The associate principals were John Korman (associate concertmaster) and Yuan Tung (associate principal cello). There were also the assistant principals: Joan Korman (assistant principal viola), Catherine Lehr (assistant principal cello), Elizabeth Enkells (assistant principal oboe), as well as Caroline White and Christopher Carson, who were to become associate and assistant, respectively, in the double bass section. Susskind had inherited three strong principals from De Carvalho's time: Max Rabinovitsj (concertmaster), Roland Pandolfi (horn), and Richard O'Donnell (percussion). As to the remaining principals, Susskind's orchestra included George Berry (bassoon), who had come into the ranks during the interim year immediately following Van Remoortel's tenure, as well as Bernard Schneider (trombone) and Henry Loew (double bass), who were still in fine form from the Golschmann days. This framework of the Susskind Orchestra (with only four changes) was to continue as the "centennial" Orchestra—the group which salutes the one hundredth birthday of the organization.

A summing up of Walter Susskind's accomplishments cannot end with a résumé of personnel. The concerts themselves call forth proud memories including highlights of the eastern tours. Three in particular come to mind. During December of Susskind's first year, the Orchestra appeared in Carnegie

Susskind conducting Mahler Symphony No. 8 (*Symphony of a Thousand*), May 1, 1975. (This was before the formation of the Saint Louis Symphony Chorus.) Choruses in concert were the Ronald Arnatt Chorale, the University Chorus and University Singers of the University of Missouri-St. Louis (Ronald Arnatt, director), the Madrigal Singers and Washington University Choir and Civic Chorus (Orland Johnson, director), Webster Groves Presbyterian Church Youth Choirs (Gene Symes, director), and the Bonhomme Presbyterian Church Youth Choirs (Aline Perkins, director).

Hall as part of the International Festival of Visiting Orchestras. Malcolm Frager was the soloist, playing Schumann's Piano Concerto. The opening work was the Susskind orchestration of Prokofiev's *Visions Fugitives*; Shostakovich's Symphony No. 10 closed the program. The New York reviews were excellent and mentioned particularly the interesting scoring and texture in Prokofiev, the competency of Frager and the orchestra ensemble, and the power of Susskind's rendition of the Shostakovich. In February 1970, another appearance of the Orchestra in Carnegie Hall featured Gina Bachauer playing the Mozart Piano Concerto No. 24. That program also presented Suk's Symphony No. 2, and the *Carnival Overture* by Dvorak. All of this music showed Susskind and the Orchestra at their best. Harold Schonberg, writing for the New York *Times*, said, "In all respects, it [the Saint Louis Symphony Orchestra] is now a major ensemble—big, confident, powerful, cohesive in ensemble. The solo playing is of high order. Clearly, the Saint Louis Symphony Orchestra has come up very fast."[4] The following year Susskind took Vaughan-Williams' *Sea Symphony* to the East coast. The Convention and Tourist Board of Greater St. Louis sponsored this trip in part, and many of the members of the St. Louis Ambassadors went along for the appearance of the Orchestra in the John F. Kennedy Center for the Performing Arts, in Washington, D.C. The St. Louis contingent—Orchestra members and patrons—was entertained at a tea at the White House. (The Orchestra played this program in Carnegie Hall and in Hartford, Connecticut, as well as in Washington.)

A final observation that should be made about the Susskind period is that it was, indeed, the Susskind-Slatkin period. In the world of high-level professional musicians, where intrigues and jealousies are often ever-present factors, theirs was an association devoid of competitive tensions. Susskind begrudged Slatkin none of his successes; he even asked his advice occasionally on contemporary music. Slatkin, on the other hand, keenly respected his mentor's ability to mould scores such as those of Mahler and Shostakovich, to handle music of the earlier periods with restraint and finesse, and to offer extraordinary orchestral support to a soloist. Susskind was generous with his expertise, and the younger associate took advantage with obvious appreciation. That Leonard Slatkin quickly became a conductor with his own style, his own interpretations, and—eventually—his own credentials was a source of pride rather than of envy to Susskind. It was a singular situation perhaps not matched before or since by any other symphony orchestra.

Walter Susskind had arrived in St. Louis with a glamorous young wife from whom he was shortly divorced. He had subsequently undergone another brief marriage and divorce, while here. Although the public evinced the usual curiosity about these news items, this aspect of Walter Susskind's image was not the dominant one. In the eyes of the music-loving citizenry, he was, most importantly, an erudite musician, a gifted and knowledgeable conductor, and an international personality with great general appeal.

Walter Susskind's last subscription concerts—his last appearances as Music Director—took place on May 23 and 24, 1975. The program was Weber's Overture to *Der Freischütz*, Beethoven's Violin Concerto in D Major (Isaac Stern, soloist), and Dvorak's Symphony No. 7. They were emotional and poignant events for both Orchestra and audience and, one imagines, for Susskind himself. Stern, much loved by St. Louis audiences in his numerous past appearances as soloist, shared the mood of the moment. Susskind is a superb conductor in accompanying a soloist and Stern relished playing with him. The Dvorak symphony closing the program was, of course, part of what is in Walter Susskind's blood. Nobody handles Czech music better, and the night of May 24 was no exception.

At the end of that Saturday night performance, there was an unexpected final touch. Someone had thought of the European custom of sending flowers to the stage at the conclusion of a special concert (regardless of whether the honored musician is male or female) and had spread the word around among Board members. After the last notes had been played, the procession of ushers delivering floral offerings onto the stage was seemingly endless. There were baskets and vases and stands of fresh flowers—florist blossoms, garden flowers and greenery. It was a stirring display of affection for the maestro who was leaving his signature so firmly inscribed on the Saint Louis Symphony Orchestra.*

---

* Walter Susskind died on March 25, 1980.

SAINT LOUIS SYMPHONY ORCHESTRA
WALTER SUSSKIND, Conductor and Music Director
FRIDAY AFTERNOON, OCTOBER 2, AT 1:30
SATURDAY EVENING, OCTOBER 3, AT 8:30
POWELL SYMPHONY HALL

WALTER SUSSKIND, Conductor
EILEEN FARRELL, Soprano

MOZART   *Overture to "The Marriage of Figaro"*

WAGNER   *Wesendonck Lieder*

"Der Engel"
"Stehe still!"
"Im Treibhaus"
"Schmerzen"
"Träume"
Miss Farrell

HINDEMITH   *Concert Music for String and Brass Instruments, Opus 50*

I.   Mässig schnell, mit Kraft
II.   Lebhaft; langsam; lebhaft
(First performance at these concerts)

INTERMISSION

MOZART   *Serenade No. 12 in C Minor for Wind Instruments, K. 388*

I.   Allegro
II.   Andante
III.   Menuetto in Canone
IV.   Allegro

WAGNER   *Immolation Scene from "Götterdämmerung"*

Miss Farrell

The Steinway is the official piano of the Saint Louis Symphony Orchestra.
NINETY-FIRST SEASON, 1970-71   THIRD CONCERT PAIR

Program page from the 1970–1971 season.

SAINT LOUIS SYMPHONY ORCHESTRA

1970-71 SEASON

WALTER SUSSKIND, Conductor and Music Director

LEONARD SLATKIN, Assistant Conductor

John Covelli and James Paul, Conducting Fellows

FIRST VIOLINS
Max Rabinovitsj
  Concertmaster

Ronald Patterson
  Assistant Concertmaster

Takaoki Sugitani
  Second Assistant Concertmaster

James Krohn
Haruka Watanabe
Wanda Becker
Robert Swain
Joseph Striplin
Rudolfs Mikelsons
Miran Viher
Helen Tung
John Lippi
Rudolph Schultz
Jacob Levine
Lawrence Diamond
Isadore Grossman

SECOND VIOLINS
Fryderyk Sadowski
  Principal

Beverly Schiebler
  Associate Principal

Charlene Clark
Carol Wolowsky
Leon Schankman
Sol Kranzberg
Ernest Walker
Louise Grossheider
Paul Schreiber
Louis Kampouris
Elizabeth Crowder
Thomas Pettigrew
Carmine Ficocelli

VIOLAS
Guillermo Perich
  Principal

Herbert Van den Burg
  Acting Assistant Principal
Margaret Salomon
Walter Riediger
Herbert Congdon
Sylvia King
Lee Gronemeyer
Anthony Verme
Charles Weiser

*Assistant Principal

VIOLONCELLOS
John Sant' Ambrogio
  Principal
Yuan Tung
  Associate Principal
*Terry Braverman
Marilyn Beabout
Richard Brewer
Aleksander Ciechanski
Kenneth Pinckney
Masayoshi Kataoka
Sallie Lydzinski
Robert Silverman

DOUBLE BASSES
Henry Loew
  Principal
*Russell Brodine
Ralph Maisel
Joseph Kleeman
Donald Martin
Richard Muehlmann
Terrence Kippenberger
Janice Roberts
Warren Claunch

HARPS
Frances Woodhams
  Principal
Ayako Watanabe

FLUTES
Jacob Berg
  Principal
Janice Coleman
*Janice Smith
John Kiburz

PICCOLO
John Kiburz

OBOES
Richard Woodhams
  Principal
Thomas Parkes
*Elizabeth Enkells
August Keller

ENGLISH HORN
August Keller

CLARINETS
George Silfies
  Principal
Christine Ward
*Robert Coleman
James Meyer

E FLAT CLARINET
Robert Coleman

BASS CLARINET
James Meyer

BASSOONS
George Berry
  Principal
Robert Wisneskey
*Robert Mottl
Bradford Buckley

CONTRA BASSOON
Bradford Buckley

HORNS
Roland Pandolfi
  Principal
*Lawrence Strieby
Carl Schiebler
Kenneth Schultz
Kaid Friedel

TRUMPETS
Chandler Goetting
  Principal
Roger Grossheider
*Gary Smith
Susan Slaughter

TROMBONES
Bernard Schneider
  Principal
Roger Davenport
Melvyn Jernigan

TUBA
John MacEnulty III

TIMPANI
Richard Holmes

PERCUSSION
Richard O'Donnell
  Principal
William Clark
Thomas Stubbs

KEYBOARD INSTRUMENTS
John Covelli
Leonard Slatkin

PERSONNEL MANAGER
Henry Loew

LIBRARIAN
Roger Grossheider

ASSISTANT LIBRARIAN
Anthony Verme

STAGE MANAGER
Leroy Stone

STAGE TECHNICIAN
Robert Fette

Walter Susskind's Orchestra during his third season. Covelli and Paul, Conducting Fellows, had come to St. Louis to participate in a session of the American Institute of Orchestra Conductors, of which Susskind was Director.

Jerzy Semkow

JERZY SEMKOW

The Symphony Years 1975–1979

"THE YEAR OF SEMKOW" was the heading on the Symphony office's 1975 news releases, and the mood was very different from those of some previous eras when the Orchestra had been in a decline and in need of a boost. The 1975 Orchestra rated well in comparison with other American symphony orchestras. The year's emphasis was on the arrival of a glamorous and dramatic personality who would carry the Orchestra to even greater heights.

Georg Semkow (his first name was spelled that way at the time) was one month short of forty-seven years old when he opened his first season in St. Louis. Born in Radomsko, Poland, he had acquired his musical training at Krakow Conservatory. At the age of twenty-two, he won a fellowship to study conducting with Eugene Mravinsky in Leningrad. After graduation from the Leningrad Conservatory, he was appointed assistant conductor, under Mravinsky, of the Leningrad Philharmonic, and conductor of the Leningrad Opera Studio. Later, he was made one of the permanent conductors of the Moscow Bolshoi Theatre, and subsequently conducted the leading Russian orchestras on tour throughout the Soviet Union. In 1959, he was named Permanent Conductor and Artistic Director of the National Opera of Warsaw. He augmented his already extensive musical education and experience through additional studies with Tullio Serafin in Rome and with Bruno Walter in Vienna. During the 1960's, Semkow conducted many of America's major symphony orchestras. He appeared on the podium of the Chicago Symphony, the Cleveland Orchestra, the Boston Symphony, and the New York Philharmonic. From 1966 to 1975, while active in his various guest-conducting appearances in this country and in Europe, he also held down the post of Permanent Conductor of the Royal Danish Symphony Orchestra.

Semkow's first exposure to the fringe obligations of conductors of American symphony orchestras came just prior to the opening of his first season in St. Louis. He was invited—in fact, more or less summoned—to appear with various Board officials at a televised interview set up to promote the season-ticket sales. He participated, but expressed the worry that everything he said under these circumstances would sound so banal, so trite. Assured that the music-loving public wanted nothing more than to see him and to hear his voice, he relaxed somewhat and acquitted himself well. This was, however, the kind of thing Semkow would clearly have rather avoided.

To point out what is perhaps obvious, the activities and responsibilities of a "Music Director" had altered gradually but radically over the almost seventy years between the first year of Max Zach and the first year of Georg Semkow. No longer was the "maestro" the principal programmer or even the actual conductor of most of the concerts. What had happened to the Saint Louis Symphony Orchestra and to all other major orchestras was that the twelve-months' employment schedule for the musicians had resulted in so many diverse series of concerts that no single conductor could possibly handle all—or even most—of them alone. While Semkow chose the music for the concerts which he himself conducted, decisions for the rest of the programs were made by others. Visiting guest conductors had, of course, a strong say-so about their own concerts. Leonard Slatkin, still conducting many of the Sunday concerts in addition to five or six subscription pairs, took an active role in choosing his own music. The programming for the subsidiary concerts—everything except the actual winter subscription series—was planned primarily by James Cain, in conjunction with the various conductors and soloists.

During Semkow's first year, he conducted ten of the subscription pairs. The date of his opening concert was September 18, 1975. The program consisted of Mozart's Overture to *The Abduction from the Seraglio*, Beethoven's Piano Concerto No. 1 (Etsuko Tazaki, soloist), and the Mahler Symphony No. 1. The sound of the Orchestra was impressive. Semkow had appeared as guest conductor with the Saint Louis Symphony Orchestra ten times since 1969 and his reputation for producing a polished performance was already established. Everyone—the audience, the musicians, the critics—applauded the performance. In a review of the concert in the *St. Louis Post Dispatch*, Frank Peters wrote, "The First Symphony of Mahler was, like a number of other Semkow performances, interesting for its tempos as well as for fastidiousness of detail. The first movement was quite deliberately paced. The scherzo moved quickly with a waltzy lilt to the rhythm of the trio section, and clean attacks by the strings to delineate the main theme. The heart of the symphony, in Semkow's account, was the third movement, the macabre funeral march of animals. Here the tempos dropped again to unusual slowness. The effect was extraordinary. So crystalline were the orchestral details—the oboe in its skipping little tune, the violins as they caressed the G-major theme from the last of the 'Songs of a Wayfarer'—that the slow march did not seem lugubrious but was filled with color and strange apprehension. Mahler had a picture in mind, the 'Huntsman's Funeral,' and Semkow re-created its dark humor vividly."[1]

The fourteen subscription pairs not conducted by Semkow were conducted by Leonard Slatkin (six), Walter Susskind (three), Gerhardt Zimmermann, Lukas Foss, Stanislaw Skrowaczewski, Charles Mackerras, and Kazuyoshi Akiyama. The array of soloists included Isaac Stern, Claudio Arrau, John

June 1975, first season of Summer Pops at Queeny Park. During that season, Orchestra was also playing summer concerts at the Mississippi River Festival. Photographed, left to right, are Robert Hyland (Regional Vice-President of Columbia Broadcasting System), Richard Hayman (Principal Conductor for Pops concerts), and Gene McNary (St. Louis County Supervisor).

Browning, André Watts, Itzhak Perlman, and Eileen Farrell, who was featured in a concert reading of *Tristan und Isolde*, which was particularly well received by the audiences and the music critics alike. Semkow, like Walter Susskind and most European trained conductors, is well grounded in the operatic tradition.

The 1975–1976 Sunday Festival series had some especially colorful moments. Walter Cronkite came to narrate *A Lincoln Portrait*—the words of Carl Sandburg, the music of Aaron Copland, Leonard Slatkin conducting. Slatkin also conducted a Sunday program featuring his own musical setting of *Absurd Alphabedtime Stories*, a children's book by Julius Hunter, KMOX-TV newscaster. David Hartman was the narrator for this. *Peter and the Wolf* was narrated by Al Hrabosky, the "Mad Hungarian" relief pitcher for the baseball Cardinals. Among the pianists appearing in the Sunday series were Abby Simon and Emanuel Ax (winner of the 1975 Michaels Award for Young Concert Artists) in his first appearance with the Saint Louis Symphony Orchestra.

Meanwhile, in 1975, a highly successful summer program had been instituted at Queeny Park in St. Louis County. The Saint Louis County Pops, performing in an air-conditioned building to an audience seated at tables cabaret style, had begun to draw large and enthusiastic audiences. The Queeny

Park location was much more accessible than had been the Edwardsville, Illinois, campus where the first summer series had been played in connection with the Mississippi River Festival. One of the conductors engaged for this new summer season was Richard Hayman, well known for his association with Arthur Fiedler, as well as for his own imaginative and crowd-pleasing podium activities. (In 1976, Hayman became Principal Pops Conductor for the Saint Louis County Pops.)

Semkow had no involvement in the County Pops. His approach to music and to conducting was serious and meticulous and no one who knew him could have imagined his participation in such musical frivolity. From the very beginning—at his first rehearsal—his musicians realized that he was, in every sense of the term, a perfectionist. Walter Susskind had been relaxed and talkative during rehearsals, especially during his later years with the Orchestra. Semkow was all business. He demanded that each musician play his notes exactly as he, Semkow, wanted them to sound. He would occasionally request the presence of each member of a given section in the conductor's suite to go through the music individually. He admired and relied upon his section principals, but he was not reluctant to tell them exactly how he wanted them to play. The musicians, for the most part, caught the fever of trying to perfect every last note. Even when they had played a piece repeatedly, they found themselves holding post-mortems after each performance and discussing at length how they might improve upon the music the next time. According to Jim Cain, one of the Mozart symphonies, played many, many times in St. Louis and on tour, came under such close scrutiny from the involved musicians that they held a discussion session after its *final* performance of the season.

Semkow studied scores with consummate thoroughness. He frequently asked Max Rabinovitsj or one of the principals to go over passages with him so that he might explain in advance the interpretation he wanted. His personal choice of repertoire was rather conservative and avoided what he considered to be shallow or showy. Semkow's hearing is amazingly sensitive, a condition advantageous to great conducting but one which has led to problems in finding acceptable hotel quarters for him. He cannot tolerate a room in which an air-conditioner duct, for instance, gives off some faint but constant sound. He immediately identifies the sound as a specific pitch and cannot then concentrate on anything else. Often on tour he would "listen to" five or six rooms before he found one that was free of miscellaneous noises.

Newly-divorced at the time of his arrival in St. Louis, Semkow lived by himself at the Chase-Park Plaza Hotel and spent a great deal of his time alone, preparing for upcoming concerts. He was never enthusiastic about attending after-concert parties and had to be persuaded before each occasion that his presence was expected and highly desired. He dreaded non-musical small talk with strangers, although when once he finally arrived at one of these receptions he was always charming and cheerful and seemed to enjoy himself. Nevertheless, he experienced the same reluctance before every party he confronted.

Those who got to know him well (and there weren't many who did) were

Semkow and Joe Weidhaas, Reservation Manager of the Chase Park-Plaza Hotel, discussing cake which Weidhaas provided to mark the opening of the 1975–1976 season. The cake is decorated as the first page of the score for Mozart's Overture to *The Abduction from the Seraglio*.

privileged to enjoy a relaxed side of Semkow rarely exposed to the public. He was able to let down completely when away from the spotlight—away from his role as "maestro." Pastreich prevailed upon him to go on a river float trip, with all the attendant primitive conditions and informality. Semkow enjoyed it thoroughly. He relished (on the few occasions when it was possible) a few hours in the country doing nothing. He delighted in the golf-cart vehicles with which he periodically came in contact on the grounds of various summer music festivals. For city exercise, he frequently rode an ancient single-speed bicycle, routing himself in and around the private streets near his hotel. He could perform fantastic feats (on his old bike) to the delight, astonishment, and envy of any children who happened to be witnesses. He could ride—arms folded across his chest—along the street, up a driveway and onto the sidewalk, back down the next driveway into the street, execute a figure eight, and then go up the next driveway—repeating the entire pattern. He would say, when his observers marvelled at his skill, "My dears, it is all in your head. You must *concentrate.*"[2]

During the summer of 1976, the Orchestra musicians played at the Mississippi River Festival, at Queeny Park, and in the Little Symphony Concerts. In addition to these regularly scheduled series, they played various special outdoor concerts including a spectacular performance on the riverfront at the Gateway Arch, on the 4th of July. Brief camera shots of this concert, which Leonard Slatkin conducted, appeared on national television in the networks' coverage of how one midwest city was celebrating the nation's two hundredth birthday in high style. (During this summer season of miscellaneous concerts and various series, the conductors were—in addition to Slatkin—Gerhardt Zimmerman, Alexander Gibson, Richard Hayman, Amerigo Marino, and Maria Tunicka.)

Symphony-goers were surprised, at the beginning of the 1976–1977 season, to find that Semkow had altered the spelling of his first name. He did this in order to have it approximate the sound of his name's Polish pronunciation. Instead of "Georg," his name appeared in the programs as "Jerzy." The change caused a little confusion but was an innocent enough request on the part of a man thousands of miles removed from the sound of his native language. He found an outlet for his use of familiar Polish in the Orchestra, in that Fryderyk Sadowski (second violin principal) and Aleksander Ciechanski (cellist), too, are Poles and when the three of them got together at an after-concert party or elsewhere, their mother tongue came into its own.

Difficult contract negotiations between the Musicians' Union and management had become almost traditional in the affairs of most major American orchestras by this period of the mid-1970's. The Saint Louis Symphony Orchestra was no exception. The musicians' contract in effect when Semkow became Music Director expired with the 1975–1976 season, hence the atmosphere in the autumn of 1976 was tense. Much had been learned about contract discussions over the preceding decade and, by 1976, meetings were undertaken by professional representatives of both factions. The Union called for a strike on September 6. A committee of young Orchestra members was actively involved but Board members and officers stayed out of it. It was a difficult period. Inflation had begun its mushroomlike growth and the musicians felt that they were caught in a painful squeeze. Disgruntled patrons threatened to withdraw their financial support. The strike lasted thirty-seven days, causing the cancellation of concert after concert scheduled for the opening weeks. Semkow, while familiar with strikes (the Venice opera house, with which he had been associated, had at that time been on strike for over a year), was disappointed and restless.

The strike was settled on October 13 with the signing of a new contract. The agreements arrived at were as follows: an escalating minimum weekly salary starting at $335, increasing to $365 the second year, and to $420 the third year; annual minimum salary to become $20,670 by the third year; pensions to be increased from $4700 to $6500 annually.

Semkow's second season, delayed by the strike, opened on October 21 with a concert featuring pianist Alicia de Larrocha playing Ravel's Concerto in G Major for Piano and Orchestra. Leonard Slatkin, who had been appointed Principal Guest Conductor with the Saint Louis Symphony Orchestra (he held the same title with the Minnesota Orchestra), conducted four of the subscription series. Walter Susskind returned as guest conductor. Soloists for this truncated season included John Browning, Claudine Carlson, Maureen Forrester, Szymon Goldberg, Eugene Istomin, Ingrid Jacoby, Susan McDuffee, Peter Pears, Leonard Rose, and Benita Valente.

The concert in which Peter Pears, the venerable British tenor, appeared was an event which attracted widespread attention. Music of Witold Lutoslawski comprised the entire program and was conducted by the composer himself. Lutoslawski had accepted a long-standing invitation from his compatriot and friend Semkow to make this St. Louis appearance. On the program were the first St. Louis performances of *Livre pour Orchestre* and *"Paroles tissees" for Tenor and Twenty Solo Instruments*, as well as *Concerto for Orchestra*. Some of the more conservative members of the audience expressed the wish that the Lutoslawski music had been "balanced" with some Beethoven or Brahms, but judged from the point of view of musicians, it was a signal event in terms of musicianship and just plain prestige.

Thanks to the experience and skill which Zimmerman, the Assistant Conductor, was rapidly acquiring, a potential crisis was avoided when Klaus Tennstedt, the guest conductor scheduled to conduct one of the subscription concerts, fell ill after arriving in St. Louis for rehearsals. Zimmermann was able to step in and produce a polished performance of the Bruckner Eighth Symphony.

A world premiere performance took place when Walter Susskind conducted the Orchestra in his own Passacaglia for Timpani and Chamber Orchestra, written especially for timpanist Richard Holmes.

A newly formed Saint Louis Symphony Chorus, with Thomas Peck as Chorus Director, made its debut in March in Colgrass' *Theatre of the Universe*

Thomas Peck, Director of the Saint Louis Symphony Chorus

and Prokofiev's *Alexander Nevsky*. The Saint Louis Symphony Orchestra was now one of only five American symphony orchestras with its own chorus. (As noted in the chapter on Vladimir Golschmann, a Saint Louis Symphony Chorus, directed by William Heyne, had been formed in 1934, but in the lean financial years following World War II, the chorus had ceased to exist.)

Two changes in first-chair players were announced as the 1976–1977 season was coming to a close. Richard Woodhams, principal oboist, resigned to accept

SAINT LOUIS SYMPHONY CHORUS

THOMAS PECK, Director
JOEL REVZEN, Associate Director
BARBARA LIBERMAN, Accompanist

Cynthia Amick
Bryan Apple
Mary Beauchamp
Milton Bennett
Phillip E. Betts
Janet F. Blees
Michele H. Bloch
Lawrence Bommarito
Marilyn Boyd
Richard F. Boyd
Jane A. Brandt
Joan Brannigan
Christine Burchyett Brewer
Thelma L. Buckley
Sr. Ruth Burkart, CSJ
Robert W. Burns
Leslie Caplan
Robert Clarke
Stephen Vance Coggeshall
Rita E. Cohen
Leonard Collier
Peggy Davenport
Veronica C. Devries
Barbara Wangerud Downs
David W. Edwards
James Ellsworth
Stanley Estrin
Merrilee Feben
Sr. Bertha Fischer, ASC
Mary Ann Flotte
Brenda Fox
Alan Freed
Doris Fridley
Roberta Fried
Fran Fulton
Roberta Gardner
Eileen Gatti
Michael L. Gibson
Gretchen Greenfield
Delores Greathouse
Suzanne Groom

Patricia Gross
Peggy Grotpeter
Emily Gruber
Mary Gyurki-Kiss
Roberta Wynn Haggerty
Laura Caroline Hartung
Nancy J. Helmich
Stephen C. Helmreich
Timothy Herbst
Linnard R. Hobler
Nancy Holtzmann
Angie Gryting Huddleston
Tom Hurd
Carol J. Hwang
Lynda K. Jesse
Jane Marie Kamp
John W. Kazee II
Warren Keller
Laura E. Kennedy
Charles H. Koehler, Jr.
Mark Anthony Koehler
Mary Krummenacher
James F. Kudrna
Julia Kunz
David Landis
John P. Landis
Eugenia K. Larson
Nancy S. Lawrence
Mary Lieber
Eleanor Mack
Betty Marlowe
Susan Mattison
Katherine Mayfield
Bob McCabe
Marguerite McCormick
Deborah Milton
Constance Moore
Elsa Toby Newburger
Jean Nunnally
David B. O'Dell
Charles Outwin
Malachi Owens

Joseph T. Page
Nancy Lee Patton
Muriel Petrovics
Linda Pleimann
Dory Potts
Lynne Powers
Roberta Lea Reese
Ron Rendleman
Mark A. Renick, Jr.
Pamela Rice
Jay Rogers
Joanne Roth
Donald C. Royse
Carole Lynn Ryan
Deborah S. Sanders
Jude Schlitt
Robert D. Slantz
M. Glenn Slates
Sr. Vicki Speno, SSND
Laverne Steinhauser
Elizabeth Ann Stevens
Margaret Strom
Marjorie Sundfors
Erickson Tankesley
Charles A. Taussig
Susan McCurry Taylor
Stephen L. Trampe
Sharon Trent
Lesley Tucker
Paul William Ullrich
David K. Ulmer
Sr. Dorothy Venhaus
Donna B. Vits
David West
Sr. Joan Whittemore, CSJ
Diane Wiel
Claudia N. Wright

Cynthia Amick, Chorus Manager
David West, Chorus Librarian

The Saint Louis Symphony Chorus is supported, in part, through the generosity of the Edward Chase Garvey Memorial Foundation Trust, the Frank G. and Florence V. Bohle Scholarship Foundation and the Missouri Arts Council.

Second season for Saint Louis Symphony Chorus.

that position with the Philadelphia Orchestra. John DeLancey, Philadelphia's principal oboist and a teacher and friend of Woodhams, had left the Philadelphia Orchestra to become the head of Curtis Institute and Woodhams was invited to replace him. And the concertmaster, Max Rabinovitsj, resigned to become director of the Conservatory of C.A.S.A. (St. Louis Conservatory and Schools for the Arts). Before the season ended, it was announced that the new concertmaster would be Jacques Israelievitch, at that time Assistant Concertmaster with the Chicago Symphony, and that the principal oboist would be Peter Bowman, from the Montreal Symphony.

Semkow's third season started on schedule September 15, 1977. The opening program featured André Watts playing the Brahms Piano Concerto No. 2. During the course of the season, three illnesses—including Semkow's—necessitated major substitutions. The first change in a planned program came about when Claudio Arrau, scheduled to play in the eighth subscription concerts, got sick and Loren Hollander was quickly engaged to take his place. Hollander gave a superb performance of the Saint-Saëns Piano Concerto No. 5, with Kazuyoshi Akiyama as guest conductor. In January 1978, Semkow himself was hospitalized in Warsaw with an acute back ailment. Walter Susskind was secured as Semkow's replacement for the Carnegie Hall concert on the Orchestra's eastern tour. Susskind, Music Advisor for the Cincinnati Symphony Orchestra, was in Cincinnati, staying at a hotel near the airport, and preparing to leave for New York, when a paralyzing snowstorm struck most of the eastern half of the country. With all ground transportation immobilized, Susskind made a heroic attempt to get to the airport on foot, on the off chance that something might be flying. Not only did his efforts prove to be in vain, he suffered a case of frostbite in his feet. Zimmermann, ever-present as a standby conductor when not scheduled to conduct himself, made his unplanned debut in Carnegie Hall conducting the Saint Louis Symphony Orchestra in a performance of the Mahler Symphony No. 4. The concert got excellent reviews.

Semkow was unable to resume his conducting until April. The subscription concerts in St. Louis were handled by Zimmermann, Susskind, and Slatkin, who was, by then, Music Director of the New Orleans Philharmonic Orchestra and, in addition to his frequent concerts in St. Louis and Minneapolis, busy all over the world. One of the St. Louis concerts which Zimmermann conducted during this period presented Isaac Stern playing the Mozart Violin Concerto No. 5—a concert at which Stern took note of his twenty-five years of association with the Saint Louis Symphony Orchestra.

The third illness which brought about a last-minute change was that of Vasso Devetzi. The Greek pianist was to have made her debut with the Saint Louis Symphony Orchestra in the twentieth subscription concerts in April. (These concerts were also to be Semkow's first appearance after his winter illness in Warsaw.) Ursula Oppens, with no more than two days' notice, performed as soloist with the Orchestra, playing Bach's Piano Concerto No. 1, and the Bach Fantasy and Fugue in D Minor. Her playing was of high quality and elicited numerous curtain calls.

Associate Conductor Gerhardt Zimmermann

The season's programs were liberally peppered with "first-performance-by-Saint-Louis-Symphony-Orchestra" music. In addition to presenting first local performances of music by Mozart, Berlioz, Rachmaninoff, Bruckner, and Ravel, the Orchestra was participating in a kind of national symphonic round-robin. The major U.S. orchestras were playing the various compositions of American composers, commissioned by the orchestras—for the Bi-Centennial Year. According to the annual report of the Music Committee, delivered in

September 1978, by Dr. Leigh Gerdine, chairman, "Of the seven American orchestras which commissioned new scores for the Bi-Centennial year, the Saint Louis Symphony Orchestra was the first orchestra to complete its obligation to the National Endowment for the Arts by performing all seven works. The project was completed during the season with performances of music by Loren Rush, Gunther Schuller, and Morton Gould. There were eight significant American works in all with several highlights worth mentioning: Gunther Schuller resurrected the *Mass* by the 19th century American John Knowles Paine, and Leonard Slatkin introduced us to the provocative *Final Alice* by David Del Tredici." (*Final Alice* requires a Herculean performance by a soprano voice, and the St. Louis audiences heard a performance that was nothing short of spectacular by Judith Kellock.)

Other soloists during the season were Abbey Simon, Ruth Laredo, Elly Ameling, Misha Dichter, Itzhak Perlman, Henryk Szeryng, Zara Nelsova, Claudine Carlson, Walter Klien, Jean-Bernard Pommier, John Browning, and seven Orchestra principals who appeared as soloists.

In May 1978, the Orchestra became involved in a new local project which rapidly became more than merely local. It was the Saint Louis Opera Theatre, then completing its third season. The Saint Louis Symphony Orchestra contracted musicians to play for a performance of Benjamin Britten's opera, *Albert Herring*, with John Moriarity conducting. The performance was telecast and has been shown over Public Television stations in this country, in England, and in parts of western Europe. The telecast was underwritten by Monsanto Co., by the BBC, and by Channel WNET in New York. (The pattern of the Saint Louis Opera Theatre, of which Richard Gaddes is General Director, has been to perform three operas in rotating sequence over a period of three weeks at the Loretto Hilton Theatre in Webster Groves, Missouri. In the few years since its inception, this Opera Theatre has developed enviable stature as one of the most outstanding American regional opera companies.)

In the spring of 1978 Peter Pastreich announced his resignation as Executive Director in order to accept a counterpart post with the San Francisco Symphony Orchestra. Pastreich had been in St. Louis for more than ten years and was highly respected in both the arts and the business communities for his keen intelligence and his effective leadership of the Saint Louis Symphony. He had seen the Orchestra through its move into Powell Symphony Hall, had worked with three Music Directors (De Carvalho, Susskind, and Semkow) and had presided over a wildfire growth of the budget. His departure left a gap that would be very difficult to fill. Following a careful and widespread search for a replacement, the Society's Board announced the appointment of David J. Hyslop as Pastreich's successor. Hyslop, who had been General Manager of the Oregon Symphony, was thirty-five years old. He started his new job with an incumbent Board president (Wells) and an established and experienced manager in Cain.

Semkow's 1979 resignation was announced at the close of the 1978 season. After much public speculation, the Society announced, on July 10, 1978, that

Mrs. William W. James, Chairman of the Junior Women's Division, presents check for $30,000 to Ben H. Wells, President of the Society's Board (left) and David J. Hyslop, Executive Director (right). Check represented money raised by the Prelude to Athens, a "gala" sponsored by the Junior Division.

the Music Director who would assume office in the fall of 1979 was Leonard Slatkin. Slatkin would be the first American-born conductor to head the Saint Louis Symphony Orchestra and one of the very few American-born conductors with any major orchestra.

At the Society's Annual Meeting in September 1978, W. L. Hadley Griffin, president of Brown Group, was elected to succeed Ben Wells as president of the Saint Louis Symphony Society. Wells became chairman.

Semkow's last season began—in a way—before the beginning. In September, before the subscription series started, the Orchestra made its first European trip. Invited to perform at the Athens Festival, the Orchestra, accompanied by family members, patrons, staff members, and stage managers (and nine bass fiddles, eleven cellos, two harps, innumerable violins, violas, brasses, woodwinds, and percussion instruments) left Lambert Field Sunday, September 3, on a chartered flight to Athens. There, the Orchestra played three concerts in the Herod Atticus Theatre at the foot of the Acropolis. Semkow conducted two of the concerts, Slatkin one. Isaac Stern appeared as soloist in two of the concerts. (The performances were dedicated to the memory of Gina Bachauer, the Greek piano virtuoso who had been such a good friend of the Saint Louis Symphony Orchestra.)

The trip was an experience which neither the musicians nor the others who went along will ever forget. The entire group of St. Louisans was taken on

Slatkin rehearsing Orchestra in Athens, September 1978. Note clothespins to secure music on the music stands.

sightseeing tours, entertained at the home of the American Ambassador to Greece and his wife, given plenty of free time to poke around the side streets of Athens, and ferried to and from the Herod Atticus Theatre for every concert. The theatre itself is overwhelming with its heroic antique proportions and six-thousand-seat capacity. Imaginative use was made of the classic architecture in the performance of Ives' *The Unanswered Question*: in a passage of the music in which a solo trumpet and the flute section are to play offstage, or at least detached from the body of the orchestra, they were stationed in the niches in the wall, above and behind the stage. The effect was dramatic both visually and musically.

Semkow's fourth and last season in St. Louis was programmed to feature Beethoven. Before the series concerts were over, the Orchestra had performed all nine Symphonies, the *Missa Solemnis*, the Incidental Music from *Egmont*, the Suite from *Prometheus*, *Calm Sea and Prosperous Voyage*, and the *Leonore* Overture No. 3. Five piano concertos had been performed by the following soloists: Charles Rosen (Piano Concerto No. 1, Gerhardt Zimmermann conducting), Emanuel Ax (Piano Concerto No. 2, Zdenek Macal conducting), Rudolph Firkusny (Piano Concerto No. 3, Semkow conducting), Anton Kuerti (Piano Concerto No. 4, Slatkin conducting), and Walter Klien (Piano Concerto No. 5, Semkow conducting).

Semkow and Isaac Stern rehearsing in Athens, September 1978, Herod Atticus Theatre at the foot of the Acropolis.

Herod Atticus Theatre in Athens filled with audience for Saint Louis Symphony Orchestra concert, Semkow conducting, September 1978.

Although Beethoven's music predominated, other composers were well represented. Walter Susskind conducted an all-Mozart program and a second concert consisting of Mahler's Symphony No. 7. Leonard Slatkin conducted an all-Rachmaninoff program (Pamela Paul, soloist) and an all-Prokofiev program, featuring *Ivan the Terrible*, with mezzo-soprano Claudine Carlson, bass Sam Timberlake, and the Saint Louis Symphony Chorus. Additional guest conductors for the year were Erich Bergel, Charles Mackerras, and Max Rudolf, who conducted the final subscription concerts.

On March 4, 1979, a concert which defies categorizing took place. It was a special concert played in honor of Morton D. May and Ben Wells. The audience (invited friends of the Mays and the Wellses) heard a sprightly concert of music selected by and conducted by Leonard Slatkin.

During the last of Semkow's years as Music Director, his tremendous self-imposed pressure seemed to let up a little. Always a taskmaster both with himself and with the Orchestra, he seemed to be somewhat less tense—a little freer in his presence on the podium. His music, always excellent, was—if anything—even better. One of his particularly outstanding concerts was the performance of the concert reading of Mussorgsky's *Boris Godunov*. His preparations for each concert were as thorough as they had been in the past: he insisted on attention to the details of every bar of the music, and all interpretive shadings were planned out and performed identically in each rendition. But his entire personality seemed more relaxed, more flexible, more at ease from the moment he appeared on the stage at the start of each concert. Perhaps this seeming change in Semkow reflected his anticipation of his future. He had accepted the post of Music Director of the official Radio Orchestra in Rome, a situation in which he would not be enmeshed in the subsidiary responsibilities attendant on being Music Director of a large orchestra in the United States. His command of the Italian language is fluent, perhaps more so than his command of English. He detested the tick-of-the-clock pressure in American recording sessions. And in general, he seems to feel more at home in Europe than he does in this country, a fact which was apparent in his relaxed behavior on the Athens trip, behavior which extended even to his public interviews. Perhaps the strain of attempting to please a diverse American audience in a varied set of subscription concerts was an unpleasant aspect which he was relieved to be leaving behind. He obviously feels extremely warmly inclined toward the Saint Louis Symphony Orchestra collectively and to many individuals in it, and in management. He grew quite close to Jim Cain, who accompanied him on tours, who argued with him over repertoire and who became, probably, his closest St. Louis associate.

Those familiar with George Szell's conducting liken Semkow to Szell. His hewing to the line, his demands for perfection from each individual musician are reminiscent of the Cleveland maestro.[3] His propensity for the most solid, time-tested music such as that of Mozart, Beethoven, and Brahms—tempered with a love for Romantics such as Schumann and Wagner—is not unusual. Nor can he be criticized for his personal dislikes—for instance, of Richard Strauss, whose music he feels to be "superficial." All of these are marks of a man who likes best the music in which he feels absolutely sure of himself, a conductor who is more meticulous than daring. His mode of conducting brought to the Saint Louis Symphony Orchestra a sense of discipline and exactitude which has served it well, indeed, and will continue to do so.

SAINT LOUIS SYMPHONY ORCHESTRA

GEORG SEMKOW, Music Director and Principal Conductor

FRIDAY AFTERNOON, MAY 7, AT 1:30
SATURDAY EVENING, MAY 8, AT 8:30

POWELL SYMPHONY HALL

GEORG SEMKOW, Conductor
ITZHAK PERLMAN, Violin

WEBER   *Overture to "Oberon"*

MENDELSSOHN   *Concerto in E minor for Violin and Orchestra, Opus 64*
I   Allegro molto appassionato
II   Andante
III   Allegretto non troppo — Allegro molto vivace
      Itzhak Perlman

INTERMISSION

SCHUMANN   *Symphony No. 1 in B-flat major, Opus 38, "Spring"*
I   Andante un poco maestoso — Allegro molto vivace
II   Larghetto
III   Scherzo: Molto vivace — Trio I: Molto più vivace
     — Trio II
IV   Allegro animato e grazioso

The Steinway is the official piano of the Saint Louis Symphony Orchestra.

The Saint Louis Symphony Orchestra records for Vox Productions, Inc.

NINETY-SIXTH SEASON, 1975-1976   TWENTY-SECOND SUBSCRIPTION CONCERTS

SAINT LOUIS SYMPHONY ORCHESTRA
1977-78 SEASON
JERZY SEMKOW, Music Director and Principal Conductor
LEONARD SLATKIN, Principal Guest Conductor
GERHARDT ZIMMERMANN, Assistant Conductor
THOMAS PECK, Chorus Director

FIRST VIOLINS
Jacques Israelievitch
  Concertmaster.
    Eloise and Oscar Johnson.
    Jr. Chair
John Korman
  Associate Concertmaster
    Louis D. Beaumont Chair
Lazar Gosman
  Second Associate Concertmaster
Takaoki Sugitani
  Assistant Concertmaster
James Krohn
  Assistant Concertmaster
Darwyn Apple
Charlene Clark
Lawrence Diamond
Silvian Iticovici
Jenny Lind Jones
Eiko Kataoka
John Lippi
Rudolfs Mikelsons
Manuel Ramos
Robert Swain
Helen Tung
Miran Viher
Haruka Watanabe
Hiroko Yoshida

SECOND VIOLINS
Fryderyk Sadowski
  Principal.
    Dr. Frederick Eno
    Woodruff Chair
Beverly Schiebler
  Associate Principal
Deborah Bloom
Elizabeth Crowder
Carol Wolowsky Denos
Lorraine Glass
Louise Grossheider
Dale Andrea Hikawa
Louis Kampouris
Raya Kodesh
Thomas LeVeck
Thomas Pettigrew
Judith Riediger
Leon Schankman
Marka Wilcox

VIOLAS
Kathleen Mattis,
  Acting Principal
*Joan Korman
Gerald Fleminger
Lee Gronemeyer
Leonid Gutman
Lynn Hague
Sylvia King
William Martin
Margaret Salomon
Anthony Verme
Charles Weiser

VIOLONCELLOS
John Sant' Ambrogio
  Principal.
    Frank Y. and
    Katherine G. Gladney
    Chair
Yuan Tung
  Associate Principal
*Catherine Lehr
Marilyn Beabout
Richard Brewer
Aleksander Ciechanski
Masayoshi Kataoka
Kenneth Pinckney
Savely Schuster
Robert Silverman
Sallie WeMott

DOUBLE BASSES
Henry Loew
  Principal
Carolyn White
  Associate Principal
*Christopher Carson
Warren Claunch
Joseph Kleeman
Ralph Maisel
Donald Martin
Richard Muehlmann
Janice Roberts Murphy

HARP
Frances Woodhams
  Principal,
    Elizabeth Elliot Mallinckrodt
    Chair
Maria Pinckney
Ayako Watanabe

FLUTES
Jacob Berg
  Principal
Janice Coleman
*Janice Smith
Jan Gippo

PICCOLO
Jan Gippo

OBOES
Peter Bowman
  Principal
Thomas Parkes
*Barbara Herr
Marc Gordon

ENGLISH HORN
Marc Gordon

CLARINETS
George Silfies
  Principal,
    Walter Susskind Chair
Christine Ward
*Robert Coleman
James Meyer

E FLAT CLARINET
Robert Coleman

BASS CLARINET
James Meyer

BASSOONS
George Berry
  Principal
Robert Wisneskey
*Robert Mottl
Bradford Buckley

CONTRA BASSOON
Bradford Buckley

HORNS
Roland Pandolfi
  Principal
*Lawrence Strieby
Carl Schiebler
Kenneth Schultz
Kaid Friedel

TRUMPETS
Susan Slaughter
  Principal.
    Symphony Women's
    Association Chair
Roger Grossheider
*Malcolm McDuffee
Gary Smith

TROMBONES
Bernard Schneider
  Principal
Roger Davenport
Melvyn Jernigan

TUBA
John MacEnulty III

TIMPANI
Richard Holmes

PERCUSSION
Richard O'Donnell
  Principal
John Kasica
Thomas Stubbs

KEYBOARD INSTRUMENTS
Barbara Liberman
  Principal.
    Florence G. and
    Morton J. May Chair

PERSONNEL MANAGER
Carl Schiebler
Joseph Kleeman, *Assistant*

LIBRARIAN
John Tafoya
David Stone, *Assistant*

STAGE MANAGER
Leroy Stone
Martin McManus, *Assistant*

*Assistant Principal

†1977-1978 Exxon/Arts Endowment Conductor
For these concerts, the Saint Louis Symphony Orchestra is utilizing the revolving seating method for section string players. Untitled string players change seats weekly and are listed alphabetically in the roster.

Semkow's Orchestra in his third season.

Leonard Slatkin (*St. Louis Post-Dispatch* photograph, November 18, 1979)

LEONARD SLATKIN

The Symphony Years 1979–

THE PLACARDS announcing "Slatkin's Back" on buses, taxis, and billboards all over St. Louis were glad tidings with which to begin the Orchestra's one-hundredth year. It is rare that the newly appointed Music Director of a major symphony orchestra is as familiar to the local musical public as Slatkin is.

Familiarity with Leonard Slatkin is not limited to St. Louis, nor—even—to the United States. In the eleven years since his first association with the St. Louis Symphony Orchestra (as a twenty-four-year-old assistant conductor) and his debut as Music Director, Slatkin's dossier had become significantly impressive, and he had grown to be a well-known figure, respected by major orchestras in this country and in Europe. He had been a regular guest conductor of orchestras in Chicago, Cincinnati, Cleveland, and Philadelphia. He had conducted in London, Vienna, Amsterdam, and Russia. He had been Music Director of the New Orleans Philharmonic as well as Principal Guest Conductor of the Minnesota Orchestra. He had accomplished all this in addition to his continuing association with the Saint Louis Symphony Orchestra, which has held his name officially on its conductors' roster (at one level or another) every year since 1968, with one exception: during the 1978–1979 season he appeared as guest conductor several times, but was not officially associated with the Orchestra.

Since the age of three, when he began to take violin lessons from Joachim Chasman, Leonard Slatkin's major involvement has been with music. His family was similarly dedicated. His father, Felix Slatkin, was a member of the first violin section of the Saint Louis Symphony Orchestra from 1933 to 1937. He resigned from the Orchestra during that period when the Saint Louis Orchestra had a woefully short employment season, and when his request for a $3-a-week raise was denied. While in St. Louis, Felix Slatkin was a member of the Orchestra's String Quartet, which built a reputation for quality. Following Felix Slatkin's resignation from the Saint Louis Orchestra, he moved to California where he and Leonard Slatkin's mother, Eleanor Aller Slatkin, a professional cellist, founded the Hollywood String Quartet. Felix Slatkin also founded the Hollywood Bowl Orchestra and was famous for his conducting and for his musical arrangements. He died suddenly in 1963. Eleanor Slatkin is still active as a cellist in Los Angeles and with occasional engagements in other parts of the world.

The second son in this musical family studied the cello and is now a soloist and principal cellist in the New York City Ballet orchestra. His professional name is Frederick Zlotkin, a name which he feels is more closely related to its Russian origins.

While still a child, Leonard Slatkin exchanged the violin for the viola, the instrument he was playing in a regional youth orchestra in California when his career took an unexpected and significant turn. The conductor of a small orchestra in which Slatkin was playing was called to the phone during a rehearsal one day. Looking at Slatkin, he asked, "Have you ever done any conducting?" In spite of Slatkin's firmly negative response, the conductor threw the score into his lap, announced that he would be back in ten minutes, and departed. Slatkin remembers being terrified but exhilarated. He remembers what the music he conducted was—Verdi's Overture to *La Forza del Destino* —but not "how it went."

For a year and a half during his teens, Slatkin dropped his music studies. However, when he was enrolled in Los Angeles City College, he recognized the irresistible pull of his family heritage, and he began to form small ensembles which he could conduct. In 1964, he was accepted as a student at the Aspen Music Festival. While studying with Walter Susskind that summer, Slatkin applied and was accepted for admission to the Juilliard School of Music in the fall. From that point on, his life revolved around conducting: in the winters at Juilliard, Jean Morel was his teacher; in the summers in Aspen he studied with Susskind. (It was during the summer of 1967 that Susskind invited him to become his assistant in St. Louis starting in 1968.)

At the end of four years of intense training and application, Leonard Slatkin had learned to avoid dissipating his energies with uncertainties. From the point of view of the St. Louis audiences, his podium appearance never seemed to be tentative or uncertain, and it was clear that the new Assistant Conductor was more than capable of taking over all the Sunday concerts of the Saint Louis Symphony Orchestra, as well as an occasional subscription pair.

Slatkin not only conducted the series of ten Sunday afternoon concerts (these series went under a variety of names, during the next few years), he also took an active part in planning the programs, and selecting the repertoire and the soloists. Occasionally, he was himself the piano soloist.[1] From the beginning, his role was an active one and the Orchestra responded energetically to his youth and to his positive approach.

During Slatkin's second year in St. Louis, he became involved in an off-beat activity which, in a roundabout way, served him well. A small "underground" radio station, KDNA-FM, interviewed him for a broadcast, liked the results, and asked him if he would like to have his own program. For three years, he broadcast live on Thursday afternoons from the Gaslight Square location of KDNA-FM. He recalls that the station was occasionally raided by the police on the suspicion that there *must* be something nefarious going on, so casual and nonchalant was its operation. Slatkin's programs consisted of playing records and then talking about the music. Sometimes he used the station's records; many times he brought along his own. One program included "An Hour of Great Endings"—during which he played the final measures of various pieces of music.

Through this unorthodox experience, Slatkin developed an ease and a sense of immediacy and accessibility in talking about music. It is a talent that has proved to be a major asset. He can deliver a lecture or conduct a master class, or even talk to a concert audience from the podium, with great effectiveness. He has a habit of presenting a few pertinent facts about contemporary music just before conducting the work. He uses this tactic judiciously and invariably his audience is more receptive than might have been the case without the introduction. Sometimes when his concert is playing in competition with a major sports event on a given evening, Slatkin has been known to announce the score from the stage.

In 1969, when he had been in St. Louis only one year, Slatkin began to conduct the Orchestra on some of its tours. He also conducted some of the subscription concerts on a regular schedule. His title changed—from Assistant to Associate Conductor during the Susskind years, to Associate Principal Conductor during the early Semkow years and, finally, to Principal Guest Conductor. As already noted, during the 1978–1979 season, he had no official title with the Saint Louis Symphony Orchestra and conducted here on the same basis as any other visiting guest conductor.

The Saint Louis Symphony Orchestra was not alone in recognizing Leonard Slatkin's growing abilities. To list a few specific milestones of recognition, in the 1973–1974 season, he made his conducting debuts with two of the giants in the world of American symphony orchestras—the New York Philharmonic and the Chicago Symphony. In 1973, he became Principal Guest Conductor of the Minnesota Orchestra. Among his innovations in Minneapolis were the "Rug Concerts," a very informal series, usually presenting contemporary music, at which the audience sat on a floor temporarily installed over the tops of the seats. This series was usually sold out, with "standing-room" only, or whatever you call it when the tickets entitle holders to sit on the floor. The same year (1973), he was appointed Principal Conductor of the Grant Park Orchestra in Chicago. During the 1976–1977 season, he conducted the Chicago Symphony on a midwest tour. In the fall of 1977, he opened the season of the New Orleans Philharmonic as its Music Director and Conductor.

In May 1979, Slatkin left the podium and entered the pit, so to speak, when he conducted the St. Louis Opera Theatre's production of *Ariadne auf Naxos*, by Richard Strauss. Slatkin had had some previous opera experience as Assistant Conductor with the Juilliard Opera Theatre and in the Opera Theatre at Oberlin. This was his opera debut, however, in St. Louis.

Leonard Slatkin is blessed with great musical talent. But another of his blessings and one that has been most evident and most welcome is his willingness to appear to his audiences and to the public as a real live human being, not an unapproachable maestro isolated by the podium. He has always taken a keen interest in enhancing the public image of his orchestra, wherever that orchestra may be. At the New Orleans opening, for instance, he insisted on standing in the foyer, after the concert, surrounded and even jostled by concert-goers, each wanting to speak to him personally.

Before the 1979–1980 season, Slatkin discussed his own feeling about his new role as Music Director of the Saint Louis Symphony Orchestra, and his aspirations for the future. He expressed his pride in having "come up through the ranks," an uncommon route for a conducting career. (Leonard Bernstein is perhaps the only other example.) He also spoke of his pride in being the first American-born conductor of the Saint Louis Symphony Orchestra, and the first conductor here since Max Zach with a background as a string player. (Van Remoortel had been a cellist, but did not have Slatkin's ability to apply this familiarity to his conducting growth.) Slatkin also discussed his ideas about the Orchestra's development of its own "sound," something professional musicians recognize as present and distinguishable among the major orchestras. "It already has the sound," he said, "but I would like to further it and define it a little more, and then get the rest of the country to recognize it."[2]

Letting his imagination run free, Slatkin scheduled a spectacular and highly unusual Centennial Celebration concert for September 8, 1979. The concert plan featured David Hartman as Master of Ceremonies for as large a group of top-level concert performers as has ever been seen on any stage at any time. The program was to lead off with the Orchestra playing Berlioz' *Roman Carnival Overture* and the *Saint Louis Symphony March* by Rudolph Ganz. These were to be followed by the Bach Concerto in C Major for Three Claviers and Orchestra (John Browning, Jeffrey Siegel, and Emanuel Ax and the three pianos) and the last movement of the Brahms Concerto for Violin, Cello, and Orchestra (Jaime Laredo, violin, and Zara Nelsova, cello).

After an intermission, the program would resume with Claudine Carlson singing "Mon Coeur S'Ouvre à ta Voix" from *Samson and Delilah* (Saint-Saëns); Seth McCoy with the "Street Singer's Aria" from *Der Rosenkavalier* (Strauss); Benita Valente with Villa-Lobos' Aria from *Bachianas Brasilieras* (Eleanor Aller Slatkin assisting on the cello); Arnold Voketaitis singing "Non più andrai" from *The Marriage of Figaro* (Mozart); and a presentation of *Two Madrigals* by "P. D. Q. Bach," to be sung by Benita Valente, Jane Marie Kamp, Claudine Carlson, Seth McCoy, and Peter Schickele. (This latter is, as most present-day concert-goers know, "P. D. Q. Bach.")

Following the singers would be conductor-composer John Williams, conducting his own music from the film *Superman*. The conclusion of the program would be a performance of Tchaikovsky's *1812* Overture, for which the Orchestra would be augmented by the Saint Louis Symphony Youth Orchestra Brass, the Saint Louis Symphony Chorus, and the Saint Louis Symphony Centennial Soloists, which meant that all the aforementioned soloists were to play the bass drums in lieu of cannon fire.

Leonard Slatkin in the doorway of his house in Saint Louis. (*St. Louis Post-Dispatch* photograph, November 18, 1979)

That was the concert scheduled for September 8. A second special concert was slated for performance on September 14, an event for the joint benefit of the Women's Association of the Symphony and for St. Louis Children's Hospital, celebrating its one-hundredth birthday in 1979. Henry Mancini was engaged to conduct this second special event.

On September 4 the Musicians' Union called a strike.

Since the musicians' contracts were due to expire September 2, and since no agreement had been reached during meetings in the summer, the strike was perhaps to have been expected. Nevertheless, it caught the St. Louis concertgoers by surprise. Both special concerts had to be cancelled. So did the opening subscription concerts scheduled for September 15 and 16. The loss of the September 8 concert was tremendous, but the loss of the benefit concert the following week stirred up the most immediate and awesome indignation among the active supporters of the Orchestra, for the women (Children's Hospital volunteers and members of the Symphony Women's Association) had sold something over $100,000 worth of advance tickets. Hell hath truly no fury like a hard-working volunteer scorned, and the Union Committee of the Orchestra announced that they would play the Benefit Concert after all, and would take no pay. Management insisted that paychecks would be forthcoming anyway, and a small dispute developed, but the concert (sponsored by Famous Barr and featuring Fashion Designer Awards) was played on schedule in Powell Symphony Hall. It was ironic that the first performance of the Saint Louis Symphony Orchestra following Leonard Slatkin's appointment as Music Director was not conducted by him. Mancini took gracious note of this fact when he spoke to the audience from the podium, thanking Leonard Slatkin for "letting him" conduct his (Slatkin's) orchestra. (Slatkin was not in St. Louis at the time.)

After the September 14 Benefit, the lights went out again in Powell Symphony Hall, and the struggle between management and the union continued. In addition to the traditional disagreement over salary, there were three principal points of contention: seniority pay, improved dental care benefits, and reduced time for specific Pops concerts and rehearsals. All of these issues fomented emotional reactions, with the seniority clause being perhaps the most heatedly argued.

In an effort to get the season back on the track, management and the Union Comittee met with a federal mediator on Monday, September 17. Both sides remained adamant in their positions, and after the meeting the musicians voted against returning to work. All concerts through October 26 were cancelled. Plans for a west coast tour, the first in many years, and recording sessions that were to have taken place in Los Angeles were dropped. Cancelled also was a Pension Fund concert in St. Louis with Nathan Milstein as soloist.

The situation appeared totally deadlocked. No meetings were scheduled. Nothing seemed to be happening. Unlike strikes in the past, this work stoppage did not generate the organization of any citizens' committees. There was talk, of course, all over the city about the absence of music at Powell Symphony Hall, but no groups were formed to try to solve the problem, as had happened in 1965 and 1968. Perhaps by this time the over-all budget figures had grown to be so seemingly astronomical that individual groups realized the impracticability of trying to raise money on their own. It was as if the community believed that the situation would get straightened out somehow without interference. Orchestra members talked and caucused among themselves, management held private meetings, and the patrons—for the most part—fumed.

It is an awkward situation when any group's incomes, working conditions, vacations, and benefits get full public exposure. The income level of any group is always higher or lower than that of some other groups. Many concert-goers have smaller incomes than those of the musicians they come to hear. (This is true in any major city, not only in St. Louis.) When the musicians' salaries and benefits are shown in black and white in the newspapers, hard feelings are inevitable. The musicians feel that they have the right to incomes that keep up with the times. They have their expensive instruments to maintain; they must devote hours each day to practice (in addition to rehearsals); they have invested a great deal in the education that got them hired to play in a major orchestra; they have irregular hours—a host of offbeat conditions that go with the job. From the patrons' point of view, the musicians are working for a not-for-profit organization which is primarily dependent on donated support from individuals, corporations, and foundations. At the same time the Saint Louis Symphony Orchestra was out, several other cities were undergoing similar labor crises: Seattle, Minneapolis, and Chicago were having their difficulties. Those strikes were settled before peace came in St. Louis.

In the midst of what appeared to be a true stalemate, a highly unusual piece of news came out. The great Russian cellist, Mstislav Rostropovich (Music Director of the National Symphony Orchestra in Washington, D.C.), offered to play a concert with the Saint Louis Symphony Orchestra on October 23 (the only possible date for him) if the strike were settled by that time. Behind this generous offer was a story. What had happened was that the chairman of the Union Negotiating Committee of the Orchestra had contacted Rostropovich and asked him if he would come to St. Louis to play a concert for the benefit of the striking musicians. Rostropovich, not willing to take that stand, telephoned Stanley Goodman, whom he knew personally, to report this development. It was out of this conversation with Goodman (former president of the Symphony Society's Board) that the offer to play a benefit concert resulted—not a benefit concert for the strikers, but a benefit concert to celebrate the settling of the strike. Rostropovich indicated that he would have to know by Saturday, October 13, in order to make his plans. Federal mediation was requested and the sessions took place between Tuesday, October 9, and Monday, October 15, when the musicians met to vote on management's offer, which included some modifications in pay and in dental insurance but no seniority. The base-pay figures were $460 per week the first year, $500 the second year, $550 the third. After a gruelling and emotional session that lasted far past midnight Monday night, the musicians voted (with a slightly over sixty per cent majority) to accept the three-year contract. The deadline for accepting Rostropovich's offer had passed, but Rostropovich announced that he *would* be in St. Louis on October 23.

And so the Saint Louis Symphony Orchestra was finally to open its one-hundredth season: not on schedule—not even with subscription concerts—but, nevertheless, it *was* to start with Leonard Slatkin conducting, and with an internationally-known celebrity as soloist. In spite of the fact that there were only six days (including two weekend days) in which to inform and remind the public of the October 23rd concert, Powell Symphony Hall was sold out.

Slatkin was asked in a television interview just before the concert if he thought that the hard feelings caused by the strike would be difficult to overcome. Slatkin's reply was that, on the stage, "it is only the music that matters." Of this first concert of the season, James Wierzbicki, of the *St. Louis Globe-Democrat* wrote, "The audience was in a festive mood and the orchestra seemed as enthusiastic as the concert-goers, who could thank world-famous cellist Mstislav Rostropovich for the concert. He had offered to perform without fee if the musicians' strike was settled in time for a concert Tuesday. Rostropovich, who has played more than 100 benefit concerts in the last five and a half years for causes from endangered animals to World War I invalids, said, 'I believe that if I don't make something good in my life, it will be bad for the way I feel.'"[3]

The Orchestra, under Slatkin's baton, played an all-Dvorak program: *Slavonic Dance* in C Major, Concerto in B Minor for Cello and Orchestra, and Symphony No. 9 in E Minor *From the New World*. It was as though the turmoil of the previous weeks had never taken place. At the start of the concert, Slatkin announced that the concerts cancelled because of the work stoppage had all been rescheduled for the 1980–1981 season. (This includes the Centennial Celebration concert, with its multitude of soloists, most of whom had been able to clear a date for the rescheduled concert.) Rostropovich received a standing ovation from the audience as he entered to perform the concerto. After the concerto, the response was so thunderous and continuing that he played an encore—the *Sarabande* from Bach's Second Cello Suite in D Minor. After the concert was over, a dinner reception for Board members, Green Room members, and the Orchestra was held on the stage. A touch of whimsy and surprise was added when two attractive young ladies, attired in top hats and tails, appeared from the "Live Wires Singing Telegrams" to sing a paean of praise, in rhyme, to Maestro Slatkin and Rostropovich. All of Rostropovich's celebrated ebullience and *joie de vivre* was evident all evening—in the performance and in the socializing onstage afterward. He has a close personal friendship with Lazar Gosman, former concertmaster of the Leningrad Philharmonic and now second associate concertmaster of the Saint Louis Symphony Orchestra, and there was much informal conversing in Russian.

The Rostropovich evening did much toward binding up the wounds of the strike and putting the past behind, where it belonged. The 1979–1980 season from this date on was scheduled to present guest conductors including Rafael

Leonard Slatkin and Mstislav Rostropovich at first concert of 1979–1980 season, performed October 23. This was a special concert for which Rostropovich donated his appearance as soloist, following the settlement of the musicians' strike. (*St. Louis Globe-Democrat* photograph, October 24, 1979)

Frühbeck de Burgos, Erich Leinsdorf, Edo de Waart, Dimitri Kitaienko, Jerzy Semkow, and Walter Susskind. A few of the scheduled soloists were Grace Bumbry, Pierre Fournier, Jean-Pierre Rampal, Isaac Stern, Philippe Entremont, John Browning, André Watts, and Jeffrey Siegel.

The Orchestra that Leonard Slatkin now heads as Music Director is awe-somely impressive. From a small choral group with a season consisting of one program (played twice) during the first year, and four programs given the second season, the Saint Louis Symphony Orchestra has grown to a complex organization that performs more than 230 concerts annually. These include twenty-four subscription weeks (each concert played two or three times), a separate Baroque Series, a Monday night chamber music series, student concerts for various age groups including the Kinder Konzerts, a summer Pops Series in St. Louis County at Queeny Park, the Little Symphony summer series, statewide touring, special touring to other areas of the United States, Christmas programs (including perennially, the *Nutcracker*), various special concerts in parks and on the riverfront, and here and there a special concert that cannot be categorized. To support these activities, an annual budget of around $6,000,000 is needed. A capital funds drive, called the "Fund for the Second Century," has a goal of $13,700,000—of which almost $8,000,000 has been raised. (This last figure— $8,000,000—is exactly one thousand times what the Choral Society paid to buy the assets of the St. Louis Musical Union in 1890.) The money, which, a hundred years ago, came from whichever interested individuals could afford to contribute, now comes from ticket sales, private foundations, corporations, the Arts and Education Fund, the National Endowment for the Arts, the Missouri Arts Council, St. Louis County, the St. Louis Convention and Tourism Bureau, the volunteer projects of the Women's Association, and—of course—which-ever interested individuals can afford to contribute. In 1979–1980, the Saint Louis Symphony Orchestra ranks twelfth (in minimum, or base, pay) out of thirty-one cities with symphony orchestras. This isn't a bad record, considering that many of the other cities in the comparison have a higher cost-of-living index, which is not taken into consideration in calculating the standings. (No valid comparison can be made with the 1880 figures, since there was only one other American symphony orchestra—the New York Philharmonic.)

The personnel of the Orchestra which Slatkin takes over now numbers one hundred, give or take one or two. This last clause is necessary because of the occasional changes that take place during any year. Within this body of approximately one hundred individuals is the largest number of married couples to be found in any American symphony orchestra. There are eleven married couples in the 1979–1980 Orchestra roster. In some cases, the women have kept their maiden (or, in this case, professional) names. The pairs, in no particular order, are John Korman (associate concertmaster) and Joan Korman (assistant principal, viola); Yuan Tung (associate principal, cello) and Helen Shklar (first violin section); Brent Akins (assistant principal, second violin) and Marka Akins (second violin section); Carl Schiebler (horn section and Per-sonnel Manager) and Beverly Schiebler (associate principal, second violin); Lawrence Strieby (assistant principal, horn) and Sylvia King (viola section); Robert Coleman (assistant principal, clarinet) and Janice Coleman (flute sec-tion); Masayoshi Kataoka (cello section) and Eiko Kataoka (first violin sec-tion); Gary Smith (trumpet section) and Janice Smith (assistant principal,

W. L. Hadley Griffin, President of Saint Louis Symphony Society since 1978, discussing Fund for a Second Century.

flute); Christopher Carson (assistant principal, double bass) and Deborah Bloom (second violin section); Roger Grossheider (trumpet) and Louise Grossheider (second violin section); and Bradford Buckley (contrabassoon) and Carolyn White (associate principal, double bass).

Almost one-third of the members of the "Centennial Orchestra" are women, a long stride from the earliest Golschmann period when there were two women string players and a woman harpist. (The presence of the handful of women added complications to accommodations on the early tours, but it is also said that Golschmann did not have much tolerance for the concept of women musicians—except, conventionally, at the harp—and surreptitiously referred to the two women string players as "the spooks."[4]) Of the women in the Orchestra, two are principals: Susan Slaughter, principal trumpet, and Frances Tietov (formerly Woodhams), principal harp. Three are associate principals: Beverly Schiebler, second violin; Kathleen Matthis, viola; and Carolyn White, double bass. Four are assistant principals: Joan Korman, viola; Catherine Lehr, cello; Janice Smith, flute; and Barbara Herr, oboe. And the official keyboard artist for the Symphony, when a score calls for one, is Barbara Liberman.

Many of the spouses of Orchestra members are professional musicians, although they are not actually part of the Saint Louis Symphony Orchestra. They, along with the Orchestra members, are an integral part of the musical life in St. Louis. Some of the musicians (and/or their spouses) are active in Young Audiences (an educational program for the local schoolchildren) and in the Rarely Performed Music series, an independent ensemble. Orchestra members and spouses are on the faculty of C.A.S.A. (St. Louis Conservatory and Schools for the Arts). Some are conductors of smaller community or school and college orchestras. They have donated their talents by offering salon concerts, to be sold at fund-raising auctions. (These donations of services are not only for the benefit of the Symphony, as is the case of the Radio Marathon, but are also given to auctions benefitting various St. Louis causes.) The impact of their presence is felt in dozens of ways in the metropolitan area.

When one talks to individual members of the Saint Louis Symphony Orchestra one is impressed by the strong conviction that this is an orchestra with an intense *esprit de corps*—a strong feeling of mutual support in all kinds of personal crises. There is, in many ways, a kind of "family" feeling. This exists, undoubtedly, in many symphony orchestras, but the members of the St. Louis Symphony Orchestra would have you believe that it is unusually strong here. The individuals have seen each other through illnesses, through divorces, through financial crises, through tragedies, and rejoiced with one another over triumphs and successes. The St. Louis community is large enough to be urbane but, at the same time, small enough to be friendly and to provide a good climate for personal relationships. This flavor prevails in the Orchestra.

The average age of the musicians in the Saint Louis Symphony Orchestra is approximately forty-one years. This is a relatively low average for an orchestra of this size, and most of the musicians are the elders of their new conductor. What's more, they all "knew him when." Slatkin has piled up enough credentials, has built his own career to such an indisputable level of excellence, that it is not difficult for the Orchestra to accept him as their "maestro." For his part, the only specific request he has made of his long-time friends is that he be called "Leonard" rather than "Lennie." And most of the principals are his long-time friends, since, with three exceptions, their association with the Orchestra dates from Walter Susskind's era, when Slatkin first came. The three exceptions are Jacques Israelievitch, concertmaster; Thomas Dumm, principal viola; and Peter Bowman, principal oboe, all of whom came into the Orchestra under Jerzy Semkow.

Changes that have come about in a century of music are obvious. What was once very modern is now conservative, a part of standard repertoire. Neglected composers such as Anton Bruckner and, more recently, Gustav Mahler, have come into their own. Some rather trifling changes have taken place. Tympani are now timpani. Battery is now percussion. Cornets have more or less disappeared. The composer who a hundred years ago was Tschaikowski is now Tchaikovsky. Later, Prokofieff became Prokofiev.

The conductor, with the help of a board of directors, can no longer take care of everything, as was true in the days of Joseph Otten. The operation requires an executive director or a manager or both.

It is no longer the Germans who make the most music in St. Louis, as it was in 1880. It is now the French, the Italians, the Chinese, the Japanese, the Russians, the Poles, the Britons, the Scotch, the Irish, *and* the Germans—to say nothing of the plain old Americans—who make the music in the St. Louis Symphony Orchestra.

This wonderful blend of backgrounds, of different styles in musical training, of diverse experiences in professional music has led to the Saint Louis Symphony Orchestra of 1980. This orchestra has come a long way since 1880 and the musicians do not intend to sit by the wayside now. Perhaps this should be amended to say that they do not intend to sit quietly on the shore, for—to mention the river again—they are like the Mississippi, growing always in size and momentum. They are part of the flow of truly great American symphony orchestras. They will not be left behind as the second century commences.

THE 100TH SEASON

LEONARD SLATKIN, Music Director and Conductor
Gerhardt Zimmermann, Associate Conductor

Thursday Evening, November 29, 1979, at 8:30
Friday Evening, November 30, 1979, at 8:30
Saturday Evening, December 1, 1979, at 8:30

Powell Symphony Hall

LEONARD SLATKIN, *Conducting*
ISAAC STERN, *Violin*

MOZART   Overture to "Così fan tutte," K. 588
          First performances by the Saint Louis Symphony Orchestra

BARTÓK   Concerto No. 2 for Violin and Orchestra
      I   Allegro non troppo
      II   Andante tranquillo
      III Allegro molto
      Isaac Stern

Intermission

SCHUBERT   Symphony No. 9 in C major, D. 944
      I   Andante; Allegro ma non troppo
      II   Andante con moto
      III Scherzo: Allegro vivace
      IV Allegro vivace

*The Steinway is the official piano of the Saint Louis Symphony Orchestra.
The Saint Louis Symphony Orchestra is featured on VOX, CANDIDE, TURNABOUT,
NEW WORLD and TELARC records.*

100TH SEASON, 1979-1980
THIRD SUBSCRIPTION CONCERTS

100th Season program.

SAINT LOUIS SYMPHONY ORCHESTRA

1979-1980 SEASON
LEONARD SLATKIN, Music Director and Conductor
GERHARDT ZIMMERMANN, Associate Conductor
THOMAS PECK, Chorus Director

FIRST VIOLINS
Jacques Israelievitch
Concertmaster,
Eloise and Oscar Johnson,
Jr. Chair
John Korman
Associate Concertmaster,
Louis D. Beaumont Chair
Lazar Gosman
Second Associate Concertmaster
Takaoki Sugitani
Assistant Concertmaster
James Krohn
Assistant Concertmaster
Haruka Watanabe
Darwyn Apple
Charlene Clark
Lawrence Diamond
Silvian Iticovici
Jenny Lind Jones
Eiko Kataoka
John Lippi
Rudolfs Mikelsons
Helen Shklar
Robert Swain
Miran Viher
Hiroko Yoshida

SECOND VIOLINS
Fryderyk Sadowski
Principal,
Dr. Frederick Eno
Woodruff Chair
Beverly Schiebler
Associate Principal
*Brent Akins
Marka Akins
Deborah Bloom
Louis Kampouris
Elizabeth Crowder
Carol Wolowsky Denos
Lorraine Glass
Louise Grossheider
Thomas LeVeck
Thomas Pettigrew
Judith Riediger
Leon Schankman

VIOLAS
Thomas Dumm
Principal,
Ben H. and Katherine
G. Wells Chair
Kathleen Mattis
Associate Principal
*Joan Korman
Gerald Fleminger
Lee Gronemeyer
Leonid Gutman
Lynn Hague
Sylvia King
William Martin
Margaret Salomon
Anthony Verme
Charles Weiser

VIOLONCELLOS
John Sant' Ambrogio
Principal,
Frank Y. and
Katherine G. Gladney
Chair
Yuan Tung
Associate Principal
*Catherine Lehr
Savely Schuster
Marilyn Beabout
Richard Brewer
Aleksander Ciechanski
Masayoshi Kataoka
Kenneth Pinckney
Robert Silverman
Sallie WeMott

DOUBLE BASSES
Henry Loew
Principal
Carolyn White
Associate Principal
*Christopher Carson
Warren Claunch
Joseph Kleeman
Ralph Maisel
Donald Martin
Richard Muehlmann
Janice Roberts Murphy

HARP
Frances Tietov
Principal,
Elizabeth Eliot Mallinckrodt
Chair

FLUTES
Jacob Berg
Principal
*Janice Smith
Janice Coleman
Jan Gippo

PICCOLO
Jan Gippo

OBOES
Peter Bowman
Principal
*Barbara Herr
Thomas Parkes
Marc Gordon

ENGLISH HORN
Marc Gordon

CLARINETS
George Silfies
Principal,
Walter Susskind Chair
*Robert Coleman
Christine Ward
James Meyer

E FLAT CLARINET
Robert Coleman

BASS CLARINET
James Meyer

BASSOONS
George Berry
Principal
*Robert Mottl
Robert Wisneskey
Bradford Buckley

CONTRA BASSOON
Bradford Buckley

HORNS
Roland Pandolfi
Principal
*Lawrence Strieby
Carl Schiebler
Kenneth Schultz
Kaid Friedel

TRUMPETS
Susan Slaughter
Principal,
Symphony Women's
Association Chair
*Malcolm McDuffee
Roger Grossheider
Gary Smith

TROMBONES
Bernard Schneider
Principal
Roger Davenport
Melvyn Jernigan

TUBA
John MacEnulty III
Gary Maske *Replacement*

TIMPANI
Richard Holmes
Principal

PERCUSSION
Richard O'Donnell
Principal
John Kasica
Thomas Stubbs

KEYBOARD INSTRUMENTS
Barbara Liberman
Florence G. and
Morton J. May Chair

PERSONNEL MANAGER
Carl R. Schiebler
Joseph Kleeman, Assistant

LIBRARIAN
John Tafoya
Carla Lebedeff, Assistant

STAGE MANAGER
Martin McManus
Gerald Eiffert, Assistant

*Assistant Principal

For these concerts, the Saint Louis Symphony Orchestra is utilizing the revolving seating method for section string players who are listed alphabetically in the roster.

Personnel of the Orchestra in its 100th season.

First Violin Section. *First row, left to right*: Jacques Israelievitch (Concertmaster), Jenny Lind Jones, John Korman (Associate Concertmaster), James Krohn (Assistant Concertmaster), Lawrence Diamond, Charlene Clark. *Second row*: Haruka Watanabe, Rudolph Mikelsons, Lazar Gosman (Second Associate Concertmaster), Eiko Kataoka, Miran Viher, Takaoki Sugitani (Assistant Concertmaster). *Back row*: John Lippi, Helen Shklar, Darwyn Apple, Silvian Iticovici, Robert Swain. (Absent from photo: Hiroko Yoshida, Peggy Andrix)

Second Violin Section. *First row, left to right*: Fryderyk Sadowski (Principal, who died on June 14, 1980, following a heart attack), Beverly Schiebler (Associate Principal), Brent Akins (Assistant Principal), Louis Kampouris, Leon Schankman. *Second row*: Thomas Pettigrew, Judith Riediger, Louise Grossheider, Lorraine Glass. *Third row*: Carol Wolowsky Denos, Marka Akins, Elizabeth Crowder. (Absent from photo: Deborah Bloom, Thomas Le Veck, and Dana Edson)

Viola Section. *First row, left to right*: Kathleen Mattis (Associate Principal), Lynn Hague, Thomas Dumm (Principal), Joan Korman (Assistant Principal), Gerald Fleminger. *Second row*: Margaret Salomon, Lee Gronemeyer, Sylvia King, Anthony Verme. *Back row*: Leonid Gutman, Charles Weiser, William Martin.

Cello Section. *Front row, left to right*: Savely Schuster, Marilyn Beabout, Aleksander Ciechanski, John Sant'Ambrogio (Principal), Yuan Tung (Associate Principal), *Second row*: Robert Silverman, Masayoshi Kataoka, Kenneth Pinckney, Catherine Lehr (Associate Principal), Richard Brewer.

Double Bass Section. *Front row, left to right*: Henry Loew (Principal), Carolyn White (Associate Principal), Christopher Carson (Assistant Principal). *Second row*: Ralph Maisel and Janice Roberts Murphy. *Back row*: Joseph Kleeman, Warren Claunch, Don Martin, Richard Muehlmann.

Barbara Liberman (keyboard) and Frances Tietov (Principal, harp).

Woodwind Sections. *Front row, left to right*: George Berry (Principal bassoon), George Silfies (Principal clarinet), Jacob Berg (Principal flute), Peter Bowman (Principal oboe). *Second row*: Robert Mottl (Assistant Principal, bassoon), Christine Ward (clarinet), Janice Coleman (flute), Barbara Herr (Assistant Principal, oboe), Marc Gordon (English horn and oboe). *Third row*: Robert Wisneskey (bassoon), Robert Coleman (Assistant Principal, clarinet), James Meyer (clarinet), Janice Smith (Assistant Principal, flute), Thomas Parkes (oboe). *Back row*: Bradford Buckley (contra bassoon) and Jan Gippo (piccolo and flute).

Brass Sections. *Front row, left to right*: Bernard Schneider (Principal trombone), Roland Pandolfi (Principal horn), Susan Slaughter (Principal trumpet). *Second row*: Roger Davenport (trombone), Lawrence Strieby (Assistant Principal, horn), Carl Schiebler (horn), Kenneth Schultz (horn), Malcolm McDuffee (Assistant Principal, trumpet), and Gary Smith (trumpet). *Back row*: Kaid Friedel (horn) and Roger Grossheider (trumpet). (Absent from photo: John MacEnulty, tuba)

Timpani and Percussion Section. *Front row, left to right*: Richard O'Donnell (Principal, percussion), Richard Holmes (timpani), John Kasica (percussion). *Standing in back*: Thomas Stubbs (percussion).

Leonard Slatkin rehearsing Orchestra.

Leonard Slatkin conducting Orchestra during performance.

John Tafoya, Librarian, and Carla Lebedeff, assistant.

Martin McManus, Stage manager, and Gerald Eiffert, assistant.

Leonard Slatkin conducting Saint Louis Symphony Orchestra in its 100th year.

THE WOMEN'S ASSOCIATION

THE WOMEN'S ASSOCIATION of the Saint Louis Symphony Society is a strong and vigorous arm of the parent organization. Women have traditionally been notable supporters of orchestras in their own cities. All of the major orchestras and most of the smaller ones have women helping to meet the budget and spreading the good word. The Saint Louis Symphony Women's Association is one of the strongest and most active in the United States. It has borrowed some ideas from other cities and it has pioneered with new trends and projects.

Before the actual beginnings of the Women's Association, the Saint Louis Symphony Society received strong support from the so-called weaker sex. There was a woman president of the Society, Mrs. John T. Davis, Jr., who held office during the period of the St. Louis World's Fair—the Louisiana Purchase Exposition of 1904. Through the 'teens and the early 1920's, the women were not organized into any official body—they were just there, helping to raise money for the "Guarantee Fund" and to increase the number of season-ticket subscribers, by word of mouth, if by no other way.

According to a statement by Mrs. Max Goldstein, an incredibly active supporter of the Saint Louis Symphony Orchestra for more than sixty years, a group of women first met in 1923 at the home of Mrs. Charles Rice (the Oak Knoll residence which is now the Museum of Science and History) to discuss the planning of a women's group to aid the Symphony.[1] They based their rules on those of the Women's Association of the Philadelphia Orchestra, which had been organized a short time previously. The group became official about a year and a half later, in 1925, and called itself The Women's Committee of the Saint Louis Symphony Society. They started listing their membership in the Symphony programs, the original list numbering something over 130 names.

The first President was Mrs. Thomas G. Ratcliffe, who served for two years, a length of service that has been followed by each of the succeeding presidents down through the years. According to one of the later historians of the group, "The requirements were: be a subscriber to the Guarantee Fund, a season-ticket subscriber, or render service to the Orchestra. The dues were $2.00 and

Past Presidents of Women's Association, posed in 1975 with Mrs. William W. Scott, President for that year, in center, with plaque. *Seated, left to right*: Mrs. Harold T. Hungerford; Mrs. Grayson Carroll; Mrs. Elmer Hilpert; Mrs. William Dee Becker; Mrs. Prince A. Gardner, Jr.; Mrs. Howard T. Bland; Mrs. Paul C. Ford. *Standing*: Mrs. J. Eldred Newton; Mrs. J. Sheppard Smith, Jr.; Mrs. J. Eugene Baker; and Mrs. Scott. Absent were Mrs. Wallace R. Persons and Mrs. Carl H. Schlapp, Jr. (President succeeding Mrs. Scott is Mrs. Frank L. Thompson, 1977–1979.)

remained so for twenty years, until 1945 when an increase of fifty cents was passed. Membership increased from 160 at the end of the first year to 465 by 1927. There was a great effort to interest other women's organizations in membership and for several years over twenty organizations were represented. One event to stimulate this interest was a mass meeting of women's organizations at the Statler Hotel, the minutes of this meeting reading that the price of the luncheon was not to exceed eighty-five cents."[2]

The women generated a large amount of support for the Symphony through this "Mass Meeting," attracting both organizations and individuals as well as campaign underwriters for the venture during the 1926–1927 season. The following season, the officers of the Women's Committee were listed formally in the program on the same page as the names of the Society's Board Members. Recognition was welcome, and spurred the Committee on to even greater efforts. The women began to sponsor young people's concerts (in addition to those which had been sponsored miscellaneously since the days of Ganz) and

MEMBERS OF THE
WOMEN'S COMMITTEE

Mrs. Charles L. Allen
Mrs. ThomasL. Anderson
Mrs. Engene Angert
Mrs. Robert Atkinson
Mrs. Howard Bailey
Mrs. Willard Bartlett
Mrs. H. H. Barton, Jr.
Mrs. Mansfield C. Bay
Mrs. Wm. Dee Becker
Mrs. W. N. Bemis
Mrs. George F. Bergfield
Mrs. Eric Bernays
Mrs. Erwin Bettman
Mrs. D. C. Biggs
Mrs. Ralph F. Bixby
Mrs. William H. Bixby
Mrs. Guy Blackmer
Mrs. R. E. Blake
Mrs. Ira L. Bretzfelder
Mrs. Margaret Chapman Byers.
Mrs. L. Wade Childress
Mrs. Perry Chrisler
Mrs. Grace Wilson Clark
Mrs. W. Palmer Clarkson
Miss Ilma Cohn
Mrs. J. Arthur Corbitt
Mrs. Ames Cushman
Mrs. W. C. D'Arcy
Mrs. J. T. Davis
Mrs. J. Lionberger Davis
Mrs. W. T. Donovan
Mrs. W. B. Douglas
Mrs. H. Chouteau Dyer
Mrs. J. T. Dyer
Mrs. Francis G. Eaton
Mrs. Louis H. Egan
Mrs. H. Worthington Eddy
Mrs. Robert R. Fauntleroy
Mrs. David Fentress
Mrs. Thomas Francis
Mrs. Rudolph Ganz
Mrs. Frederick D. Gardner
Mrs. Russell Gardner, Jr.
Mrs. Clifford W. Gaylord
Miss Pearl E. Gehner

Mrs. Warren Goddard
Mrs. M. A. Goldstein
Mrs. Evarts Graham
Mrs. Louis M. Hall
Mrs. John A. Haskell
Mrs. George Hitchcock
Mrs. Lon O. Hocker
Miss Lucile Howard
Mrs. Wm. B. Ittner
Mrs. D. O. Ives
Mrs. Paul V. Janis
Mrs. J. Forbes Johnson
Mrs. Clay E. Jordan
Mrs. Alden Kimball
Mrs. J. O. King
Mrs. Harry G. Koerber
Mrs. Carl W. Koop
Mrs. David Kriegshaber
Mrs. Ernest R. Kroeger
Mrs. Louis LaBeaume
Mrs. Carl H. Langenberg
Mrs. J. A. Latzer
Mrs. William Lemp
Mrs. George S. Levis
Mrs. Joseph W. Lewis
Miss Alves Long
Mrs. Louis F. Lumaghi
Mrs. Edward Mallinckrodt, Jr.
Mrs. Charles W. Martin
Mrs. W. N. Matthews
Mrs. Morton May
Mrs. Esmeralda Berry Mayes
Mrs. James McCluney
Mrs. Mildred McCluney
Mrs. Stewart McDonald
Mrs. N. A. McMillan
Mrs. S. B. McPheeters
Mrs. George D. Markham
Mrs. H. C. Meister
Mrs. Adolph A. Meyer
Mrs. Leo Moser
Mrs. Henry S. Miller
Mrs. D. H. Mudd
Mrs. Harvey G. Mudd
Mrs. Robert Mueller

Mrs. Jesse Myer
Mrs. J. M. Nelson, Jr.
Mrs. Hayward Niedringhaus
Mrs. C. C. Pangman
Mrs. Everett W. Pattison
Mrs. Charles P. Pettus
Mrs. W. J. Polk
Mrs. Harry Potter
Mrs. Aaron S. Rauh
Mrs. Charles M. Rice
Mrs. Oliver F. Richards
Mrs. Minnie H. Roever
Mrs. Virgil Rule
Mrs. Horace Rumsey
Mrs. Lewis M. Rumsey, Jr.
Mrs. Wm. Scheville
Miss Adele Schmitz
Mrs. S. I. Schwab
Mrs. J. F. Shoemaker
Mrs. Wallace D. Simmons
Miss Eunice C. Smith
Mrs. H. W. Soper
Miss Edith E. Souther
Mrs. H. E. Sprague
Mrs. H. J. Steinbreder
Mrs. Albert I. Stix
Mrs. Charles A. Stix
Mrs. Harry F. Stix
Mrs. John B. Strauch
Mrs. Royall Switzler
Mrs. B. J. Taussig
Mrs. Frederick J. Taussig
Mrs. N. David Thompson
Mrs. P. Y. Tupper
Mrs. W. T. Treadway
Mrs. F. W. A. Vesper
Mrs. H. Von Schrenk
Mrs. E. J. Walsh
Mrs. Clinton L. Whittemore
Mrs. W. H. Whitton
Mrs. Letticia Parker Williams
Mrs. Raymond Wilber
Mrs. Edward Worcester, Jr.
Mrs. Thomas Crane Young
Mrs. Vertrees Young

Women's Committee listing in concert program, 1925–1926 season. This was the first year of the organization which became, in 1937, the "Women's Association."

THE WOMEN'S COMMITTEE

OF THE

ST. LOUIS SYMPHONY SOCIETY

A TEA will be given in honor of Mr. Lawrence Tibbett, following the concert, on Friday, December thirteenth, at four-thirty o'clock, at the St. Louis Woman's Club. Members may procure guest cards in advance by applying to Miss Charlotte Gerhard, GRand 1359.

The privilege of membership in the Women's Committee is open to the women of Saint Louis upon application to the Chairman of the Membership Committee, Mrs. William Dee Becker. The annual dues of two dollars are used by the organization for numerous entertainments, musical scholarships, for prizes in connection with the Student Concerts, and for aiding various other musical enterprises.

We cordially invite your cooperation in this movement for the advancement of musical interest.

JOIN THE WOMEN'S COMMITTEE!

MRS. CHARLES M. RICE	. . . . President
MRS. CHARLES MULLIKIN	. . . 1st Vice-President
MRS. ERIC BERNAYS	. . . . . . 2nd Vice-President
MRS. W. N. MATTHEWS	. . . . Treasurer
MRS. FRANK A. HABIG	. . . . Recording Secretary
MRS. M. HAYWARD POST	. . . Corresponding Secretary

THE JUNIOR WOMEN'S COMMITTEE

Members of the Junior Women's Committee enjoy the same privileges as those in the Senior group and, in addition, they have the privilege of attending the Pre-Symphony Program discussions, conducted each Friday morning under the direction of Miss Martha Love. Membership applications should be addressed to Miss Frances Conant, 19 Portland Place (Forest 4934), Chairman of the Membership Committee.

MRS. CHARLES LAMY President	MISS MARY CARPENTER Treasurer
MISS ADELAIDE MAHAFFEY 1st Vice-President	MRS. ARTHUR FEUERBACHER Recording Secretary
MISS FRANCES BATES 2nd Vice-President	MRS. DUNCAN I. MEIER, JR. Corresponding Secretary

From program in the 1935–1936 season. This includes one of the earliest mentions of the Juniors.

offered various prizes to students. During the early 1930's, the Committee for Young People's Concerts offered awards for all manner of youthful efforts—efforts inspired by the concerts. There was an award for the best booklet describing the instruments of the orchestra. There were awards for the best poem, the best carving (soap, wood, etc.), and the best musical composition suggested by something in the concerts. The schools in the area became more involved than ever before and sold blocks of tickets to their own students.

The printed programs for the student concerts during this period had some very interesting features, in addition to the usual comments and analyses of the music. In the back of each program was a quiz for the listeners to give themselves, offering such relatively erudite questions as "In what country did the Sonata Form begin to grow?" and "Which composer likes to describe with music what is invisible in nature?" If you had read your program notes carefully, you were able to answer the first with "Italy," having heard Vivaldi's Allegro Movement from the Concerto in D Minor. The answer to the second question was "Debussy." (Excerpts from his *Petite Suite* were part of the program and the notes had waxed lyrical about his impressionism.)

Not only were the students encouraged to pay attention and to learn something, they were given a tempting blank page, in the back of the program, headed "This is Your Page." Underneath the title was printed, "Write, draw, or paste anything the music suggests. Keep it neat and attractive."

The Women's Committee sponsored social gatherings honoring the Symphony soloists. Frequently these took the form of teas following the Friday afternoon matinees—tea at the Wednesday Club or the St. Louis Woman's Club. Mrs. Oscar Johnson, Sr. (whose son, Oscar, Jr., was President of the Symphony Society) was president of the St. Louis Woman's Club and also quite active in the Women's Committee of the Symphony.

The redoubtable Mrs. Goldstein was head of the women's newly formed Educational Committee and a suggested reading list appeared in the concert programs. The women prevailed upon Harry Burke,[3] who was then writing the program notes, to compile the list. The recommendations were impressive, including such suggested reading as Thayer's *Life of Beethoven* and Ernest Newman's *Wagner, Man and Artist*.

Early in the 1930's the Association began to offer a music scholarship, originally for attendance at the summer high school camp at Interlochen, Michigan. The use of the scholarship has varied through the years, sometimes being a purse for participation in the Aspen Music Festival, and sometimes being financial aid to attend a conservatory or music school.

In 1936, one of the many projects which have continued with vitality was instituted—the Young Artist Auditions. This competition (still very much in effect) is open to students of voice, piano, winds, strings, and percussion. The winners receive cash awards and an opportunity to perform in a concert.

In the 1935–1936 season, a junior division of the Women's Association sprang up, calling itself the "Junior Women's Committee." These younger women arranged their own pre-concert lectures and, occasionally, their own

THE WOMEN'S COMMITTEE
OF THE
ST. LOUIS SYMPHONY SOCIETY

A TEA will be given in honor of Mr. Lawrence Tibbett, following the concert, on Friday, December thirteenth, at four-thirty o'clock, at the St. Louis Woman's Club.. Members may procure guest cards in advance by applying to Miss Charlotte Gerhard, GRand 1359.

The privilege of membership in the Women's Committee is open to the women of Saint Louis upon application to the Chairman of the Membership Committee, Mrs. William Dee Becker. The annual dues of two dollars are used by the organization for numerous entertainments, musical scholarships, for prizes in connection with the Student Concerts, and for aiding various other musical enterprises.

We cordially invite your cooperation in this movement for the advancement of musical interest.

JOIN THE WOMEN'S COMMITTEE!

The newly-formed Educational Committee, under the Chairmanship of Mrs. M. A. Goldstein, offers a new service to music-lovers and Symphony patrons:

SUGGESTED READING ON NEXT WEEK'S SYMPHONY PROGRAM

ORCHESTRAL MUSIC: *Symphonic Masterpieces,* by Olin Downes: Human, justly appreciative, authoritative and with its feet on the ground, it is the best of its kind. *Masters of the Symphony,* by Percy Goetschius: A technical study with musical illustrations, it is easy to follow, admirable for beginners, and has a living quality. *Standard Concert Guide,* by George P. Upton and Felix Borowski: A sound and scholarly verbal analysis of the symphonic repertory. *Symphonies and Their Meaning,* by Philip H. Goepp: An excellent standard work.

OPERA: *Stories of the Operas,* by Ernest Newman: Admirably combines the story with an excellent and easily understandable illustrated musical analysis. *The Complete Opera Book,* by Gustav Kobbé: Stories and histories of the standard operas with biographical fact, musical comment and illustrative themes in popular form. *One Thousand and One Nights of Opera,* by Frederick H. Martens: A compact and comprehensive story outline.

BEETHOVEN: *Life of Ludwig van Beethoven,* by Alexander Wheelock Thayer, translated by E. H. Krehbiel: The ultimate authority. *Beethoven, the Creator,* by Romain Rolland: A scholarly and sympathetic study of the life and music of the period of these works. *Beethoven, the Man Who Freed Music,* by Robert Haven Schauffler: An excellent study of man and music. *Beethoven and His Nine Symphonies,* by Sir George Grove: Pioneer and Victorian but perceptive and valuable. *St. Louis Symphony Orchestra Program: Notes on Fourth Symphony,* April 5-6, 1929; on *Fidelio* overture, March 2-3, 1934.

HANDEL: Romain Rolland's essay, *A Portrait of Handel* in *A Musical Tour of the Land of the Past* is suggested as admirable background reading.

WAGNER: *Life of Richard Wagner,* by Ernest Newman: Authoritative and comprehensive, but not yet all published. *My Life,* by Richard Wagner: Fascinating and revealing, but not always entirely trustworthy nor innocent of pose. *The Truth About Wagner,* by Philip Dutton Hurn and Waverly Lewis Root: Though rather biased and sensational it affords material not otherwise easily accessible. *Wagner as Man and Artist,* by Ernest Newman: A splendid study of Wagner's personality, aesthetics and art. *St. Louis Symphony Program Notes,* March 9-10, 1928, and March 11-12, 1932.

Compiled by HARRY R. BURKE

119

From 1935–1936 program. The women were expected to bone up on the music before each concert.

Women's Committee Activities

NOW IS THE TIME TO JOIN THE WOMEN'S COMMITTEE! Telephone the Membership Chairman, Mrs. William Dee Becker (FOrest 3622). Annual membership dues $2.00.

The first Program-Tea of the Season will be given next Thursday, Nov. 19th, at three o'clock at the Wednesday Club. Mr. William B. Heyne, Chorus Master of the Symphony Chorus, will lecture on "The Damnation of Faust." This will be followed by a Tea in honor of the Assisting Artists, Miss ROSE BAMPTON, Mr. PAUL ALTHOUSE and Mr. CHASE BAROMEO. Members may obtain Guest Tickets at 75c.

SYMPHONY HIGH-LIGHTS. Tune in on Station KWK each Thursday evening at 5:45 for this very interesting and informative program, presented by the Educational Committee and sponsored by the Security National Bank. The speaker for the program of Nov. 19th will be Mr. William B. Heyne.

SYMPHONY RECORD HOUR. You and your friends are cordially invited to the Aeolian Hall, 1004 Olive St., every Wednesday morning at 10:30. Miss Edith Gordon will be the speaker for Nov. 18th.

FUTURE CONCERT DATES AND ARTISTS

"DAMNATION OF FAUST" (Hector Berlioz)	November 20-21
SERGE RACHMANINOFF, *Composer-Pianist*	November 27-28
Special Orchestral Features	December 4- 5
SCIPIONE GUIDI, *Violinist*	December 11-12
ALEXANDRE TANSMAN, *Composer-Pianist*	December 18-19
RUTH SLENCZYNSKI, *Pianist* . . . . (Saturday and Sunday)	December 26-27
DALIES FRANTZ, *Pianist*	January 8- 9
GREGOR PIATIGORSKY, *Violoncellist*	January 15-16
SERGE PROKOFIEFF, *Composer-Pianist-Conductor*	January 29-30
CORINNE FREDERICK, *Pianist*	February 5- 6
Special Orchestral Features	February 12-13
VLADIMIR HOROWITZ, *Pianist*	February 26-27
"BELSHAZZAR'S FEAST" (WILLIAM WALTON)	March 5- 6
St. Louis Symphony Chorus Soloist—Arthur Fear, *Baritone*	
ALBERT SPALDING, *Violinist*	March 12-13
Gala Closing Concerts	March 19-20

TICKET INFORMATION

Tickets for any of the future concerts listed above may be purchased at any time at the Symphony Box Office in the Municipal Auditorium Ticket Lobby.

Single concert admission prices for all individual concerts during the season, regardless of the artist or special attraction, are as follows:

ORCHESTRA—$2.50, $2.00; LOWER BALCONY—$2.00, $1.50; UPPER BALCONY—$1.00, 75c; BOXES—(Seating four) $14.00; BOX SEATS—$3.50; MEZZANINE—(Rear of Boxes) $3.00.

On Monday morning of each week, tickets for the current week's concerts will be placed on sale at the Aeolian Company Ticket Office, 1004 Olive St., (CHestnut 8828) as well as at the Symphony Box Office (Auditorium Ticket Lobby), (CHestnut 8590). Mail orders filled as received when accompanied by check payable to St. Louis Symphony Society. Enclose stamped, addressed envelope if tickets are to be mailed.

From 1936–1937 season. Mr. William B. Heyne, who was to deliver the lecture on *The Damnation of Faust*, was the founder of the first Symphony Chorus which dated from 1934. Note the names of Rachmaninoff, Piatigorsky, Prokofiev (with earlier version of spelling), Horowitz, and Spalding as artists to be presented during the season.

WOMEN'S COMMITTEE ACTIVITIES

JOINT RECITAL! The Women's Committee, the Junior Women's Division and the Men's Auxiliary Committee will present Mlle. Lucienne Radisse, Violoncellist, and Gari Shelton, pianist, in a joint recital on Monday night, December 7th, at 8:30 o'clock, at the Wednesday Club, Taylor and Westminster Avenues. Mlle. Radisse, who is a native of Paris, is in this country filling concert engagements. She is an intimate friend of Mr. and Mrs. Vladimir Golschmann. Mr. Shelton needs no introduction, as he is a well-known St. Louis pianist and has been soloist with the orchestra.

A PERMANENT YOUNG MEN'S AUXILIARY has been organized in order that men may attend the concerts and entertainments presented by the Junior Women's Division during the year. The dues are $2, and any young man is invited to join. One PRE-SYMPHONY lecture each month will be given on Thursday evening, and it will be under the direction of a member of the newly-formed auxiliary.

SYMPHONY RECORD HOUR will be held at the Aeolian Hall, 1004 Olive Street, every Wednesday morning, at 10:30 o'clock. The speaker for December 2 will be Mrs. Frank Neal.

WEEKLY RADIO PROGRAM. In anticipation of the concerts of December 4th and 5th, The EDUCATIONAL COMMITTEE will present Mrs. Joseph Mayes and a woodwind ensemble, under the direction of John F. Kiburz, on Radio Station KWK, at 5:45 o'clock, Thursday afternoon, December 3. The Security National Bank are sponsors of this weekly program.

NOW IS THE TIME TO JOIN THE WOMEN'S COMMITTEE! Telephone the Membership Chairman, Mrs. William Dee Becker (FOrest 3622). Annual membership dues $2.00.

FORM OF BEQUEST

Music, in its highest form as exemplified by the ST. LOUIS SYMPHONY ORCHESTRA, has its place among the great cultural and educational influences of St. Louis.... An adequate Endowment Fund assures permanency ... A suggested form of Bequest:

"I hereby give and bequeath to the St. Louis Symphony Society for its

Endowment Fund the sum of $.."

From program in 1937. Note the formation of a "Permanent Young Men's Auxiliary" so that the Juniors could have co-educational gatherings.

Officers of the Junior Division of the Women's Association in 1939. (Organization went out of existence later and was refounded in 1959.) Their names in 1939 were (*left to right*): Mrs. Robert A. Black, Jr.; Miss Adelaide Mahaffey; Mrs. Mahlon Hale; Mrs. Arthur Gaines; and Mrs. Lawrence Stern. (*St. Louis Post-Dispatch* photograph, May 14, 1939)

parties for visiting artists. (During the 1940's, the Juniors faded out of the picture, to be revived in 1959.)

In the late 1930's, the Educational Committee sponsored weekly broadcasts by members of the Saint Louis Symphony Orchestra on Radio Station KWK—fifteen minutes every Wednesday night, during the season.

In 1937, the women adopted the official name "Women's Association of the Saint Louis Symphony Society." As their projects multiplied, the women never neglected their two primary aims: the selling of season tickets and the enlisting of more donors to the Guarantee Fund, later called the Maintenance Fund. In the lean years of the Depression and the hard-pressed years of World War II, they worked like the proverbial beavers trying to help fill the hall and reduce the deficit.

The good works carried on by the Women's Association break down into two categories: musical activities and fund-raising projects. In the present day, the musical activities are numerous. In addition to the Student Concerts (which, since 1966, have included the Kinder Konzerts for ages 4 to 8), the Young Artists sponsorship, and the awarding of scholarship funds, the women offer, each season, an "On Stage" program. This is a series of six presentations,

Student Concerts
Project Contest Awards

ᴄ⌒ᴐ

The Committee in charge is highly gratified at the interest in this year's contest, as evidenced by the entry of 193 objects in the contest. The Committee wishes to express its warm appreciation to the judges who so kindly gave their time in the difficult task of selecting the winners.

NOTE BOOKS—
    1st Place—VILLA DUCHESNE
    2nd Place—GOODALL SCHOOL (Webster Groves)

Honorable Mention
Ritenour High School (Overland)
Webster Groves Junior High School
Webster Groves Senior High School

Judged by ten members of the Women's Association

POSTERS—
    1st Place—ADAMS AVENUE SCHOOL (Kirkwood)
    2nd Place—ACADEMY OF THE VISITATION

Honorable Mention
The Principia

Judges—Charles Galt
          Tanasko Milovich
          Mercer Orwig, *Chairman*

MODELING AND CARVING—
    (TIE)
    1st Place—GOODALL SCHOOL (Webster Groves)—imagination and originality.
    1st Place—ADAMS AVENUE SCHOOL (Kirkwood)—Knowledge of musical instruments and excellence of execution.

Honorable Mention
Villa Duchesne
Academy of the Visitation
St. Margaret's Parochial School

Judges—Mrs. David B. Ewing, *Chairman*
          Mrs. Amy L. Isaac
          Mrs. Scott MacNutt

SCHOOL ENTRY—CENTRAL SCHOOL (Ferguson)

The Committee expresses its warm appreciation to the competing students and the school officials for their interest and cooperation.

STUDENT CONCERT COMMITTEE,
Mrs. O. K. Bovard, *Chairman*

From 1936–1937 season program. All of this activity was sponsored by the Women's Committee, later called the Women's Association.

Women's Association members preparing for annual Maintenance Fund Campaign, 1940. *Seated, left to right*: Mrs. Hugh McKittrick Jones; Mrs. William N. Matthews; Mrs. William Dee Becker (President); and Mrs. Max Goldstein. *Standing*: Mrs. James K. Vardaman and Mrs. Eric Bernays.

each one by a conductor, an Orchestra member, a guest artist, or a recording expert. In other words, the speaker is someone involved, one way or another, in the world of professional music. These programs, as the name implies, take place on the stage of Powell Symphony Hall (on Monday mornings) and offer fare various enough so that many individuals, men and women, sign up year after year, and feel no sense of repetition. Another musical activity in the present Women's Association is the Docent program wherein volunteers are trained to go forth into the area schools and speak to groups of children in ways that enhance their enjoyment of the Student Concerts.

One of the major musical activities projects which has been taken up and underwritten by the Women's Association in more recent years (1970) is the Saint Louis Symphony Youth Orchestra. Sponsored and financed by the Association, this group of young musicians, between twelve and twenty-one years of age, numbers approximately 125 members. They audition, rehearse, and perform with the same diligence and sense of professionalism as does the Saint Louis Symphony Orchestra, albeit the number of their performances is considerably smaller—usually three concerts a year. Leonard Slatkin was a co-

DEBUT PERFORMANCE
of the
Saint Louis Symphony Youth Orchestra
Friday Evening, December 4, at 8:30
Powell Symphony Hall

LEONARD SLATKIN, Conductor and Music Director
WALTER SUSSKIND, Guest Conductor
JOYCE MATHIS, Soprano

Program

BACH-STOKOWSKI	Passacaglia and Fugue in C Minor
MOZART	Dove Sono from "The Marriage of Figaro"
PUCCINI	Vissi D'Arte from "La Tosca"
GERSHWIN	Summertime from "Porgy and Bess" Miss Mathis
MILHAUD	Suite Provençale Conducted by Mr. Susskind
COPLAND	Suite from "Billy the Kid"

General Admission: $1.50

Phone JE 4-1700 for ticket information

The Saint Louis Symphony Youth Orchestra made its debut during the 1970–1971 season.

founder (with the Women's Association) of the Youth Orchestra and was the first Music Director, but as his commitments grew more and more pressing, he surrendered his responsibility to Gerhardt Zimmermann, present Associate Conductor of the Saint Louis Symphony Orchestra. The young musicians, first under Slatkin, now under Zimmermann, turn out astonishingly professional-sounding music. Their repertoire, chosen to bring out the superb best in them, rather than to "make them look good," is sophisticated and difficult to play.

How do the women support all these musical activities? By the other half of their projects, the fund-raising ones. Fund-raising activities not only underwrite the projects described above, but they also produce a surplus which is given to the Symphony Society, an amount sufficient to have endowed a chair in the Orchestra—the principal trumpet chair, held at present by a woman (Susan Slaughter). In 1979, they pledged an additional $300,000 to endow the principal string bass chair (occupied by Henry Loew) and made their first payment on the pledge.

The fund-raising projects vary greatly, offering enough choice to tempt volunteers into helping no matter what the particular volunteer's bent may be. Their cookbook—*The Symphony of Cooking*—was first issued and sold during the 1954–1955 season. Its compilation required an enormous amount of work, but resulted in what is now an ongoing money-maker.

Four annual project events take place. Although in the minds of the public they are "annual events," they are actually planned for and worked toward the year round. The first of these, the "Gypsy Caravan," is a colossal antiques-and-crafts fair held each Memorial Day since 1974. Part of this venture is underwritten by Famous Barr Company, and its annual yield is somewhere in the neighborhood of $30,000. Merchants and individuals pay a fee to park their vehicles or set up small shops on an allotted spot in a huge parking lot. They proceed to sell their wares to the thousands of people who stroll up and down the aisles, looking for whatever catches their fancy.

The second of the annual events is the newly instituted (1978) Radio Music Marathon, organized so that listeners can telephone in to buy something that has been offered in a predistributed catalog. The items may vary from a private concert donated by Orchestra musicians to a hand-embroidered table cloth. Various Symphony officials and local celebrities keep a kind of talk show going on the air during the several days of the sale. This enterprise has brought in over $28,000 annually.

A third event is the appearance of the Symphony Rotogravure Section, published yearly in the *St. Louis Post-Dispatch*. This multipage spread features photographs of St. Louis individuals posed with the product of some local sponsor, everything from automobiles to edibles and potables. This nets something over $70,000 each year. The fourth special event involves a Symphony-planned trip, usually featuring cultural events not available on an ordinary tour. The Women's Association makes the claim, "Our trips have become legendary, with galas in embassies, palaces, theaters, and restaurants; there are concerts, recitals, opera, ballet, and modern dance; there is always planned

"Gypsy Caravan" scene, photographed through empty antique frame. (*St. Louis Post-Dispatch* photograph, May 28, 1973)

Women's Association's "Tours of Distinction" takes sightseeing group to riverfront in chartered bus.

sightseeing and free time for shopping." Returns from each Symphony Trip benefit the Orchestra to the tune of around $10,000.

A money-maker that operates three days a week, fifty-two weeks a year, is the shop on Grand Boulevard (across from Powell Symphony Hall) called "Second Fiddle Fashions." This store carries used furs, clothing, jewelry, and accessories for men, women, and children—all for sale for the benefit of "The Cause." The store is well-patronized and earns over $20,000 a year. "Tours of Distinction," offering sightseeing bus tours of the city for convention visitors, as well as for local groups, is run by trained volunteer guides, all members of the Women's Association. Each tour is arranged specifically to suit whatever the particular group wants to see or do. This yield is modest—several thousand dollars each year—because the call for sightseeing tours tends to be sporadic and seasonal.

Finally, there is the Tribute Fund. While its income is not significant, it offers a dignified, pleasant service to members and friends. Through the Fund, gifts to the Symphony are made not only in memory of someone, but to honor a friend's birthday, to say "thank you" for some favor, and for a variety of other reasons. The individual in whose name the gift is made receives from the Symphony Society a card reporting the gift and the name of the donor. This very formal card is illustrated, on its front cover, with an elegant photograph of one of the crystal-hung sconces in the Grand Foyer of Powell Symphony Hall.

Orchestra members eating lunch, between rehearsals, on steps in Powell Symphony Hall Grand Foyer, courtesy of the Junior Division, Women's Association. The Juniors sponsor this special luncheon once a year. (*St. Louis Post-Dispatch* photograph, January 28, 1973)

One other contribution which the Women's Association makes must be included: the help which the volunteer workers give to the Arts and Education Fund of St. Louis. The Arts and Education Fund was instituted in 1963. The Women's Association began the first of their annual solicitations for it immediately thereafter. They have been active in this endeavor ever since, working primarily in the Residential Division. Although the Arts and Education Fund obviously does not exist solely for the good of the Symphony, it is so beneficial that the Women's Association has embraced the solicitation effort as one of its projects.

The Junior Division has, in general, supplemented the labors of the Seniors. While they have conducted their own meetings, mailings, membership drives, etc., they have also generously lent their members to augment the work forces of the various pursuits of their elders, such as the Second Fiddle Shop, the Youth Orchestra, and the Arts and Education Fund solicitation. They have frequently engaged in fund-raising galas. These occasions are advised by the Senior members but conducted independently by the Juniors. These galas have included special evenings on one of the river boats docked on the St. Louis waterfront, fashion shows, and fund-raising concerts. Shortly before the Orchestra embarked on its first trip to Europe to play three concerts in the Athens Festival, the Junior Division sponsored a "Prelude to Athens" affair, a formal supper and concert in Powell Symphony Hall.

Saint Louis Symphony Youth Orchestra embarking for Vienna to play a concert in 1976. Conductor Gerhardt Zimmermann and Mrs. Zimmermann (with large white shoulder bag) in center. Manager Edith Hougland on other side of Zimmermann. (Public Relations department blocked out "TWA" name on plane for photograph.)

Busloads of school children arriving for student concert in Powell Symphony Hall, 1979.

President Jimmy Carter greets conductor Gerhardt Zimmermann on St. Louis riverfront after Youth Orchestra performance for President Carter's arrival on *Delta Queen*, August 24, 1979.

The Women's Association and its Junior Division now have almost twelve hundred members, the Junior Division accounting for just under two hundred. There may have been a time when membership was looked upon primarily as "social position," but there has never been an era when the women weren't serving as an indisputable aid to the ledger-book credit entries. Many of the members have had some musical education, either in music history and appreciation or in the playing of an instrument. This has, however, never been the sole factor that attracted women to devote volunteer time to the Association. The element which draws women into the operation seems to be that strangely American phenomenon—the startling achievements that can be brought about by groups of women pulling in harness for a specific and common interest, in this case the Saint Louis Symphony Orchestra. And the turning over of some $200,000 to $250,000 annually to the treasury is a startling achievement.

THE **10**TH ANNIVERSARY SEASON

of the

Saint Louis Symphony Youth Orchestra

Gerhardt Zimmermann, Music Director and Conductor

The Saint Louis Symphony Youth Orchestra will celebrate its tenth anniversary during the 1979-1980 season. Founded in 1970 to acquaint young musicians with the atmosphere of a professional orchestra, the Youth Orchestra has rapidly acquired an international reputation.

In August, 1979, the Youth Orchestra returned from a trip to Aberdeen, Scotland, where it served as the honored host at the International Festival of Youth Orchestras. An Aberdeen critic praised the performance saying the musicians "set standards of orchestral playing that will be difficult to surpass." Three years earlier members of the Youth Orchestra toured Vienna, Austria and Switzerland. A recording was made from tapes of their performances in Lausanne, Switzerland, and at Powell Symphony Hall. *

Sponsored by the Women's Association of the Saint Louis Symphony Society, the Youth Orchestra also receives numerous requests to perform for organizations in the St. Louis area. Recently the young musicians played for President Carter when he arrived in St. Louis aboard the Delta Queen.

More than a score of Youth Orchestra members have won local, regional and national music competitions, and many have continued their music education — after leaving the Youth Orchestra — at American and European conservatories. One former Youth Orchestra member is now a violinist with the Saint Louis Symphony Orchestra.

Members of the Youth Orchestra are selected by audition. They range in age from twelve through twenty-one and attend schools throughout the greater St. Louis area. They rehearse weekly under the direction of their conductor, Gerhardt Zimmermann — an outstanding successor to the Orchestra's founder and first conductor, Leonard Slatkin. Mr. Slatkin, who is now the Saint Louis Symphony Orchestra's Music Director and Conductor, will guest conduct the Youth Orchestra in a concert this season.

The Youth Orchestra record album may be obtained by contacting the office of the Saint Louis Symphony Orchestra, at Powell Symphony Hall, 533-2500.

POWELL

Friday Evening,

GABRIELI
MILHAUD

R. SCHUMANN
SMETANA

KHACHATURIAN

Friday Evenin

SAINT-SAËNS
TIPPETT

STRAUSS
BEETHOVEN

Friday Even

WAGNER

MOZART

ELGAR

ALL PROGR

*The Steinu
Saint Louis*

TENT

Y HALL

23, 1979, at 8:30
ni Toni No. 2
ncerto
, soloist
. 4

skind, Conductor
. 3
enam, Organ
estra Alumni

1980, at 8:30
a Princesse jaune"
te
remiere)
nsfiguration
ano, Chorus and
80
estra Piano
winner, soloist

1980, at 8:30
e
tkin, Conductor
in G major
soloist
ons

CHANGE
no of the
Orchestra
1980

Saint Louis Symphony Youth Orchestra

GERHARDT ZIMMERMANN, Music Director and Conductor
EDITH HOUGLAND, Manager

VIOLINS I

Donald Boyer
Co-Concertmaster
Becky Boyer
Co-Concertmaster
Margaret Jones
Co-Concertmaster
Robert Brownfield
Katherine Emblom
Steven Grant
Joseph Kaminsky
Eunice Kwak
Karry Krohn
Kimberly Meier
Jeff Peng
Lucia Piaskowiak
Jan Reinert
Mark Rothman
Bruce Shu
Libby Triplett
Caroline Youngermann
Kathleen Youngermann

VIOLINS II

Dean Schramm
Principal
Anne Beitel
Craig Caesar
Liz Cain
Mary Carter
Eric Delente
Edward Emblom
David Friedlander
Charles Gladney
Ann Hirschl
Laura Holtgrewe
Beth Johnson
Mike Kraus
Nancy Kwon
Amy Macy
Emilie Morgenthaler
Larry Neuman
Geralyn Schneider
Julie Spengel
John Tafoya
Amy Tremain
Kem Williams

VIOLAS

Leslie Sonder
Principal
Melody Archer
Chris Bruening
John Dowden
Alan Eynon
Charlotte Gordon

Thoraya Halhoul
Misha Kavka
John Posey
Lisa Sinden
Bettina Zastrow

CELLOS

Gena Taylor
Principal
Ann Bregitzer
Scott Cook
Timothy Dumm
Kristine Gabriel
Richard Hirschl
Brad James
Kristin Kaminsky
Linda Marshall
Kim Percival
Philip Polster
Carol Van Eenam
Julie Zupan

DOUBLE BASSES

Karen Katzen
Principal
Christopher Allen
Leanne Butts
Jim Mayer
Kathy Rebe
Tim Rickmeyer
Jim Schultz
Barbara Stark
Andrew Tinge

FLUTES

Sherry Lile
Principal
Susan Elkins
Erin Overton
Susan Rueter

OBOES

Sue Stebbins
Principal
Ann Homann
Robin Mazo

CLARINETS

Eve Danna
Co-Principal
Jeanine York
Co-Principal
Dave Sparks
Bill Tierney

BASS CLARINET

Gabriel Golliday

BASSOONS

Karen Gabriel
Principal
Chris Kilpatrick
Robin Robertson

HORNS

Jon Gustely
Principal
Kathy Bowman
Catherine Fox
Bill Hinson
Lisa Walter

TRUMPETS

Jim Stewart
Principal
Steven Frew
Paul Levin
Penelope Perkins

TROMBONES

Alan Skrainka
Principal
Keith Barrett
Doug Bert
James A. Martin

TUBA

Jeff Chronister

TIMPANI

Henry Claude

PERCUSSION

Matthew Furfine
Robin Hendry
Randy Max
Ted Rubright

HARP

Gwen Riles

KEYBOARD

Sue Ryan

STAGE MANAGER

Gerald Eiffert

POWELL SYMPHONY HALL

Floor by Floor

IT SEEMS LOGICAL to start a verbal tour of Powell Symphony Hall on the main floor, in the entrance foyer. This area with its white marble floors, glass-enclosed ticket windows, and framed concert announcements on the wall is a fitting entryway, but gives only a hint as to what lies beyond.

Passing through the doors into the Grand Foyer, one is surrounded by pure splendor. Crystal and bronze chandeliers that smack of old Vienna hang suspended from a thirty-foot-high ceiling, illuminating a white marble floor which, in turn, is set off and brightened by red velvet and gilded chairs, ranked along the perimeter. In the daytime, natural light floods in through immense windows. Red-carpeted stairs at one end of the expanse swirl upward to what might have been called, in an earlier era, the mezzanine. Now, it is the level of the Grand Tier boxes, each with its own small private anteroom. On this level is a large bar, salvaged from the Metropolitan Opera House in New York and given to the Saint Louis Symphony Society for installation in Powell Symphony Hall.

Returning to the ground level of the Foyer, an oval-shaped island bar separates the white marble floor from the red-carpeted floor immediately behind the doors leading into the Hall proper. Inside the Hall, the almost three thousand red seats (including the Orchestra seats, the Grand Tier boxes, and above them the Dress Circle boxes and the Balcony) face a stage simple in appearance but actually quite sophisticated in design. The ornamental ivory background, with its intricate mouldings etched in gold leaf, is actually a carefully planned acoustical shell. Red dominates the stage, too, with the red and black chairs for the musicians and the red-padded podium for the conductor.

Outside the enclosure of the Hall are the aisles, right and left, carpeted in the red that is the signature of the decor. Lining these outside aisles are multiple cubbyholes for wraps. To call them lockers doesn't quite tell the story, for they present a quite different appearance from the expected "locker" look. They, too, are red—slender doors which can be unlocked and relocked by inserting a twenty-five-cent piece, in an operation that not only gives the user private space for coat, hat, umbrella, etc., but does away with a wait in the check-out line.

All of this is convenient, beautiful, and familiar to anyone who has attended concerts in Powell Symphony Hall. From here, the tour now goes backstage to an area which may or may not have a familiar look, depending on whether or not one has ever been taken to the Green Room or has attended the On Stage programs sponsored by the Women's Association.

The backstage area contains the stage door, opening onto Delmar Boulevard, a door invariably under the scrutiny of a security guard. In the daytime, an unfamiliar visitor entering here signs in with the guard, stating the purpose of the visit. In the evening, on concert nights, the guard merely scrutinizes the entering stream of orchestra personnel and staff, sorting out the unfamiliar faces, if any there be.

This stage door entryway leads to many different sectors of backstage in Powell Symphony Hall. It leads to the stairwell, to the elevator, to a conductor's dressing room, to the true backstage area, and to the Green Room. The most logical area to look at first is the Green Room, a reception room comparable to those in many of the opera houses and theaters in this country and in Europe. The name "Green Room" is the traditional name for such a room, and this one happens to be decorated in green. Furnished to look like a dignified private drawing room or salon, it contains chairs, tables, mirrors, a couch, and a grand piano.

It is a room in constant use whenever the soloist is a pianist, for this is the room in which the artist may practice. The Green Room has its own door into the conductor's room so that a visiting conductor can also utilize the privacy of the Green Room to meditate, study the scores, or whatever. It is in this room that the soloist stands after a concert, greeting his close friends and orchestra members, although the room is not large enough to accommodate a mass reception. A discreet bar at one end of the room can be brought into service for a small reception.

Although the Green Room is the epitome of glamor backstage, it can be transformed radically during a recording session, with all of the machinery of the recording engineers being set up amidst the formal furnishings.

Across the hall from the Green Room is the actual backstage area of the stage. Here is a space, closed off from the stage, where the soloist or conductor can wait until time to go before the audience. A large bulletin board commands the attention of orchestra personnel, for here they may post notices or find announcements which apply to them. Off this area are two cubicles, one an office for the Personnel Manager (at present, Carl Schiebler) and the other a small office for the Stage Manager and his assistant (at present, Martin McManus and Gerald Eiffert). Neither office is formally furnished, to indulge in understatement. Each has a utilitarian desk, but classic decor is lacking. Nor is it needed. The Stage Manager's office has a maze of electronic devices whereby he can identify all mechanical or electrical problems immediately, and a small television set with which the men can catch up on sports events while the concert is going on—not that they are ever really detached from what is going on on the stage. They have a small closed-circuit television screen in sight at all times, and are conditioned to be aware as the program draws near to intermission or to the end. The stage managers have never—at least, up to this time—been caught napping. One is invariably there to open the door for the conductor and/or soloist who may be leaving the stage, and, of course, to hold the door open for the grand entrance.

The other side of the backstage area (the south side, on the audience's right) is mainly used for storage. It is not a large area. In fact, Powell Symphony Hall cannot be used for productions which require room backstage for scene flats or stage properties. For these reasons (in addition to the fact that there is no orchestra pit) the building is not suited for productions of ballet, for instance, or for musical theater. The two backstage areas, right and left, are connected by a narrow walk-through aisle behind the stage shell.

Taking the tour upstairs next, one finds that the second floor offers a small room or office for the concertmaster as well as a "soloist's room," a small dressing room and lavatory exclusively available for the singer or instrumentalist of the moment. These rooms are both north of the stairwell and elevator. There is nothing south of this small hallway. Nor is there anything south of the hall on any of the floors up to the sixth. This seeming oddity is immediately explained when the visitor realizes that the vaulted dome—the ceiling over the hall proper—is five stories high.

To continue upstairs to the third and fourth floors, there are rooms (with lavatories) for women members of the Orchestra, four or five sharing a room. The rooms are small but provide closets, each to be shared by two musicians.

The fifth floor, still on the Delmar side, contains an office for the Associate Conductor (at present Gerhardt Zimmermann) and a room for the Orchestra Committee.

The sixth floor has many more square feet of floor space, for we are now over the top of the dome. When one gets out of the elevator on the sixth floor, one finds doorways on both sides. The door to the north leads into the private domain of the Music Director. This room, for Leonard Slatkin's use, is a large room, with many windows, furnished to serve as a living room-office. It, too, has its own lavatory and, in this case, includes a shower room. It is through a small doorway from this office that the stage managers or an electrical crew can crawl onto a flyway on top of the dome, in order to adjust lighting or handle some emergency. The top of the dome, in the shadowy light here, looks somewhat like the rough exterior of a giant plaster cast, which is, in a way, what it is. The refined, contoured side is beneath, forming what the audience sees.

Across the hallway from the conductor's suite, still on this sixth floor, is the doorway leading to the executive offices. Here, beyond a receptionist's desk, are the offices of the Executive Director, the Manager, and their secretaries. Still farther beyond these are the mail room and the rooms housing the various copying machines, etc.

The seventh floor provides space for the ticket office staff, bookkeepers, and the comptroller. Immediately above these offices are the eighth-floor quarters of the Public Relations department (with its boxes and bundles and stacks of promotional material everywhere), an office for the Women's Association, the Development office, and the Library. This last is a sanctuary housing hundreds and hundreds of scores and orchestra parts, a copying machine, and a large drafting table where the librarian or the conductor or a section principal can mark the scores and parts.

The elevator, which was installed by the Symphony Society, goes only as high as this eighth floor. From here on up, one must take the stairs. The ninth floor is full of miscellany: red-cushioned chairs which need repair repose here until reconditioned, records and scrap books and outdated public relations materials are stored on metal shelves and in boxes on the floor. For pure attractiveness and interest, this ninth floor would rank far down the scale except for one dramatic feature: a leaded-glass skylight in the center of the ceiling allows natural light to illumine the materials being stored. In the days of the St. Louis Theatre, this skylight arched above a nine-story column straight down to the stage. Obviously the glass ceiling was not needed to light up the stage so many feet below, but being constructed with operating windows, it could serve as ventilation. The nine-story shaft was also space in which to hoist the scenery, in the days when vaudevillians instead of concert musicians were on the stage.

As Powell Symphony Hall, the building does not need the facilities for hoisting things up—it needs the mechanics for lowering things, mainly the concert piano. This takes us, on the tour, to the nether regions, the subterranean floor which sees as much, if not more, activity as any of the other floors. In the basement, or underground floor, are the areas which serve the most members of the Orchestra. The space into which the piano is lowered when offstage is the least of it. For on this same level are the musicians' lounge (co-educational) the men's dressing room, and the ladies' room. (You may recall that the ladies' dressing and locker rooms are on the upper floors. Down here is their communal washroom). The men's dressing room is enough to astonish a newcomer to the ranks of the Orchestra. To call it a locker room would be a gross insult. The room is lined not with lockers but with bona fide closets, each to be shared by two men. Down the center of the room are two rows of long, day-bed style couches, where one may sit to change shoes, or lie down to relieve an aching back.

Of course, the most admired room on this level is the musicians' lounge which has occasionally been mentioned or written up in the newspapers. Here, the musicians have various card tables, a pool table, kitchenette facilities where coffee can be heated up and snacks served. The room includes a candy machine, a soft drink machine, and a cigarette machine, although there is a constant war of nerves and of words between the smokers and the nonsmokers.

One other area on this lower level is important to the musical activities of the Orchestra. That is the not-too-large room where the Saint Louis Symphony Chorus assembles and warms up. When all are present, the room bulges at the

Passing the time in the musicians' lounge in Powell Symphony Hall. Left to right: John Lippi, Lee Gronemeyer, Roland Pandolfi, Thomas LeVeck, Louis Kampouris. Center (back to camera) is Fryderyk Sadowski. (*St. Louis Post-Dispatch* photograph, February 19, 1978)

scams, but for the present, it must serve. (Incidentally, behind the wall of this room are remnants of the woodwork, including a mantlepiece, of what was once the large formal lounge of the St. Louis Theatre. Two flights of stairs, still decorated with Art Deco handrails, lead down to this, although they are now concealed by closed doors in the ground floor foyer.)

Powell Symphony Hall has been mentioned many times in accounts of restorations, conversions, and the building of present-day concert halls. It is regarded as a highly successful adaptation of the old to serve the new, while preserving some of the grace of the past. Its acquisition in 1968 by the Society has had a tonic effect on the Orchestra, the management, and the concert-goers alike.

NOTES ON THE CHAPTERS

DA CAPO – BEFORE 1880

1. Walter B. Stevens, *The History of St. Louis–The Fourth City 1764–1911* (St. Louis & Chicago: The S. J. Clarke Publishing Co., 1911) Vol. II, p. 657. (Missouri Historical Society.)

2. Ibid.

3. Ernst C. Krohn, *Missouri Music* (New York: Da Capo Press, 1971), p. 255. This reference from Dr. Krohn's book is contained in a segment titled "The Autobiography of William Robyn, Edited and Annotated by Ernst C. Krohn." This was originally published in the *Bulletin of the Missouri Historical Society*, Vol. IX, Nos. 2 and 3.

4. Ibid., p. 265.

5. Stevens, *History of St. Louis*, Vol. II, p. 658.

6. Krohn, *Missouri Music* ("Autobiography of William Robyn"), p. 273.

7. J. Thomas Scharf, *History of St. Louis City and County* (Philadelphia: Louis H. Everts and Co., 1883) Vol. II, p. 1630. (Missouri Historical Society.)

8. William Hyde and Howard L. Conard, *Encyclopedia of the History of St. Louis* (New York, Louisville, St. Louis: The Southern History Company, 1899) Vol. III, p. 1603. (Missouri Historical Society.)

9. Krohn, *Missouri Music*, pp. 183, 184. Also see last paragraph, p. 185. (From a segment entitled "Some Notes on the Philharmonic Orchestra and Related Amateur Orchestras in St. Louis," originally published in the *Bulletin of the Missouri Historical Society*, Vol. IV, No. 3.)

10. Hyde and Conard, *Encyclopedia*, Vol. III, p. 1604.

11. Krohn, *Missouri Music*, p. 170.

JOSEPH OTTEN

1. Dena Lange and Merlin M. Ames, *St. Louis, Child of the River – Parent of the West* (St. Louis, Mo.: Webster Publishing Co., 1939) p. 284.

2. Krohn, *Missouri Music*, p. 171.

3. This clipping from *Adelaide Kalkman Musical Scrapbook III 1872–1924*, in Missouri Historical Society Archives. According to Krohn, in *Missouri Music*, p. 113 (Index), Adelaide Kalkman, born in 1858, was a soprano, a vocal teacher who studied in London, Paris, Dresden, and Munich. She taught for ten years at Strassberger's Conservatory of Music in St. Louis and was a soloist with the St. Louis Choral-Symphony Society in 1889, 1891, 1892, 1895, 1897, and 1902.

4. Ibid. Clipping undated and unidentified as to source.

5. *Spectator*, Vol. II, No. 66, December 17, 1881, pp. 235–236, review signed "G." The *Spectator* was published every Saturday morning by the Spectator Publishing Co., 212 Pine Street, St. Louis, with a New York Office at 150 Nassau Street. Among regular columns appearing in each issue was a Music Column. The issue preceding a concert by the St. Louis Choral Society carried an advance announcement, and the issue following carried a critical review. (Missouri Historical Society.)

6. *Spectator*, Vol. III, No. 117, December 9, 1882, p. 305. Review has no signature.

7. *Spectator*, Vol. III, No. 130, March 10, 1883, p. 556. Review signed "Fra Angelico."

8. *Spectator*, Vol. III, No. 141, May 26, 1883. Review signed "Fra Angelico."

9. This announcement appeared in the Music Column of the *Spectator* under "Notes," Vol. LV, No. 170, p. 277.

10. *Spectator*, Vol. IV, No. 189, April 26, 1884, p. 610. Review signed "W.W.P."

11. Krohn, *Missouri Music*, p. 171.

12. Hyde and Conard put the date at 1886 (*Encyclopedia of the History of St. Louis*, p. 1604.) Krohn puts it at 1890 (*Missouri Music*, p. 172).

ALFRED ERNST

1. Krohn, *Missouri Music*, p. 173. Krohn lists the number of first violins as ten, in 1894 when Ernst took over. Earliest printed lists of personnel (1904) indicate that there were then eight firsts.

2. *Reedy's Mirror*, Vol. VII, No. 47, January 6, 1898, p. 5. William Marion Reedy, after working in St. Louis as a newspaper reporter, became publisher of the *Sunday Mirror* in 1891. The paper, regarded originally by many as a disreputable gossip sheet, became—under Reedy— a periodical which took a keen interest in the arts and in presenting the works of little-known young writers. Edgar Lee Masters' "Spoon River Anthology" made its debut, in serial form, in *Reedy's Mirror*. A weekly, it was published every Thursday from 316 Rialto Bldg. in St. Louis; subscription cost was $2.00 per year, single copies five cents. Reedy died in 1920, and his personal influence (in spite of a somewhat scandalous private life) was so effective that the periodical known by his name succumbed a few months after his death. (Missouri Historical Society.)

3. Ibid, Vol. VII, No. 50, January 27, 1898, p. 14. Review signed "A.C.W."

4. Ibid., Vol. VII, No. 48, January 13, 1898, p. 14. Review signed "A.C.W."

5. Missouri Historical Society *Bulletin*, Vol. XXXVI, No. 1, October, 1979. Article entitled "Music at the Louisiana Purchase Exposition," by Jane Anne Liebenguth, p. 29.

6. St. Louis Symphony Orchestra Diamond Jubilee Souvenir Program.

7. Krohn, *Missouri Music*, p. 108 (Index).

MAX ZACH

1. Krohn, *Missouri Music*, pp. 174–175.

2. John H. Mueller, *The American Symphony Orchestra* (Bloomington: Indiana University Press, 1951) p. 149.

3. Ibid., pp. 89–90.

4. *Reedy's Mirror*, Vol. XXIII, No. 40, November 27, 1914. Review signed "Victor Lichtenstein."

5. Conversation with Elmer Gesner, December 1978.

RUDOLPH GANZ

1. Mueller, *American Symphony Orchestra*, p. 147.

2. Ibid., p. 149.

3. Conversation with Elmer Gesner.

4. *St. Louis Post-Dispatch*, July 11, 1971. Article by Frank Peters.

AFTER GANZ

1. Mueller, *American Symphony Orchestra*, p. 147.

VLADIMIR GOLSCHMANN

1. *St. Louis Post-Dispatch*, December 29, 1931. Article by Thomas Sherman.

2. Ibid., January 1, 1932. Article by Thomas Sherman.

3. Conversation with Herbert Van den Burg, November 1978.

4. Ibid.

5. Conversation with Oscar Johnson, September 1977.

6. *St. Louis Globe-Democrat*, December 7, 1943. Article on Sol Hurok, by James R. Treverton. Hurok is quoted: "The Saint Louis Symphony was among the few organizations to agree that Ballet was really coming into its own, though it was little more than a novelty so far as American theater-goers were concerned. It took the Russian Ballet to the little Odeon Theater on Grand Avenue in 1933, right after the first New York performances, and has presented it every year since then."

7. Conversation with Oscar Johnson.

8. The Farbman Sinfonietta made its debut in New York's Town Hall in 1940. The group

engaged in extensive touring. When Farbman came to St. Louis, he kept the Sinfonietta going, with many musicians from the Saint Louis Symphony Orchestra. The soloist was pianist Edith Schiller (Mrs. Harry Farbman). The Sinfonietta continued with its travelling concerts through the 1940's. In 1949, Edward O'Gorman, writing in the *New York Times*, said, "The group of nineteen men, a girl and a conductor . . . deserts St. Louis each Spring and Fall for a breezy six weeks' tour of the States and Canada." Edith Schiller had made her debut in Town Hall with a piano recital in 1946. The press clippings of this period indicate the high quality of the conducting, the ensemble playing, and the solo piano.

9. Conversation with Herbert Van den Burg.

10. Conversation with John Edwards, May 1979.

11. Ibid.

12. Virgil Thomson, *Music Right and Left* (New York: Henry Holt and Company, 1979), pp. 14, 15. Used by permission of Virgil Thomson. The review, titled "Expert and Original," first appeared in the *New York Herald Tribune* on the morning after the concert. In 1950, Dr. Thomson was celebrating his tenth year as music critic for the *Herald Tribune*. The book, *Music Right and Left*, is a compilation of his music reviews from 1947 through the spring of 1950.

13. David Wooldridge, *Conductor's World* (New York, Washington: Praeger, 1970), pp. 149–150.

14. *St. Louis Globe-Democrat*, January 23, 1958.

EDOUARD VAN REMOORTEL

1. *St. Louis Post-Dispatch*, July 24, 1958.

2. An award given by the St. Louis Newspaper Guild.

3. *St. Louis Post-Dispatch*, November 9, 1958.

4. Ibid., March 1, 1959.

5. Ibid., March 2, 1959.

6. *St. Louis Globe-Democrat*, November 1, 1960.

7. Conversation with Herbert van den Burg, November 1978.

ELEAZAR DE CARVALHO

1. Gordon Binkerd, on the faculty of the University of Illinois, was described in Leigh Gerdine's program notes for this concert as "a tonal composer, who admits the 12-tone system as part of the contemporary composer's vocabulary, but attributes to classical counterpoint a greater importance." Binkerd's Symphony No. 1 was recorded for Columbia Masterworks by the S.L.S.O., Edouard Van Remoortel conducting.

2. Robert Wykes, composer-in-residence at Washington University in St. Louis since 1955, has had five works performed by the S.L.S.O., with a sixth scheduled for May 1980. His works performed by the Orchestra have been *Density III* (1958), *The Shape of Time* (1965), *Letter to an Alto Man* (1967), *Toward Time's Receding* (1972), and *Adequate Earth* (1976). In addition to his symphony orchestral music, he has written film scores and documentary soundtracks. He composed the music for the biographical film on John F. Kennedy, which is shown in the new Kennedy Library, opened in Boston in October 1979.

3. Leigh Gerdine, in program notes of May 19, 20 (1967) referring to *The Shape of Time*, performed two years previously.

4. Robert Wykes interviewed De Carvalho in connection with a Spring Festival of Contemporary Music held at the University of Illinois at Urbana in 1965. Interview was taped and played over local radio.

5. Ibid.

6. *St. Louis Globe-Democrat*, Saturday-Sunday issue May 6, 7, 1967. Article by Clark Mitze.

WALTER SUSSKIND

1. In October, 1968, an article about the S.L.S.O. Kinder Konzerts, signed by Lowell McKergan, was sent out by the Associated Press. The press-clippings scrapbook of the S.L.S.O. contains clippings from newspapers in the following cities: Alva, Oklahoma: Augusta, Maine; Anderson, Indiana; Baltimore, Maryland; Bridgeport, Connecticut; Bristol, Virginia; Colorado Springs,

Colorado; Columbus, Ohio; Crawfordsville, Indiana; Gardner, Massachusetts; Greeley, Colorado; Greenville, South Carolina; Homestead, Pennsylvania; Lubbock, Texas; Midland, Michigan; Paducah, Kentucky; Pasco, Washington; Port Arthur, Texas; Riverside, California; Richmond, Virginia; Twin Falls, Idaho; Waynesboro, Pennsylvania; Winchester, Kentucky; and Youngstown, Ohio. Undoubtedly there were many more cities where local newspapers carried the story.

2. *St. Louis Post-Dispatch*, October 20, 1968. Article by Frank Peters.

3. Conversation with Carl Schiebler (Personnel Manager and French horn player. S.L.S.O.) in May 1979.

4. Review by Harold Schonberg, music critic for the *New York Times*, appeared in the *Times* February 27, 1970, and in the *St. Louis Post-Dispatch* on the same date. This quote was reprinted in the S.L.S.O. programs during the spring of 1970.

JERZY SEMKOW

1. *St. Louis Post-Dispatch*, September 19, 1975. Review by Frank Peters.
2. Personal experience of K. G. Wells and her grandchildren, May 1977.
3. Conversation with George Silfies (principal clarinet, S.L.S.O.) August 1979.

LEONARD SLATKIN

1. Slatkin is a gifted and accomplished pianist, although he has not pursued a career as a soloist playing concerti with orchestras. Since coming to St. Louis in 1968, he has played the piano in chamber ensembles and has accompanied singers in, for instance, the "Musical Offering" series. His maternal grandfather started giving him piano lessons when he was five years old. Slatkin says that further piano instruction was given him years later by pianist Jeffrey Siegel in exchange for Slatkin's giving Siegel conducting lessons. To date, Siegel has not tried his wings as a conductor.

2. Conversation between Leonard Slatkin and K.G.W., August 1979.

3. *St. Louis Globe Democrat*, October 24, 1979.

4. Conversation with Herbert Van den Burg.

THE WOMEN'S ASSOCIATION

1. *St. Louis Post-Dispatch*, January 22, 1961. Article not signed.
2. Excerpt from brief history of the Women's Association prepared in 1972 by Lucille Papendick, a member.
3. Reporter and Music Critic for the *St. Louis Star-Times*.

APPENDICES

APPENDIX I

Principal Conductors, Saint Louis Symphony Orchestra

The title has varied through the years. It was originally "Permanent Conductor," and has been, in later years, either "Principal Conductor" or "Music Director."

Joseph Otten   1880–1894
Alfred Ernst   1894–1907
Max Zach   1907–1921
Rudolph Ganz   1921–1927
  Guest Conductors   1927–1931
Vladimir Golschmann   1931–1958
Edouard Van Remoortel   1958–1962
Eleazar De Carvalho   1963–1968
Walter Susskind   1968–1975
Jerzy Semkow   1975–1979
Leonard Slatkin   1979–

APPENDIX II

Concertmasters of the Saint Louis Symphony Orchestra

Frank Gecks, Jr.   1888–1898 (?)[1]

Christ Jacob   1904–1907[2]

Hugo Olk   1907–1917

Michel Gusikoff   1917–1926

Sylvain Noack   1926–1929

Alexander Thiede   1929–1931

Scipione Guidi   1931–1942

Harry Farbman   1942–1961

Melvin Ritter   1961–1965

Max Rabinovitsj   1965–1977

Jacques Israelievitch   1977–

1. Records are sketchy concerning the orchestra personnel during the period from 1880 to 1904. According to Ernest Krohn in his book, *Missouri Music*, page 110, Gecks was concertmaster of the S.L.S.O. for ten years. This same entry in Krohn's book states that Gecks earned his M.A. in 1884 (from Christian Brothers College in St. Louis) and that he was in Europe during 1886–1887.

2. Jacob may have been concertmaster prior to 1904, but as stated above, no records of orchestra personnel before 1904 were preserved.

APPENDIX III
Managers of the Saint Louis Symphony Orchestra

Arthur J. Gaines   1912–1922
S. E. Macmillen   1922–1925
George R. Robinson   1925–1930
William Walter   1930–1931
Arthur J. Gaines   1931–1938
Donald S. Foster   1938–1939
John Edwards
   Acting Manager   1939–1940
   Manager   1940–1942
William Zalken   1942–1965
Leigh Gerdine   1965–1966
Peter Pastreich   1966–1970
   Executive Director   1970–1978[1]
James N. Cain
   Assistant Manager   1968–1970
   Manager   1970–1979[2]
David J. Hyslop
   Executive Director   1978–

APPENDIX IV
Stage Managers

Clarence and Elmer Gesner   1925–1945
George Buermann   1945–1960
William McCarthy   1960–1968
Leroy Stone   1969–1978
Martin McManus   1978–

1. Since 1970, the Saint Louis Symphony Orchestra has had both an Executive Director and a Manager.
2. On January 1, 1980, James Cain joined the Saint Louis Conservatory and Schools for the Arts as vice-president in charge of performance.

APPENDIX V
Presidents of the Saint Louis Symphony Society

L. L. Tebbets   1880–1881

Nat Hazzard   1881–1882

W. S. Stuyvesant   1882–1884

Robert S. Brookings   1884–1896

John T. Davis   1897–1899

William McMillan   1899–1901

Corwin Spencer   1901–1902

John Schroers   1902–1903

Mrs. John T. Davis, Jr.   1903–1907

Hanford Crawford   1907–1914

James E. Smith   1914–1916

John Fowler   1916–1924[1]

Mrs. John Fowler (Honorary)   1927–1928

L. Warrington Baldwin   1928–1932

J. D. Wooster Lambert   1932–1933

Oscar Johnson   1933–1955

Edwin J. Spiegel   1955–1958

Orrin S. Wightman, Jr.   1958–1964

Stanley J. Goodman   1964–1970

Ben H. Wells   1970–1978

W. L. Hadley Griffin   1978–

APPENDIX VI
Additional Board Executives

In 1941, at the start of World War II, Oscar Johnson—President of the Board for nine years by then—was a Lieutenant in the United States Navy. A new executive title on the Board was created, that of "Chairman of Directors," distinct from and not to be confused with "Chairman of the Board." During the War and for a period thereafter, this title or office was retained in the Board's structure. The individuals who held this title had considerable responsibility, handling many of the affairs of the Society.

CHAIRMEN OF DIRECTORS

Harry S. Koerber 1941–1942	Alfred Fleischman 1955–1957
Mrs. Clifford Gaylord 1942–1951	Roland Richards 1957–1961

1. Mr. Fowler died in 1924. His name was listed for two years following his death. There was no president listed for the year 1926–1927.

APPENDIX VII
Presidents of the Women's Association

Mrs. Thomas G. Ratcliffe   1925–1927
Mrs. Harry E. Sprague   1927–1929
Mrs. Edgar R. Rombauer   1929–1931
Mrs. H. Blaksley Collins   1931–1933
Mrs. Clifford W. Gaylord   1933–1935
Mrs. Charles M. Rice   1935–1937
Mrs. M. Hayward Post   1937–1939
Mrs. William Dee Becker   1939–1941
Mrs. Leicester B. Faust   1941–1943
Mrs. Robert W. Otto   1943–1945
Mrs. Grayson Carroll   1945–1947
Mrs. J. Sheppard Smith, Jr.   1947–1949
Mrs. John C. Tobin   1949–1951
Mrs. Lawrence T. Post   1951–1953
Mrs. Gerald A. Goessling   1953–1955
Mrs. J. Eugene Baker   1955–1957
Mrs. J. Eldred Newton   1957–1959
Mrs. Harold T. Hungerford   1959–1961
Mrs. Wallace R. Persons   1961–1963
Mrs. Carl H. Schlapp, Jr.   1963–1965
Mrs. Prince A. Gardner, Jr.   1965–1967
Mrs. Joseph Glaser, Jr.   1967–1969
Mrs. Elmer E. Hilpert   1969–1971
Mrs. Howard T. Bland   1971–1973
Mrs. Paul C. Ford   1973–1975
Mrs. William C. Scott   1975–1977
Mrs. Frank L. Thompson   1977–1979
Mrs. Robert C. West   1979–1981

APPENDIX VIII

Chairmen of the Junior Division of the Women's Association

Mrs. Ernest A. Eddy, Jr.   1959
Mrs. Sanford N. McDonnell   1959–1960
Mrs. William F. Trent, Jr.   1960–1962
Mrs. William J. Oetting   1962–1963
Mrs. William R. Cady, Jr.   1962–1963
Mrs. Henry T. Niedringhaus   1964–1965
Mrs. Herbert C. Phillips, Jr.   1965–1967
Mrs. Richard A. Glenn   1967–1969
Mrs. James M. Pierce, III   1969–1971
Mrs. Donald L. Fleming   1971–1973
Mrs. Charles H. Perkins   1973–1975
Mrs. Paul E. Fox   1975–1976
Mrs. Brian E. Smith   1976–1978
Mrs. William W. James   1978–

APPENDIX IX

Program Annotators

1907–1908, notes were written by William Schuyler, an educator, writer, and composer who was Principal of McKinley High School.

Before 1910, program notes were usually passages taken from published works.

1910–1911, notes were signed "G.M.B." This possibly was George Buddeus, a concert pianist who appeared as soloist with the S.L.S.O. frequently during this period and was teaching at this time at Strassberger's Conservatory in St. Louis.

1911–1912, notes were signed "Mc."

1913–1914, notes were written by William John Hall, an organist and the Supervisor of Music at Soldan High School.

1914–1918, notes were written by Charles Allen Cale, a member of the second violin section of the S.L.S.O., and husband of Rosalie Balmer Cale, pianist and teacher.

1918–1925, notes were written by Richard Stokes of the *St. Louis Post-Dispatch* staff.

1925–1939, notes written by Harry Burke, of the *St. Louis Star*, later *St. Louis Star-Times*.

1939–1943, notes written by John Edwards.

1943–1948, notes written by Bateman Edwards (no kin to John Edwards).

1948–1950, notes written by Frank Llewellyn Harrison.

Starting in 1950, program notes were written by Leigh Gerdine, at that time Chairman of the Music Department of Washington University, and later to become President of Webster College. Dr. Gerdine continued to prepare the notes single-handedly until the late 1960's, at which time notes written by others were interspersed with his. A regular contributor was composer and writer Arthur Custer. During the early 1970's, the program notes had various authors, including Shirley Fleming (of *Musical America*).

Since 1974, notes have been written by Richard Freed.

APPENDIX X
Significant Dates in the History of The Saint Louis Symphony Orchestra

1880 Orchestra founded as St. Louis Choral Society.

1893 St. Louis Choral Society incorporates in the name of "St. Louis Choral-Symphony Society."

1907 Constitution of the St. Louis Choral-Symphony Society amended to rename the Society "The Saint Louis Symphony Society."

1910 Musicians hired for regular season of twenty weeks.

1913 Orchestra starts tours (under Zach).

1922 Concerts for school children instituted (under Ganz).

1925 Founding of Women's Association.

1934 Orchestra begins playing concerts in Kiel Auditorium.

1950 Orchestra performs first time in Carnegie Hall.

1968 Orchestra moves into Powell Symphony Hall.

1973 Orchestra expands season to fifty-two weeks of concert activity.

1975 Beginning of nationwide radio broadcasts of Orchestra concerts to more than thirty-five U.S. cities.

1976 Beginning of present Saint Louis Symphony Orchestra Chorus (150 voices).

1978 First European tour; Orchestra played three concerts in Athens Festival.

1980 Orchestra is 100 years of age.

APPENDIX XI
Founding Dates of Twenty-six American Symphony Orchestras

Atlanta   1945
Baltimore   1916
Boston   1881
Buffalo   1936
Chicago   1891
Cincinnati   1895
Cleveland   1918
Dallas   1900[1]
Denver   1922
Detroit   1914[2]
Houston   1913[3]
Indianapolis   1930
Kansas City   1932
Los Angeles   1919
Milwaukee   1959
Minneapolis (Minnesota
   Orchestra)   1903
New Orleans   1935
New York Philharmonic   1842
Philadelphia   1900
Pittsburgh   1895[4]
Rochester   1923
San Antonio   1939
San Francisco   1911
Seattle   1926
Washington, D.C.   1930
Utah   1940

1. No orchestra 1942–1944. Resumed 1945.
2. No orchestra 1942, nor in 1949–1950.
3. No orchestra 1918–1929.
4. No orchestra 1909–1925.

APPENDIX XII
Saint Louis Symphony Orchestra Discography

I. CONDUCTED BY RUDOLPH GANZ

E. GERMAN Three Dances from *Nell Gwyn* (78) (Victor 9009)

MENDELSSOHN *Fingal's Cave* Overture (Hebrides) (78) (Victor 9013)

E. LASSEN *Festival* Overture (78) (Victor 55202)

II. CONDUCTED BY VLADIMIR GOLSCHMANN

BARTOK Piano Concerto No. 3 (Leonard Pennario) (with Prokofiev Concerto No. 3) (Capitol P-8253)

BIZET "Carmen" Suite (with Gounod: *Faust*, ballet music) (Capitol P-8288; reissued on Pickwick S-4020)

CHOPIN "The Romantic Music of . . . (Etudes, etc.)" (Columbia ML 5161)

CORELLI Adagio from Sonata Op. 5, No. 5, arr. Amadeo de Filippi (final side in 78 album of Schoenberg's *Verklärte Nacht*) (Victor M/DM-1005)

COUPERIN *La Sultane, see under* MILHAUD

DEBUSSY *La Mer* (with two Ravel titles) (Columbia ML-5155)

DELIBES Suites from the ballets *Coppelia* and *Sylvia* (with Easdale, Weber titles) (Columbia ML-5254/MS-6028; reissued on Odyssey 32 16 0338)

DVORAK Slavonic Dances Op. 46, Nos. 1 and 3 (78) (Victor 11-8566)

B. EASDALE Ballet music from *The Red Shoes* (with Delibes and Weber, *see under* DELIBES *for numbers*)

FALLA "Nights in the Gardens of Spain" (Artur Rubinstein) (with Mozart K. 488) (Victor LM-1091)

FALLA *Three-Cornered Hat*—ballet suite (with Prokofiev *Chout*) (Capitol P-8257)

FALLA *La Vida breve* – Spanish Dance No. 1 (with Shostakovich *Age of Gold*) (78) (Victor 11-8592)

FRANCK Symphony in D Minor (Capitol P-8221; reissued on Pickwick S-4012)

GOUNOD Ballet Music from *Faust* (with Bizet, above) (Capitol P-8288; reissued on Pickwick S-4020)

HAYDN Symphony No. 103 in E-flat *Drum Roll* (78) (Columbia M-221)

KABALEVSKY Suite from *Colas Breugnon* (with Shostakovich Symphony No. 1) (Columbia ML-5152)

LALO *Symphonie Espagnole* (Nathan Milstein) (with Prokofiev Violin Concerto No. 1) (Capitol P-8303)

MILHAUD *Suite Provençale* (78) (Victor DM-951; reissued with Schoenberg *Verklärte Nacht* on Camden CAL-178)

MILHAUD *La Sultane*, after Couperin (78) (Victor 11-8238)

MOZART Piano Concerto in A, K. 488 (Rubinstein) (Victor LM-1091)

MOZART Symphony No. 38 in D, K. 504 *Prague* (78) (Victor M/DM-1085; reissued on Victor LM-27; reissued with Sibelius Symphony No. 7 on Bluebird LBC-1067)

PROKOFIEV *Chout* ballet (with Falla *Tricorne*) (Capitol P-8257)

PROKOFIEV Piano Concerto No. 3 (Leonard Pennario) (with Bartok Piano Concerto No. 3) (Capitol P-8253)

PROKOFIEV Violin Concerto No. 1 (Nathan Milstein) (with Lalo *Symphonie Espagnole*) (Capitol P-8303)

PROKOFIEV Symphony No. 1 *Classical Symphony* (78) (Victor M/DM-942; reissued minus most of finale with recordings by other orchestras on Camden CAL-215)

RACHMANINOFF Concerto No. 2 (Leonard Pennario) (Capitol P-8302; reissued on Pickwick S-4030)

RAVEL *La Valse*; *Valses Nobles et Sentimentales* (with Debussy *La Mer*) (Columbia ML-5155)

SCHOENBERG *Verklärte Nacht* with Corelli Adagio (78) (Victor M/DM-1005; reissued with Milhaud *Suite Provençale* on Camden CAL-178)

SHOSTAKOVICH Symphony No. 1 (with Kabalevsky Colas) (Columbia ML-5152)

SHOSTAKOVICH Symphony No. 5 (Capitol P-8268; reissued on Pickwick S-4016)

SIBELIUS Symphony No. 7 (78) (Victor M/DM-922; reissued with Mozart Symphony No. 38 on Bluebird LBC-1067)

TANSMAN Triptych for String Orchestra (78) (Columbia X-47)

TCHAIKOVSKY *Francesca da Rimini*; *Romeo and Juliet* (Capitol P-8225; reissued on Pickwick S-4002)

TCHAIKOVSKY *Swan Lake* excerpts (78) (Victor M/DM-1028; reissued on Victor LM-1003)

WEBER *Invitation to the Dance*, arr. Berlioz (Leslie Parnas) (*See under* DELIBES *for numbers*)

III. CONDUCTED BY LEONARD BERNSTEIN

BERNSTEIN *Jeremiah* Symphony (with Nan Merriman) (78) (Victor M/DM-1026; reissued on Camden CAL-196)

IV. CONDUCTED BY EDOUARD VAN REMOORTEL

BINKERD Symphony No. 1 (with Wagner "Siegfried Idyll," by Columbia Symphony Orchestra) (Columbia ML-5691/MS-6291)

PROKOFIEV *The Love for Three Oranges* Suite; *Scythian* Suite (Columbia ML-5462/MS-6132; reissued on Odyssey 32 16 0344)

V. CONDUCTED BY ANDRÉ PREVIN

BRITTEN *Sinfonia da Requiem* and

COPLAND *The Red Pony* Suite (Columbia ML-5983/MS-6583; reissued on Odyssey Y-31016)

VI. CONDUCTED BY WALTER SUSSKIND

DVORAK Works for Solo Instrument and Orchestra (Cello Concerto, Rondo and "Silent Woods," Zara Nelsova; Piano Concerto, Rudolf Firkusny; Violin Concerto, Romance and Mazurek, Ruggiero Ricci) (Vox Box QSVBX 5135)

DVORAK Piano Concerto in G minor (Rudolf Firkusny) (Turnabout QTVS 34691)

HOLST *The Planets* (Turnabout QTVS 34598)

SMETANA *Ma Vlast* and Overture and Dances from *The Bartered Bride* (Turnabout QTVS 34619/34620)

STRAUSS *Thus Spake Zarathustra* (Turnabout QTVS 34584)

VII. CONDUCTED BY LEONARD SLATKIN

GERSHWIN All the Works for Orchestra and for Piano and Orchestra (Jeffrey Siegel) ("Catfish Row" from *Porgy and Bess, An American in Paris, Rhapsody in Blue, 2nd Rhapsody,* Concerto in F, *Cuban Overture, Promenade,* "I Got Rhythm" Variations, "Lullaby") (Vox Box QSVBX 5132)

GERSHWIN *Rhapsody in Blue,* Piano Concerto, Variations on "I Got Rhythm" (Jeffrey Siegel) (Turnabout QTVS 34703)

GERSHWIN *An American in Paris,* "Catfish Row" from *Porgy and Bess, Promenade* (Turnabout QTVS 34594)

MUSSORGSKY *Night on Bald Mountain,* arr. Rimsky-Korsakov, Mussorgsky/ Ravel *Pictures at an Exhibition* (Turnabout QTVS 34633)

PROKOFIEV[1] *Alexander Nevsky* (Claudine Carlson, Saint Louis Symphony Chorus, Thomas Peck, Director) (Candide QCE 31098)

RACHMANINOFF Piano Concerto No. 2 and *Rhapsody on a Theme of Paganini* (Abbey Simon) (Turnabout QTVS 34658)

RACHMANINOFF[1] Symphony No. 1 (Candide QCE 31099)

RACHMANINOFF All the Works for Piano and Orchestra (Abbey Simon) (The 4 Piano Concerti and *Rhapsody on a Theme of Paganini*) (Vox Box QSVBX 5149)

RACHMANINOFF The Three Symphonies (Vox Box QSVBX 5152)

PROKOFIEV Film music: *Ivan the Terrible* (Claudine Carlson, Arnold Voketaitis, Samuel Timberlake, Saint Louis Symphony Chorus, Thomas Peck, Director); *Lieutenant Kije* (Arnold Voketaitis); *Alexander Nevsky* (Claudine Carlson, Saint Louis Symphony Chorus, Thomas Peck, Director) (Soon to be released by Vox Productions)

BIZET *Carmen* Suite and GRIEG *Peer Gynt* Suite (TELARC 10048 Digital process)

1. received Grammy nomination, 1978.

VIII. CONDUCTED BY WALTER SUSSKIND AND LEONARD SLATKIN

A Slavonic Festival: DVORAK Slavonic Dance, Op. 46, No. 1; SMETANA *The Moldau* and "Dance of the Comedians" from *Ma Vlast* (conducted by Walter Susskind); MUSSORGSKY Introduction to Act I, *Dawn on the Moskva River*—Entr'acte, Scenes 1 and 2, Act IV—"Dance of the Persian Slaves" from *Khovanshchina*; BORODIN *In the Steppes of Central Asia* and KHACHATURIAN "Sabre Dance" (conducted by Leonard Slatkin) (Turnabout QTVS 34718)

IX. CONDUCTED BY JERZY SEMKOW

BEETHOVEN "Choral Fantasy", Rondo in B-flat, "Elegiac Song", "Calm Sea and Prosperous Voyage" (Walter Klien, Saint Louis Symphony Chorus, Thomas Peck, Director) (Candide QCE 31111)

RIMSKY-KORSAKOV *Scheherazade* (Turnabout QTVS 34667)

SCHUMANN Four Symphonies and *Manfred* Overture (Vox Box SVBX 5146)

WAGNER Overture to *Rienzi*; Preludes to Acts I and III of *Lohengrin*; Prelude to *Die Meistersinger von Nürnberg*; "Good Friday Spell" from *Parsifal*; "Ride of the Valkyries" from *Die Walküre* (Turnabout QTVS 34719)

X. CONDUCTED BY GUNTHER SCHULLER

PAINE Mass in D, Saint Louis Symphony Chorus, Thomas Peck, Director (Carmen Balthrop, soprano; Joy Blackett, contralto; Vinson Cole, tenor; John Cheek, bass) (New World Records NW262/263)

XI. CHAMBER MUSIC RECORDINGS

BEETHOVEN Quintet for Piano and Winds (Abbey Simon, piano; Richard Woodhams, oboe; George Silfies, clarinet; George Berry, bassoon; Roland Pandolfi, horn)

BEETHOVEN Serenade for Flute, Violin and Viola (Jacob Berg, flute; Max Rabinovitsj, violin; Darrel Barnes, viola) (Turnabout TVC 37004)

BRAHMS Clarinet Quintet (George Silfies, clarinet; John Korman, violin; Jonathan Beiler, violin; Darrel Barnes, viola; John Sant'Ambrogio, cello) (Turnabout TVC 37000)

MOZART Quintet for Clarinet and Strings in A Major, K. 581 (George Silfies, clarinet; John Korman and Jenny Lind Jones, violin; Joan Korman, Viola; John Sant'Ambrogio, cello)

MOZART Quintet for Piano and Winds in E Flat Major, K.452 (Walter Klien, piano; Peter Bowman, oboe; George Silfies, Clarinet; George Berry, bassoon; Roland Pandolfi, horn) (Turnabout TVC 37013)

INDEX OF PROPER NAMES

GENERAL INDEX

ABOUT THE AUTHOR

Katherine Gladney Wells is a native St. Louisan who has been an appreciative supporter of the Symphony Orchestra's programs ever since her attendance at the concerts for school children. Mrs. Wells refers to herself as a lifelong "closet" writer of poetry, prose, and music, although occasionally her efforts have indeed been public. She has compiled histories for various women's organizations in St. Louis and has written innumerable scripts for volunteer organizations, scripts occasionally involving original music. She researched and wrote the St. Louis historical material used by the volunteer guides on the sightseeing Tours of Distinction, conducted by the Women's Association of the Symphony. In 1969 she was designated by the St. Louis *Globe-Democrat* as a "Woman of Achievement," her category being Creative Achievement.

Her husband, Ben H. Wells, was president of the Symphony Society's Board from 1970 to 1978. During this period, both Mrs. Wells and her husband developed personal friendships with many individual members of the Orchestra. For several summers they have made a cottage on their Mississippi River farm available for "rest and relaxation" for Orchestra personnel.

Through annual auctions of goods and services for the benefit of both the Arts and Education Fund and the Saint Louis Orchestra, Mrs. Wells and her husband have, for several years, "bought" the right for her to conduct the Orchestra in one selection at a special concert. The music which she has conducted has been her own, fully-orchestrated work; and her program notes have been characteristically lively. She says she regards these events as the most colossal combination of exhilaration and fright that she has ever experienced. Some of the music presented at these special concerts has been in the form of songs, with orchestral accompaniment, based on her own poems or the poems of others. In the Centennial year, Mrs. Wells' music was a "Mississippi River Suite" for orchestra. This would seem natural enough, considering the analogy made in her book between the course of the Mississippi River and the first hundred years of the Saint Louis Symphony Orchestra.

SYMPHONY AND SONG was designed by Freeman Keith;
composed by The Stinehour Press, Lunenburg, Vermont, in Linoterm Sabon;
printed by the Universal Printing Company, St. Louis, Missouri;
and published for the Saint Louis Symphony Orchestra
by The Countryman Press, Woodstock, Vermont.